P9-CML-015

Table of Contents

Monuments

such as these could

not be erected by men

who consider the racer

as a means of gambling;

rather, by men who loved

courage, strength, speed

and will – and found

these qualities incarnate

in the Thoroughbred.

-Joe Palmer

Introduction

Many years had passed since I had last visited Domino's grave. But on a warm July day in 1994, I was in Lexington with a friend and wanted to show her the site. Although I was uncertain of the exact location, something drew me directly to the spot. We were struck silent by the haunting beauty of Domino's headstone standing close by an unused stable, his ghost almost palpable in the steamy summer air.

This visit spurred me on a quest to learn more about the Thoroughbred burial sites of the "inner" Bluegrass region and to document their whereabouts. My fascination with the subject became the genesis of *Etched in Stone: Thoroughbred Memorials*. The book contains information about many important horses which inspired memorials and markers as well as brief histories of the farms which were their homes. I also have included short biographies of horses with interesting stories or historical significance.

During the course of my research, I discovered that equine graveyards range from single markers to large, formal burial areas, some including sculptures of notable individuals. I learned that the tradition of erecting monuments began with the death of the great stallion Lexington in 1875. I also learned that horses are buried and memorialized in many different ways. Some are not always buried in their entirety — many times the head, heart, and hooves are symbolically interred. Neither are the memorials always on the actual grave site. Frequently, markers are placed in a cemetery, while the actual remains of the animal might be buried elsewhere on the farm or at another location entirely. At Calumet, for instance, there are markers representing some of the farm's great horses which were later sold and died abroad.

Some people may look askance at the idea of memorializing a horse, and to them I offer these words from Domino's obituary in the sporting publication *Turf, Field and Farm*: "The animal which possesses intelligence and affection and which brings to us fame and fortune is worthy of remembrance in death."

More than one hundred years have passed since Domino's death, and today his grave stands alone by the roadside. The small stable no longer exists, and horses no longer graze the nearby pastures. Graves of other great horses, unmarked, are long forgotten; other memorials may have been lost to the ever increasing development of farm lands. *Etched in Stone* was conceived in hopes of educating the casual observer and entertaining the devotee to encourage the preservation of existing memorials and the continuation of a great Bluegrass tradition.

Lucy Zeh
Louisville, Kentucky

ETCHED IN STONE

THOROUGHBRED MEMORIALS

By Lucy Zeh

THE BLOOD-HORSE, INC. ❧ LEXINGTON, KENTUCKY

Copyright © 2000 The Blood-Horse, Inc.

All rights reserved. No part of this book may be reproduced in any form by any means, including photocopying, audio recording, or any information storage or retrieval system, without the permission in writing from the copyright holder. Inquiries should be addressed to Publisher, The Blood-Horse, Inc. Box 4038, Lexington, KY 40544-4038.

Library of Congress Card Number: 99-68802

ISBN 1-58150-023-8

Printed in China
First Edition: April 2000

ETCHED IN STONE

Part One: The Beginning of a Tradition

Chapter 1 – Early Memorials

The tombstones of Nantura Farm's two great sons, Longfellow and Ten Broeck, are the oldest of the more than 400 Thoroughbred memorials which grace the Bluegrass. No trace remains today of a monument reportedly erected in memory of the great stallion Lexington in 1875, as the horse's skeleton was exhumed just months after his death and given to the Smithsonian Institution for public display.

Other early memorials to Thoroughbreds include the single stones honoring the renowned runners Domino and Ornament; the small cemetery at Hartland Farm; and the headstone of Merrick, no great racer but a valiant competitor and the nation's longest-lived Thoroughbred.

NANTURA FARM

Jacob Harper founded Nantura Farm in 1795 when he purchased 700 acres adjoining R. A. Alexander's Woodburn Stud. When Harper died, his four children inherited the farm, and each played a role in its operation. Harper's son John, and later his grandson Frank, helped make Nantura one of the region's leading Thoroughbred operations.

In its heyday, Nantura Farm encompassed more than 2,000 acres on either side of Old Frankfort Pike, near Midway. Its proximity to the railway at Spring Station was convenient for shipping horses. In 1885, *The Kentucky Livestock Record* described Nantura's Thoroughbred facilities: two training stables, stallion barns, and a one-mile training track that was "a little up and down hill and slow in comparison with many others."

Nantura Farm produced many good racers, among them Drake Carter, Endorser, Fellow Play, Freeland, Jenny Lind, and Marksman, but Longfellow and Ten Broeck were its two finest. Harper named his farm for the race mare Nantura, whom he had purchased as a broodmare.

LONGFELLOW

John Harper's favorite horse was foaled in 1867. The huge (nearly seventeen hands) brown son of the good race mare Nantura was sired by the imported stallion Leamington, who stood just a few miles away at Bosque Bonita.

Longfellow's exploits on the racetrack made him a popular favorite. *The American Turf* wrote: "He rivaled even the immortal Lexington in popularity. Throughout his long and brilliant career he was the equine idol of the United States, and was elevated to a pinnacle of admiration, such as it has been the fortune of but few thoroughbreds to attain…Old turfmen and even those who have had no more than the merest acquaintance with the race course, hold him in fond remembrance."

His great size, plus an injury kept Longfellow off the track during his two-year-old season. He made his three-year-old debut in April of 1870 at the Kentucky Association meeting, and was soundly beaten. He was away from the races until September, when he returned to win the Produce Stakes at the Lexington track. He captured his final three starts of the season: the Ohio, Citizens, and Post Stakes.

But it was at ages four and five that Longfellow's greatness became evident. He was shipped East for the first time at the age of four and easily conquered Helmbold in the Monmouth Cup and Kingfisher in the Saratoga Cup. (Helmbold gained a measure of revenge by defeating Longfellow in their next meeting, on a heavy track the giant Longfellow simply couldn't handle.) Back to Kentucky, Longfellow was

victorious in his final start of the season, a match race against Pilgrim at the Lexington track.

At age five, after two easy victories, Longfellow was

again sent East to tackle a new foe, Harry Bassett, winner of the Belmont and Travers Stakes and holder of a fourteen-race winning streak. In the Monmouth Cup, Longfellow romped home an easy winner. Two days later, he scored another facile win in the Jersey Jockey Club Purse. Longfellow's final engagement was a rematch with Harry Bassett at Saratoga. In a valiant effort, Longfellow fell a length short of victory, despite bending a racing plate before the start and injuring his hoof. He never raced again.

Retired to stud at Nantura, Longfellow sired the champions Thora, Freeland, Longstreet, and The Bard as well as Kentucky Derby winners Leonatus and Riley. In 1891, Longfellow was named leading sire. When he died on November 5, 1893, at the age of twenty-six, *The Live Stock Record* wrote: "Longfellow has served his day well, and died full of honors, but his name, through his descendants, will long be kept fresh in the minds of turfmen."

TEN BROECK

Ten Broeck was a striking bay stallion, about 16.2 hands, with a muscular frame and excellent legs but with a rather plain head. *The Kentucky Livestock Record* described Ten Broeck as "the most perfect and grandest model of a race horse that was ever foaled." His sire, the imported Phaeton, stood in Louisville at the Hurstbourne Stud of Richard Ten Broeck, for whom the colt was named. Ten Broeck's dam, Fanny Holton, was a daughter of Nantura, herself the dam of Longfellow.

During his four-year racing career, Ten Broeck won twenty-three of his twenty-nine starts. A good three-year-old, he improved with age, losing just twice in his final three seasons: at age four, to Aristides (who at three had won the inaugural Kentucky Derby, in which Ten Broeck was unplaced); and at age five, to the Saratoga Cup winner Parole.

Ten Broeck, in addition to speed, also possessed outstanding stamina, setting American records at five distances: one mile in 1:39 3/4, two miles in 3:27 1/2, two and five-eighths miles in 4:58 1/2, three miles in 5:26 1/2, and four miles in 7:15 3/4. His one-mile record stood for thirteen years.

Ten Broeck retired to a successful career at stud in 1878. His son Drake Carter lowered his sire's record for three miles to 5:24. Other successful get included Ten Strike, Bersan, Ten Booker, Free Knight, Tennessee,

Field and Farm expressed a heartfelt sentiment:

Longfellow lives, but Ten Broeck is dead. The daughters of producing lines which neigh for the son of Phaeton are answered by silence. A great horse, wearing a name distinguished in the annals of the turf, has passed away, and no one would blame Frank Harper if he should put crape on his hat.

Ten Broeck and Longfellow lie in adjacent graves under the sod that once felt the drum of their hoofbeats. Thoroughbreds no longer play in Nantura's pastures; today, cattle graze the land. But a few visitors still come to pay their respects to Ten Broeck, once holder of five American records; and to Longfellow, "King of Racers and King of Stallions."

EARLY GRAVE SITES

DOMINO

Domino, nicknamed "the Black Whirlwind" by his followers, was foaled at Hira Villa, a small farm north of Lexington leased by Major Barak Thomas to accommodate the overflow from his larger and more famous Dixiana Farm. Foxhall Keene bought the son

and Ten Stone. At the time of his death, Ten Broeck's offspring had earned more than $200,000.

In June 1887, the great bay died of paralysis. *Turf,*

Domino excelled as a racehorse and had a lasting influence as a sire.

of Himyar and Mannie Gray as a yearling in 1892 for $3,000. The following year, Foxhall and his father, James R. Keene, merged their racing stables and Domino began his career for both of them.

The Thoroughbred Record described Domino as "the color of highly polished rosewood."[1] About 15.3 hands, he was well-made with powerful shoulders and quarters, short-coupled, with an alert, intelligent expression. Domino's fame was his astounding speed;

he was defeated only once at distances of a mile or less. Like Longfellow, Domino was a favorite of racing fans, *The Thoroughbred Record* noting that "His prestige and the proud, dashing way in which he ran all of his races endeared him to the hearts of race-goers as did few other horses."[2]

Domino was undefeated as a two-year-old — although a match race with the colt Dobbins ended in a dead heat. Despite injuring a hoof at age three, he won important races that year and at age four, though his stamina limitations became apparent when tried at distances of more than a mile. He won nineteen of twenty-five starts, amassing then-record earnings of $193,550. His stakes victories included the Great American, Hyde Park, Futurity, and Matron (not then restricted to females) as a two-year-old; the Withers Stakes and Culver and Ocean Handicaps as a three-year-old; and the Coney Island and Sheepshead Bay Handicaps as a four-year-old.

Domino retired to James R. Keene's Castleton Stud for the 1896 breeding season. In July of 1897, Domino had completed his second season at stud. Turned out one morning, he was found down in his paddock a short time later by his groom. Despite efforts by the best veterinarians, the great horse died the next day. The cause was attributed to meningitis, but a paddock accident might have been the cause, as Domino was known to rear in play when first turned out.

At Keene's request, Domino was returned to his birthplace for burial. He was laid to rest next to Hira, the dam of Domino's sire, Himyar. As *Turf, Field and Farm* reported:

> On Friday, July 30, a wide and deep grave was dug on the Thomas place and the body of the great Domino, brought from Castleton in a two-horse wagon, was lowered into it. Major Thomas stood at the head and Major Daingerfield at the foot of the grave with uncovered heads, while some 40 people were grouped around them, and the sadness that was plainly felt was revealed in faces as the earth fell upon the form of the once great racer. It was a strange and impressive scene, but no one who sincerely admires fleetness, gameness and other desirable qualities in the horse will find fault with it. The animal which possesses intelligence and affection and which brings to us fame and fortune is worthy of remembrance in death.

Of Keene, *The Thoroughbred Record* noted:

> Of Domino he was passionately fond. Not so much because as a colt he won him about $200,000, but on account of the beauty of his lines, his extraordinarily high turn of speed…and his gameness. Mr. Keene is a con-

HERE LIES THE FLEETEST RUNNER THE AMERICAN TURF HAS EVER KNOWN, AND ONE OF THE GAMEST AND MOST GENEROUS OF HORSES.

DOMINO

noisseur, and to him a horse like Domino was as a rare jewel to an expert in precious stones.[3]

A headstone of Barre granite was erected over the grave. Keene dictated the inscription: "Here lies the fleetest runner the American Turf has ever known, and one of the gamest and most generous of horses." The nearby grave of Hira was never marked, nor that of Domino's dam, Mannie Gray.

Despite Domino's untimely demise, he exerted a tremendous influence as a sire. Of his nineteen named foals, an incredible forty-two percent went on to become stakes winners. His offspring included Epsom Oaks winner Cap and Bells, and the 1907 leading American sire Commando. Today, Domino's male line

MERRICK
GOLDEN GARTER — BIANCA
JAN. 25, 1903 — MAR. 13, 1941
NOBLE IN CHARACTER, WORTHY IN DEEDS.

lives on in the stallion Broad Brush, whom race fans hope will sire an heir capable of carrying on Domino's legacy.

MERRICK

The tombstone of Cal Milam's gallant gelding lies under the trees in front of the Lexington restaurant, Merrick Inn. Surrounded by a maze of apartment complexes, it is difficult to believe the site was once on the 500-acre farm, Merrick Place. The inscription on Merrick's tombstone reads: "Noble in character, worthy in deeds."

Bred by James Ben Ali Haggin (later of Elmendorf fame), Merrick was foaled in 1903 at Haggin's Rancho del Paso in California. Newton Bennington purchased the yearling son of Golden Garter and Bianca, campaigning him at two and three before selling him to Cal Milam in the fall of the colt's three-year-old season.

Merrick had not done much to distinguish himself at the time Milam bought him, but the colt went on to race until the age of twelve, compiling a record of sixty-one wins in 208 starts. He finished in the money an additional sixty-four times to amass career earnings of $26,785. His most notable achievement was a track record at Latonia for seven furlongs in 1:25 2/5, which remained the standard until after his death.

Twice Merrick was claimed from Milam, and twice his devoted owner bought him back. Retired after the 1915 season to the farm Milam had named in his honor, Merrick became something of a local celebrity, attracting many visitors. He died in 1941 at the remarkable age of thirty-eight, making him the longest-lived Thoroughbred on record. He was buried in a small plot with the Thoroughbred mare Anna M. Humphrey and an Arabian, whose graves are unmarked.

ORNAMENT

George Washington Headley founded Beaumont Farm near Lexington in 1880. A 1901 article in Lexington's *Morning Herald* praised the farm's "eight hundred and twenty-five acres of rolling uplands, at times almost hilly, again stretching out three hundred yards before the eye as level as a plain, with open country here and yonder woodland, beautiful in its virgin forest, a spot upon which the God of the sun smiled in the beginning a blessing which has been ful-

filled until now." Headley's son, Hal Pettit Headley, carried on the operation of the farm and also bred Ornament, one of the best horses of his day.

Photographs of the chestnut son of the imported stallion Order and Victorine show a smallish, rather light-bodied but attractive colt, who was said to resemble his maternal grandsire, Onondaga.

Racing under the colors of owners Charles T.

Patterson, Ornament was a good two-year-old in 1896, but his losses to Ogden led that colt to be named champion of the division. Ornament had an outstanding three-year-old season, setting a track record in his seasonal debut and winning the Latonia, St. Louis, and Oakley Derbys — the latter two run just five days apart. He was generally regarded as unlucky to have narrowly lost the 1897 Kentucky Derby to Typhoon II. He again made the expedition East from Kentucky to take on the best of that region's colts, meeting with mixed success but doing well enough to finish the year with ten wins from sixteen starts, earning the three-year-old championship. Among his Eastern victories were the Sheepshead Bay and Twin City Handicaps and the Brookwood Stakes.

In April of his four-year-old year, Ornament's breeder bought him back from Charles Patterson. The colt went on to win the Brooklyn and Brighton Handicaps in the East and the Country Club Handicap at Memphis. By the time he retired to stud at Beaumont Farm, he had amassed a record of twenty wins in thirty-two starts and career earnings of $99,276.

Despite high expectations, Ornament was not particularly successful at stud. A 1973 article in *The Blood-Horse* stated that "Ornament's legacy was that he was credited with securing the breeding operation of Hal Pettit Headley, and the ramifications of that transcend his misfortune at stud."

Today, much of the old Beaumont Farm has been developed, and Ornament's grave lies in the parking lot of an office complex, at the top of a small rise. The flat headstone is not visible at pavement level; one must climb the rise to see Headley's tribute to the horse. Beaumont was home to many outstanding Thoroughbreds — particularly during the farm's later years, when Hal Pettit's son, Hal Price Headley, was in charge — but only Ornament was honored with a headstone.

HARTLAND STUD

The equine cemetery at Hartland Stud is today on property owned by the University of Kentucky near Versailles. Five flat stones in a shaded, grassy area mark the resting places of the best of Hartland's Thoroughbreds, not far from the main house.

The oldest stone marks the grave of the stallion Esher, who died in 1901. A quick horse by Claremont, Esher won several races in England before he was imported to the United States. Esher's best-known off-spring is probably 1903 Kentucky Derby winner Judge Himes. Esher also sired Champagne Stakes winner Garry Herrmann, Suburban Handicap winner Alcedo, and Lady Schorr, victress in the Kentucky, Tennessee, and Latonia Oaks.

Also buried at Hartland are Peter Quince, a son of James R. Keene's great sire Commando and himself the sire of Papp and other good stakes winners; the great sire Ben Brush; and champion filly Rose of Sharon and her dam, Rosa Mundi.

Johnson N. Camden, who later became a U.S. Senator, took over the estate belonging to his wife's family and established Hartland Stud in the early 1890s. The farm was known for its cattle and sheep as well as for its Thoroughbreds. The stallion Spendthrift was among Camden's earliest purchases, along with several mares bought from Keene. Camden later bought Ben Brush when Keene dispersed his stock.

Camden lost money in the stock market crash of 1929, resulting in the dispersal of the Hartland Stud in 1931. In later years, Camden returned to Thoroughbred breeding and racing, this time at Runnymede Farm near Paris, Kentucky.

Ben Brush counted the 1896 Kentucky Derby among his victories.

BEN BRUSH

The smallish brown horse — who was longer than he was tall — was foaled in 1893. He was sold to Eugene Leigh and Ed Brown before the start of his racing career, and was sold again in the fall of his two-year-old season to Mike Dwyer, in whose name he raced thereafter.

A son of Bramble out of Roseville, Ben Brush won twenty-four of his forty starts, with ten placings and earnings of $65,108. In 1895 as a two-year-old, he won the Cadet, Harold, Emerald and Diamond, Nursery, Albany, and Champagne Stakes and the Holly and Prospect Handicaps. At three, he won the Kentucky Derby by a nose. *The Thoroughbred Record* described the race:

> The Kentucky Derby is over and Ben Brush wears the crown, but his victory was obtained only by the narrowest of margins, and while his neck was clothed with flowers after the race,

his sides were sore and bleeding from the marks of the spur, and his giant muscles ached as they never did before…At the turn from the back stretch Simms leaned over his mount's neck and urged him to the front…but the white face of Bed Eder had followed him like a ghost and was coming on the outside like a flash of light. For one fleeting instant the white face showed before the red. But Ben Brush, too, came from an unconquered race and the blood of Bramble and Old Bonnie Scotland surged through his veins as responding to the touch of steel his extended nose was thrust again an inch in front…On they came nose and nose until with an expiring effort Simms struck the wire first. It was probably the only point in the last fifty yards at which a difference could be detected between the two horses.[4]

Ben Brush also won the Schulte Stakes, Buckeye Stakes, and the Latonia Derby at three. His four-year-old season was perhaps his best, capped by his thrilling finish in the Suburban Handicap, where he won a desperate half-length victory from The Winner and Havoc.

Dwyer sold Ben Brush to Keene after the colt's four-year-old season, and he retired to stud at Castleton Farm, where he stood until Keene's death in 1913. Camden then bought the horse and moved him to Hartland Stud. Ben Brush excelled at stud and was named the nation's leading sire in 1909. Two of his sons also became leading sires: Broomstick, who earned the honor three times; and Sweep, twice. Ben Brush died in June of 1918 at the age of twenty-five (his gravestone reads 1917 in error) and was laid to rest near Esher.

ROSE OF SHARON

Rose of Sharon had a brief yet successful career on the turf, winning ten of her fourteen starts and earning $64,069. She was considered the champion of her three-year-old division in 1929, her only season to race. She was by Light Brigade out of Rosa Mundi, a half-sister to the gelding Helios who won the Breeders' Futurity and other stakes. Rosa Mundi was a daughter of John Madden's Kentucky Derby winner Plaudit and the mare Hindoo Rose.

Rose of Sharon was described as a giant chestnut filly, standing a full seventeen hands. Her tremendous size kept her from racing at two. She finished second at Lexington in her maiden race and won her next outing, the Ashland Oaks. Later that year, she won the Kentucky, Latonia, and Illinois Oaks. *The Blood-Horse* of July 6, 1929, reported that Senator Camden refused an offer of $50,000 for his great filly. Her only poor race was a twelfth-place finish in Chicago in the Classic Stakes, where she was beaten by the top colt Blue Larkspur. She defeated colts in the Chicago Test Stakes, among them Preakness Stakes winner Dr. Freeland. Her final start was in Maryland at Havre de Grace, where she scored her final victory in the Potomac Handicap on September 21.

Rose of Sharon became ill with pneumonia on the trip from Baltimore to Kentucky, and died on November 7, 1929. Her owner was devastated by the loss, as the filly's value as a broodmare was beyond price. She was buried in the Hartland Stud cemetery, and just a year later her dam was buried next to her.

Chapter 2 – Hamburg Place

*H*amburg Place founder John Madden rose from humble beginnings to become America's leading Thoroughbred breeder for eleven consecutive years. He bred 182 stakes winners and also enjoyed considerable success in the breeding and racing of Standardbreds, the breed with which he began his career as a horseman. He also was a noted trainer and a superb horse trader — one savvy enough to situate his farm close enough to downtown Lexington that prospective buyers could be whisked to Hamburg Place to look at horses while in a spending frame of mind.

Madden named his farm for his first champion, the great horse Hamburg, a $1,200 purchase whom Madden resold for $40,001 (so Madden could say that he sold the colt for more than $40,000). Madden purchased the farm on Winchester Road east of Lexington with the profits, and his land holdings grew rapidly as he acquired adjacent acreage. Eventually, Hamburg Place encompassed more than 2,000 acres of prime Kentucky bluegrass.

Madden, extolled as the "wizard of the turf," died of a heart attack on November 3, 1929. Neither of his two sons shared his passion for Thoroughbreds, and so it was left to his grandson Preston to return Hamburg Place to the stature it enjoyed under his grandfather's watch. Preston began by managing two sons of Man o' War, War Admiral and War Relic, in the late 1950s for the estate of Samuel Riddle. He later purchased T. V. Lark, a good turf horse who would become America's leading sire in 1974, and still later added another Kentucky Derby winner, Alysheba, to the roster of five bred at Hamburg Place.

The cemetery at Hamburg Place is the oldest formal

The cemetery at Hamburg Place is the oldest formal Thoroughbred burial ground in the Lexington area.

Thoroughbred burial ground in the Lexington area. It lies a stone's throw from the interstate highway, enclosed by a limestone wall, the surrounding trees dappling the turf with their shade. John Madden's tribute to his horses was mentioned in a 1929 article in *The Thoroughbred Record*: "There was a real vein of sentiment beneath his burly exterior and persistent quest of wherewithal. It demonstrated itself in many ways — his kindness to employees and attachés, his devotion to the fame and memory of many a great horse or horseman…His 'equine graveyard' at Hamburg Place was celebrated. It contained the graves of both thoroughbreds and trotters, horses he kept enshrined in his 'heart of hearts' forever, it being unendurable to him that they should pass into oblivion when their race was run."[1]

The cemetery's centerpiece is the grave of the Standardbred mare Nancy Hanks, which once was topped by her bronze likeness. It also contains the graves of four additional Standardbreds as well as the Thoroughbreds Sir Martin, Plaudit, Star Shoot, Ogden, Imp, Ida Pickwick, T. V. Lark, Pink Pigeon, Miss Kearney, Princess Mary, and Lady Sterling — the last three being dams of Kentucky Derby winners. The stone markers with their bronze plaques form a horseshoe shape around Nancy Hanks' grave. Ida Pickwick, granddam of Kentucky Derby winner Old Rosebud, is remembered as "The Queen of the West." Ogden's marker proclaims him as "winner of two races in one day." But of the horses memorialized here, perhaps the most interesting stories are those of Imp, the superb racehorse Sir Martin, and leading sires Star Shoot and T. V. Lark.

IMP

Imp was neither a product of the Hamburg Place breeding program nor a great producer for the farm — Madden had purchased her as a broodmare after the death of her owner and breeder, Daniel Harness. She was, however, a superb racer and the darling of racing fans — who dubbed her "My Coal Black Lady." A daughter of Wagner and the Fonso mare Fondling, Imp was foaled at Harness' farm in Chillicothe, Ohio, in 1894. In his definitive work *The History of Thoroughbred Racing in America*, William Robertson called Imp "the embodiment of the spirit of the Gay Nineties." According to an 1899 article in *The Thoroughbred Record*, she had "a broad, intelligent

IMP
1894 – 1909
"THE BLACK WHIRLWIND"
STAKES WINNER
OF 62 RACES

nine thirds for earnings of $70,069. She started an amazing fifty times as a three-year-old, winning fourteen races. At five, she scored perhaps her most famous victory when she became the first mare to win the Suburban Handicap. Charles Trevathan, author of *The American Thoroughbred*, declared: "Her Suburban was a grand race. The mile and a quarter was run in 2:05 4/5, and she had behind her Bannockburn, Warrenton, and thirteen others…She received such an ovation as had not been seen on the Sheepshead Bay track since Salvator beat Tenny."

After the Suburban, the town of Chillicothe, Ohio, declared a holiday when the popular mare returned to the farm for the winter. *The Thoroughbred Record* of October 14, 1899, carried this report:

Today is "Imp Day" in Chillicothe, and it is a big day for Chillicothe as Dewey Day for New York city. The business part of the city was decorated with flags, and there is only one subject of conversation — Imp. The game little mare, crowned with the glory of her performances in the East this season, arrived home yesterday evening at 7 o'clock…Imp, ridden by little Pete Clay, her jockey…followed the band. She

head, patterned much after that of Wagner. Imp is a big-framed, raw-boned mare. There is nothing flashy or sensational in either her appearance or her style of running. On the contrary, she lopes along with head down and in an easy going, matter of fact way that is very deceptive to the eye, but which at the same time carries her over the ground at racehorse speed."[2]

During Imp's six-season racing career, she faced the starter 171 times. Although her marker notes sixty-three victories, several sources credit her with sixty-two wins, along with thirty-five seconds, and twenty-

was almost covered with orange and black ribbons, while Clay wore his orange and black racing colors. Tom Tand, who rubs Imp, walked at her side to see that nobody "woke her up."[3]

Imp retired from racing in 1901, at the close of her seven-year-old campaign. She had set track records at four distances, from one and one-sixteenth miles to one and three-quarter miles. She was sold to Madden in 1902, and spent the rest of her days in the lush pastures of Hamburg Place, but her racetrack success did not follow her to the breeding shed. She produced only six foals, the best of which was her 1904 colt Faust, winner of the Southampton, Ramapo, and King's County Handicaps. Nevertheless, she was given a place of honor in the Hamburg Place cemetery when she died in 1909.

SIR MARTIN

Sir Martin was one of the best horses produced at Hamburg Place. Madden owned his sire, Ogden, champion two-year-old of 1896 who went on to a successful career at stud. Sir Martin was the second foal of the Hanover mare Lady Sterling, who later produced Sir Barton and Lady Doreen, a full sister to Sir Martin.

Lady Doreen's daughter Princess Doreen was the best of her day, becoming the leading money-winning filly and a three-time champion.

Sir Martin began his racing career in the United States and was the champion two-year-old of 1908. He won eight of thirteen starts, including the Saratoga Special, Great American, Flatbush, Great Trial, and National Stallion Stakes. Madden's horses were always for sale, and Sir Martin was sold at the end of his two-year-old season to Louis Winans and sent to England to race.

America's hope for the 1909 Epsom Derby, Sir Martin started as the favorite. Many observers thought he would have won had it not been for an unfortunate fall at Tattenham Corner. He went on to win four of his nine races abroad, including the Coronation Cup, Challenge Stakes, and Durham Stakes. Sir Martin entered stud in England, but was bought back by Madden in 1919. Wrote *The Thoroughbred Record*: "The homecoming of Sir Martin must be regarded as most auspicious, for he is outbred from the already overworked lines of Galopin, Bend Or, Leamington, Hampton, Isonomy and the like…Bloodstock breeders will have, in days to come, cause to bless the happy inspiration which prompted the purchase and return of Sir Martin."[4]

Sir Martin was moderately successful at stud, siring stakes winners Spinach, Happy Thoughts, and Revenue Agent, among others. None of his sons could carry on his male line, but his daughters were more successful. Sir Martin died on July 26, 1930, after breaking a bone in a stall accident. According to his obituary in *The Blood-Horse*, "Sir Martin was the late John E. Madden's favorite horse, and in his will he made provision for his retention as a pensioner after the sale of all other Thoroughbreds of the establishment." Sir Martin's sire and dam also rest in the cemetery at Hamburg Place.

STAR SHOOT

Star Shoot was Madden's most successful stallion, becoming the leading sire in America on five occasions, a record at that time surpassed only by the great Lexington. Foaled in 1898, the son of Isinglass and Astrology, by Hermit, was bred and raced in England. His two-year-old campaign indicated that he had some ability, but a wind infirmity surfaced at the age of three and precipitated his sale and exportation to the United States.

Star Shoot began his career in the stud at Raceland near Paris, Kentucky, and led the sire list in 1911. Madden bought him in 1912 and had him shipped to Hamburg Place, where the horse lived until his death on November 19, 1919. His most successful offspring were Sir Barton, America's first Triple Crown winner (although the series was not named as such at the time), Grey Lag, and Uncle. Although Star Shoot's daughters proved good broodmares, his sons met with little success at stud; and his male line has not continued to the present day. Still, he sired a total of sixty-one stakes winners, thirty-four of which were bred in Madden's name.

T. V. LARK

T. V. Lark was born in 1957, a son of the Nasrullah stallion Indian Hemp out of Miss Larksfly, by Heelfly. A decent two-year-old, he won three of his fourteen starts, including the Arlington Futurity over Bally Ache. His real ability surfaced at age three, when he was tried on the turf. His victories that year included a stunning upset in the United Nations Handicap, in which he defeated Sword Dancer, First Landing, and Intentionally.

The following year, owner C. R. McCoy sold the colt to a syndicate headed by Preston Madden for $600,000. That season, he scored in the Santa Catalina, Los Angeles, and Knickerbocker Handicaps, plus the Hawthorne Gold Cup and Washington, D.C., International. He was named champion grass horse for 1961. T. V. Lark raced through age five, retiring with nineteen wins in seventy-two starts and earnings of $902,194.

T. V. Lark had a successful career at stud and was

America's leading sire in 1974. His fifty-three stakes winners included Quack, Pink Pigeon, Buffalo Lark, and Golden Don. In March of 1975, T. V. Lark died as a result of an allergic reaction and was buried alongside Hamburg Place's other leading sires.

T. V. Lark excelled as a turf runner, and later became a top sire.

Part Two: The Great Farm Cemeteries

Chapter 3 – Whitney Farm

In the late 1890s, Cornelius Vanderbilt Whitney's grandfather, William Collins Whitney, founded a racing stable and breeding operation that his son and grandson continued with unparalleled success for nearly a century. W. C. Whitney died in 1904, cutting short his involvement in racing, but his contributions were significant nonetheless: He campaigned Jean Beraud, Ballyhoo Bey, Kilmarnock, and Yankee in the United States, plus Epsom Derby winner Volodyovski and others in England. He also bred the top fillies Artful and Tanya.

Many famous horses lie in the Whitney cemetery, including the Kentucky Derby winner Regret.

Whitney's stock was dispersed after his death, but his son, Harry Payne Whitney, acquired some of his father's best horses. In 1917, H. P. Whitney purchased 600 acres on the east side of Lexington's Paris Pike, which had once been part of James Ben Ali Haggin's Elmendorf empire. He went on to breed 192 stakes winners, nineteen of which were champions. His death in 1930 left his son, Cornelius Vanderbilt Whitney, to carry on the stud, which he did with remarkable success, breeding 176 stakes winners of his own.

Most of the Whitney family's horses are buried on land that Gainesway Farm acquired before C. V. Whitney's death in 1992. The equine cemetery occupies a peaceful knoll overlooking the Elkhorn Creek, with thirteen headstones evoking the memories of some of the finest American Thoroughbreds in history.

BROOMSTICK

In *The Great Ones*, Kent Hollingsworth noted, "Broomstick was not a champion race horse. He was a nice horse which, like Fair Play and Bull Lea, developed into a great sire." Breeder Colonel Milton Young had purchased Broomstick's dam — thought barren to Ben Brush — from James R. Keene's Castleton Stud.

Captain Samuel Brown bought Broomstick as a yearling in 1902 and raced him for three seasons, during which he won fourteen of his thirty-nine starts and a total of $74,370. At two, he captured the Juvenile, Great American, and Expectation Stakes and at three, the Brighton and Flying Handicaps and the Travers Stakes.

The Blood-Horse of 1932 wrote: "He was little more than a pony. But, he had a big heart — and that is what really counts. The only thing about him physically that indicated any unusual quality was his head — a beauty. He was smooth and well made from nose to tail...A horse doesn't have to have size to be a champion, as also witness Equipoise and Gusto. He must have something else. Something one cannot see — that innate spark which lends wings to his heels, and indomitable courage..."

Broomstick was retired to stud in 1906 at Brown's Senorita Stud near Lexington. Brown died later that same year, and in 1908, Brown's heir sold the bloodstock at a dispersal. H. P. Whitney bought the horse on the advice of his trainer, who had in his stable Whisk Broom II, a promising colt by the stallion. Subsequently, Broomstick was shuttled between

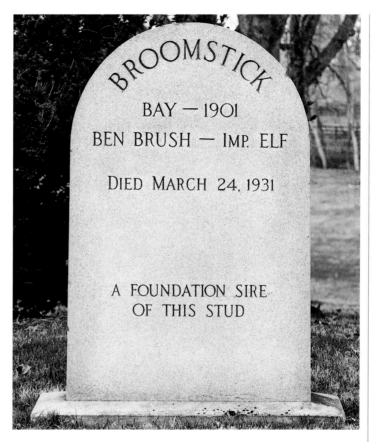

Brookdale, Whitney's stud in New Jersey, and the Whitney Farm in Kentucky.

Broomstick was a remarkable sire: seventy-four percent of his foals were winners, and twenty-five percent (a total of sixty-nine) were stakes winners. He was the country's leading sire for three years running (1913-1915) and ranked in the top ten a total of seventeen times. Among his get were Kentucky Derby winners Regret and Meridian and Preakness winners Holiday, Broomspun, and Bostonian. Whisk Broom II won

Equipoise, a star of his era, was known as the Chocolate Soldier.

important races in England before returning to the United States to capture the "Handicap Triple Crown" of the Metropolitan, Brooklyn, and Suburban Handicaps.

Broomstick died on March 24, 1931, at the age of thirty, and was buried near Whisk Broom II. His obituary in *The Blood-Horse* of April 4 read, "Broomstick, a small horse, usually got small horses, possessed of high speed and moderate stamina, full of courage, easily handled and easily trained, and sufficiently precocious for 2-year-old racing. But their chief characteristic, perhaps, in the minds of the people of the Turf, is their durability, their long resistance to the rigors of the track. Broomstick never got a horse which had the outstanding position of a Sysonby, Colin, Sir Barton, Man o' War, Reigh Count, Blue Larkspur, or Gallant Fox, but he filled the books with stout racers which could give and take with the best."

EQUIPOISE

The death of the gallant performer and crowd favorite Equipoise in 1938 at the age of ten was a blow to the racing world and yet another tragedy in the star-crossed line of Domino. In *The Blood-Horse*,

Joe A. Estes wrote:

> As always happens when a great horse passes away in the midst of a splendid career, a universal grief was stirred last week by the unexpected death of Equipoise. Next to Man o' War he was the horse most often asked for and visited among the thousands of Thoroughbreds in Kentucky. As much as any horse of his day he symbolized for his admirers the fleetness, the strength of heart, the unfailing courage which are the highest virtues of his race.

Dubbed "The Chocolate Soldier" by racing fans — in part because of his dark chestnut coloring — Equipoise won twenty-nine of his fifty-one starts in a career extending from 1930 to 1935, netting the Whitney Farm $338,610. He was co-champion two-year-old in 1930 and champion handicap horse from 1932 to 1934. His record is even more remarkable when one considers that he suffered from chronic hoof problems. In *The Great Ones*, William H. Rudy wrote that Equipoise "went every place, met every rival of consequence, asked no favors, and gave none...Plagued by shelly feet, he raced with a chronic quarter crack and, as much as any horse in history, it may be said that no one could know how good he might have been if he had been sound..."

As a two-year-old, Equipoise won the Youthful, Keene Memorial, Juvenile, National Stallion, Great American, Eastern Shore, and Pimlico Futurity. In the last-named, he gave what many considered the best performance of his career, as he encountered numerous problems but still pulled off the victory. Physical problems limited his three-year-old season to just three starts and a single victory, though he finished fourth in the Preakness to Mate. At four he returned in championship form, beginning the season with a string of victories in the Toboggan, Harford, Metropolitan, Delavan, and Stars and Stripes Handicaps. He also added the Whitney and Wilson Stakes and the Arlington Gold Cup later that year. His best performance of his four-year-old season was his world record-setting victory in the Delavan Handicap, which he won in a remarkable 1:34 2/5 while carrying 128 pounds.

At five, Equipoise again won the Metropolitan Handicap — carrying 128 pounds — and was victorious in the Suburban Handicap under a 132-pound impost. He also won the Arlington Handicap, the Hawthorne

Gold Cup, and the Saratoga Cup. At six, he again finished first in the Metropolitan Handicap but was disqualified; however, he did tally wins in the Philadelphia and Dixie Handicaps and the Whitney

IMP. MAHMOUD

IMP. BLENHEIM II—MAH MAHAL

1933 — 1962

FAMOUS RACE HORSE
AND
ILLUSTRIOUS SIRE

Gold Trophy. His finale came at the age of seven, when he finished unplaced in the Santa Anita Handicap.

Equipoise entered stud at the Whitney Farm with the highest of expectations. At the time of his death, his first foals were two-year-olds who were just beginning their racing careers. Of Equipoise's seventy-four foals, nine (twelve percent) went on to become stakes winners, including 1942 Kentucky Derby winner Shut Out.

Equipoise died on August 4, 1938, from enteritis. He was buried with the other Whitney greats, his tombstone proclaiming him "An Illustrious Son of This Stud." At one time, a bronze likeness occupied a niche in the stone; the bronze later was removed to prevent its theft.

MAHMOUD

With the death of Equipoise, the Whitney Stud needed a top-class stallion — preferably one unrelated to Domino and Ben Brush, whose lines permeated the operation. In 1940, C. V. Whitney purchased abroad the Epsom Derby winner Mahmoud for $85,000.

Bred in France by the Aga Khan, Mahmoud was a very good two-year-old, although he was ranked below his stablemate, Bala Hissar. In 1936, at the age of three, the gray colt won England's Epsom Derby, setting a course record that stood until after his death. He also finished second in the Two Thousand Guineas and third in the St. Leger. He was retired to stud in Ireland the following year and was an immediate success.

Mahmoud was lucky to arrive in America, as the ship on which he originally was loaded was torpedoed by the Germans. Fortunately, the stallion had been transferred to another vessel and made the voyage uneventfully.

At the Whitney Farm, Mahmoud sired seventy stakes winners, including Grey Flight, Oil Capitol, Snow Goose, Cohoes, The Axe II, Almahmoud, and champion First Flight. In 1946, Mahmoud was named America's leading sire. He and his get did much to erase the Thoroughbred industry's long-standing prejudice against gray horses.

Around midnight on September 18, 1962, Mahmoud died at the age of twenty-nine from the infirmities of old age. Mourned by all who knew him, he was remembered by the Whitney Farm personnel in *The Thoroughbred Record*: "Mahmoud was very much an individual and he seemed to delight in being one. One of his idiosyncrasies was that he refused to be ridden across the Elkhorn Creek bridge though was willing to go when led. Those of us who have grown fonder of Mahmoud with each of the passing years will miss him more than words can express…He knew human affection but he did not exploit it. He was never too preoccupied to walk to his paddock fence to receive a pat. He was kind and gentle, uncomplicated; any living thing was allowed in Mahmoud's paddock."[1]

PETER PAN

Another outstanding runner bred by James R. Keene, Peter Pan was one of the best members of the 1904 foal crop, earning championship honors as a three-year-old, and went on to a successful career at stud. One of just twenty-four foals sired by Domino's son Commando, Peter Pan was produced from the imported mare Cinderella, by Hermit. According to the book *Thoroughbred Types 1900-1925*, "He had a fine head and a stout neck, good shoulders, deep in the chest; his barrel was noted for the roundness of his ribs. He had fine development of quarters, big arms, and was in all, a sturdy one."

In two seasons, Peter Pan won ten of seventeen

races, earning $115,450. He won the Surf, Flash, and Hopeful Stakes as a two-year-old. At three, he captured the Belmont, Standard, Tidal, and Advance Stakes, plus the Brooklyn Derby (known today as the Dwyer Stakes), and the Brighton Handicap. In *The Great Ones*, Hollingsworth quotes Peter Pan's rider, Joe Notter: "Peter Pan was one of the best horses I ever rode. There was nothing horses are asked to do that Peter Pan couldn't do. He could carry weight, he could sprint, and he could stay with the best of them."

Peter Pan was retired at the close of his three-year-old campaign, entering stud at his owner's Castleton Stud, where he sired Pennant and Black Toney in his third crop. Keene's death in 1913 led to the dispersal of the Castleton horses, and Peter Pan was sold to H. P. Whitney for $38,000. At the Whitney Farm, he sired Prudery (herself a champion racer and dam of Kentucky Derby winner Whiskery and Preakness winner Victorian), and major producer Cherokee Rose. Pennant, a full brother to Cherokee Rose and another of Whitney's studs, sired the great Equipoise.

Through Black Toney, Pennant, and numerous daughters, Peter Pan's influence has continued to this day, although his male line has practically died out. He was retired from stud duty in 1931 and died on December 9, 1933. His final resting place is near Broomstick and Prudery, beneath a headstone proclaiming him as "a foundation sire of this stud."

REGRET

Regret made history by becoming the first filly to win the Kentucky Derby, in 1915, a feat not achieved a second time until Genuine Risk's victory sixty-five years later in 1980. In eleven starts, Regret won nine and was once second, and earned champion two- and three-year-old filly honors. She began her career as a two-year-old of 1914 by soundly defeating the year's best colt, Pebbles, in the Saratoga Special. That same year, she won the Sanford and Hopeful Stakes.

The Kentucky Derby was Regret's first start as a three-year-old, and again she easily beat the boys. In her only other race at three, she won the Saranac Handicap over the good colt The Finn. At four she again started only twice. The Saratoga Handicap marked the only time she finished unplaced, as she faded to finish last after leading early. She returned to win an overnight event in her only other start.

Regret went postward four times as a five-year-old. She won the Gazelle Handicap and finished second in the Brooklyn Handicap, a scant nose behind her stablemate, the late-charging Borrow.

Regret enjoyed far less success in her second career as a broodmare. Her only stakes-winning produce was

Regret was the first filly to win the Kentucky Derby.

Revenge. Her daughters produced stakes winners First Fiddle, Easter Hatter, Red Rag, Avenger, Blot, and Rhadamanthus (the last two steeplechasers). Regret died of a hemorrhage on April 14, 1934, at the age of twenty-two. Her obituary in *The Thoroughbred Record* recalled her racing days: "Peerless Regret she was hailed and peerless she undoubtedly was, and to this day, we have never been able to think of her without that descriptive adjective affixed."[2]

Chapter 4 – Greentree Farm

Today the cemetery where the Greentree Stable greats sleep, like the Whitney Farm cemetery, is part of the 1,600-acre Gainesway Farm complex, occupying an expansive lawn in front of the barn once called Cherry Lodge. A hedge separates the two rows of headstones, and set apart on each side are islands containing two graves each. The island on the left marks the graves of Tom Fool and The Axe II, two of Greentree's most influential stallions; on the right are those of Bebopper and Dunce Cap II, two of the farm's finest mares.

Greats such as Tom Fool and The Axe II rest in the Greentree Stable cemetery, now located on Gainesway Farm property.

Helen Hay Whitney's involvement in racing began with the ownership of steeplechasers in the early days of the 20th Century, and she always had a soft spot in her heart for jumpers. Soon, her Greentree Stable began racing horses on the flat, with equal success. She established Greentree Farm in the late 1920s when she purchased some 600 acres from the Haggin and John T. Hughes estates.

The racing world mourned Mrs. Whitney's passing in 1944. *The Thoroughbred Record* noted, "Her unfailing devotion to the best in racing and her true love of the sport have done much toward placing American racing in the trustworthy and honorable position that it enjoys today."[1]

Mrs. Whitney's two children, John Hay Whitney and Joan Whitney Payson, continued to operate Greentree after their mother's death, with John Hay later acquiring his sister's interest in the farm and the racing stable. After John Hay died in 1982, his widow, Betsey, carried on the Greentree tradition for a number of years, but in 1994 she made the decision to sell the farm and the horses.

Although Greentree was named the nation's leading Thoroughbred breeding farm just once, in 1942, it bred a total of 183 stakes winners, and raced 202, among them Racing Hall-of-Famers Jolly Roger, Tom Fool, Twenty Grand, and Devil Diver. But it was not just the stable's top money earners who were accorded places of honor in the farm cemetery. Helen Hay Whitney's favorite horses — including three of her beloved 'chasers — also lie there. More recently, the Gainesway mares Polite Lady and Jedina have been interred near the Greentree greats.

BIMELECH

Although he is buried in the Cherry Lodge cemetery, Bimelech was a product of Idle Hour Farm. The mating of Bradley's great stallion Black Toney and La Troienne had already produced the grand race mare Black Helen. As a result, Black Helen's brother, Bimelech, was highly regarded from the outset. He was described as a well-balanced, elegant colt with beautiful action and a perfect temperament. And his

two-year-old season saw him unbeaten in six starts, with the Hopeful, Saratoga Special, and Belmont and Pimlico Futurities among his victories.

The champion two-year-old of 1939, Bimelech was widely regarded as a shoo-in to give Idle Hour its fifth Kentucky Derby victory. After winning the Blue Grass

Bimelech was the best racehorse produced from his dam, the great La Troienne.

Stakes and the Derby Trial, Bimelech could not hold off Gallahadion and finished second in the Derby — his third race in nine days. He turned the tables on

Gallahadion in the Preakness with a resounding victory, leaving Gallahadion some four lengths in his wake. A loss in the Withers Stakes followed, but Bimelech claimed the Belmont in a stirring finish. John Hervey, in *American Race Horses* of 1940, wrote of the race: "Bimelech's Belmont deserves to rank among the best three-year-old performances in our turf history. From the start he was on the pace. Attacked in succession by Andy K., Gallahadion, and Corydon, he one after the other raced them into submission. Being then challenged by Your Chance, who had been reserved for the stretch, he stood him off and decisively outfinished him."

Bimelech next finished third in the Classic at Arlington in what turned out to be the final race of his three-year-old campaign. Injured just prior to the Travers at Saratoga, he was sidelined for the rest of the year.

Although Bimelech had not demonstrated the same dominance over his contemporaries as he had at two, he again was named champion of his age group.

Bimelech returned to the races at four, but only managed two starts with one win. He was retired to Idle Hour after he finished fourth in the Widener

Handicap. All told, he won eleven of fifteen starts for earnings of $248,745. He stood at Idle Hour until his owner's death, when he was moved to Greentree. His thirty stakes winners included Better Self, Be Faithful, and Bimlette. His daughters proved good producers, and it is primarily through them that Bimelech's influence has continued in modern pedigrees. He died on July 21, 1966, at the advanced age of twenty-nine, and was buried alongside the Greentree heroes.

CHERRY MALOTTE

Cherry Malotte, one of the first horses to carry Helen Hay Whitney's colors, was foaled in 1909 and raced over fences from 1913 to 1918. She is featured in the book *Thoroughbred Types 1900-1925* section on steeplechasers: "She proved her quality with the best. Her entire record brings thoughts of hard fought contests in various parts of the country and under all sorts of conditions, and whether she won or lost, her performances were always creditable."

Cherry Malotte won eighteen races, including the Meadow Brook Steeplechase Handicap of 1918, and earned $25,335. After her retirement, she joined Mrs.

Whitney's fledgling broodmare band and later produced the gelding Cherry Pie, the first of Greentree's good flat racers. Cherry Pie won twenty-one races, including the Saranac, Jerome, and Long Beach Handicaps. Mother and son are buried near each other in the Greentree cemetery.

JOLLY ROGER

Another of Greentree's outstanding steeplechasers, Jolly Roger won eighteen of forty-nine starts and earned $143,240 — a record for a 'chaser at that time. His earnings record stood for nearly twenty years before being eclipsed by Elkridge. Among Jolly Roger's victories were the Glendale, Grand National (American, twice), Charles L. Appleton Memorial, Wheatley, and Brook Steeplechase Handicaps. He was voted into racing's Hall of Fame for his accomplishments.

A great favorite of his owner, Jolly Roger also was well loved by the children at Greentree, who would pass off the flashy chestnut with the white stockings as one of Lexington's more famous equine residents (such as Man o' War) and collect tips from impressed tourists. Jolly Roger died in 1948 at the age of twenty-six — ironically, the day after his earnings record fell.

LA TROIENNE

The Blood-Horse reported the death of La Troienne in its February 6, 1954 issue: "On Saturday, January 30, the 28-year-old *La Troienne was consigned to a

IMP.
LA TROIENNE

1926 — 1954

merciful death at Greentree Farm, Lexington. She was buried near the stallion paddocks, within sight of her best son, Bimelech. A stone will be erected in memory of the most notable broodmare of her time."

La Troienne's lackluster racing career in France and England did nothing to foreshadow her success as a broodmare. She started seven times, never once hitting the board. Nor did she appear the ideal matron; a 1940 article in *The Blood-Horse* described her as "light-barreled and comparatively delicate." Nonetheless, Colonel E. R. Bradley bought her at Newmarket in December 1930 and imported her to join the other broodmares at his Idle Hour Farm. After Bradley's death, the Ogden Phipps-Greentree-King Ranch partnership acquired the Idle Hour stock, and La Troienne was sent to her new home at Greentree.

Five of La Troienne's foals — eleven bred in Bradley's name — were stakes winners: Bimelech (undoubtedly the best of her offspring), Biologist, Bee Ann Mac, and Bimelech's sisters Black Helen and Big Hurry. La Troienne's daughters proved prolific producers, and their descendants have continued to produce numerous high-class runners, among them Buckpasser,

Allez France, Straight Deal, Caerleon, Easy Goer, and a host of other stakes winners. La Troienne's importance in the pedigrees of modern Thoroughbreds ranks her as one of the century's most influential mares.

SHUT OUT

A member of the great Equipoise's fourth and final foal crop, Shut Out carried high hopes from the farm to the track. John Hervey described the colt in the 1942 volume of *American Race Horses*:

> When foaled, Shut Out was considered to resemble strongly his sire, without, however, approaching him in beauty. About the head the likeness if anything is strongest. The irregular strip in the face of the son is almost a duplicate of his progenitor's, while the entire facial expression is strikingly similar. But Shut Out's chestnut coat is not of the deep, rich, glowing hue that won for Equipoise his famous sobriquet of "the Chocolate Soldier" and was one of his chief beauties. It is lighter, softer and duller in hue, and in comparison lacks lustre and satiny texture. Nor is his conformation comparable to that of Equipoise. He is a bigger horse, rangier, less smooth, symmetrical and close-knit.

Although he showed promise as a two-year-old,

Shut Out won the 1942 Kentucky Derby and Belmont Stakes.

43

Shut Out was overshadowed by his stablemate, Devil Diver. Still, he won the Grand Union Hotel Stakes; was second to another stablemate, Amphitheatre, in the Saratoga Special; and was second to Devil Diver in the Hopeful. Despite his less-than-stellar record, Shut Out's connections and other astute observers continued to regard him as a bright prospect for the spring classics.

As a three-year-old of 1942, Shut Out rewarded his faithful following by winning first the Blue Grass Stakes at Keeneland, then the Kentucky Derby — outrunning Devil Diver and thirteen others in the process. He finished a disappointing fifth in the Preakness, won by Alsab in a record-setting performance, but rebounded to claim victory in the Belmont Stakes in near record time. That same year, he also set a track record in the Yankee Handicap and won the Travers and Classic Stakes.

Shut Out was unable to recapture his best form at the ages of four and five, although at four he won the Wilson and Laurel Stakes, and the Pimlico Special. Retired to stud at Greentree, he had limited success. His best offspring included the two-year-old champion Evening Out, plus stakes winners Social Outcast and One Hitter. He died on April 23, 1964, at the age of twenty-five.

TOM FOOL

In 1949, the Bull Dog mare Gaga produced a bay colt by Menow at the Manchester Farm of Duval Headley. The colt was sold privately as a yearling to Greentree, whose colors he carried throughout his remarkable racing career. Not an overly large colt, he was described by Joe A. Estes in *American Race Horses* as "robust, sound, and possessed of an extraordinary equanimity of disposition." Later, he retired to Greentree to become one of its best stallions.

At two, Tom Fool made his debut at Saratoga, winning a maiden event. He followed up with stakes scores in the Sanford and the Grand Union Hotel, defeating Cousin and Jet Master — who, at the time, were considered the best of the two-year-olds — in the latter race. He was second in each of his next two races, dropping the Hopeful to Cousin and finishing behind Hill Gail in a prep for the Futurity. He capped his season with victories in the Futurity and East View Stakes and was named champion of his division.

At three, Tom Fool missed the classics as the result of an illness. His first stakes victory of the season came in the Wilson Stakes at Saratoga. Next, he took the Jerome by seven lengths, then added triumphs in the Sysonby, Greg Lag, and Westchester Handicaps.

Tom Fool was at his best as a four-year-old. In its August 30, 1976 issue, *The Blood-Horse* stated in his obituary: "Prelude was really what Tom Fool's career was prior to 1953. In that year he was four — mature, knowing, willing, a courageous competitor blessed with commanding physical strength and trained with precision."

Few horses survive the handicap races without encountering defeat, as their burden is increased with each victory. Tom Fool was able to do just that, going undefeated in ten starts at four. He became only the second horse (after H. P. Whitney's Whisk Broom II) to sweep New York's "Handicap Triple." He won under 130 pounds in the Metropolitan Handicap and under 128 in the Suburban. He topped off the Triple by carrying a staggering 136 pounds home first in the Brooklyn Handicap. In his year-end review for *American Race Horses*, Estes noted, "It would have

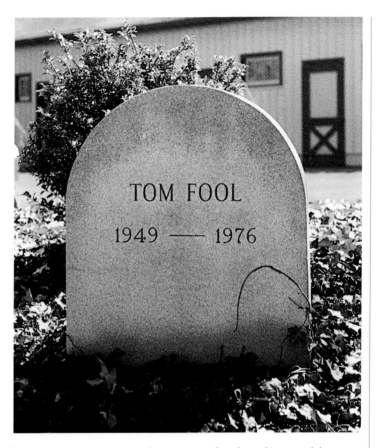

been interesting to discover whether he could carry two jockeys and still win, but John Hay Whitney and his sister Mrs. Charles S. Payson, owners of Greentree, were not that curious."

After a win in the Carter Handicap to close out his

A Horse of the Year and handicap champion, Tom Fool also was a successful sire.

summer campaign, Tom Fool was aimed for the fall, weight-for-age events. He added victories in the Wilson, Whitney, and Sysonby Stakes and in the Pimlico Special. He was named Horse of the Year in 1953. His final record stood at thirty starts, twenty-one wins, and earnings of $570,165.

After a shaky beginning, Tom Fool's stud career at Greentree was as successful as his racing career. His progeny included the brilliant Buckpasser as well as Tim Tam, Jester, Dunce, and Cyrano. His daughters produced such outstanding runners as Foolish Pleasure, Stop the Music, and Hatchet Man. He was pensioned from stud duty in 1972. In 1976, Tom Fool was euthanized due to the infirmities of old age and buried in front of Cherry Lodge.

TWENTY GRAND

A son of the imported stallion St. Germans and the mare Bonus, Twenty Grand was foaled in 1928 and became one of the best runners to carry the Greentree colors of watermelon pink with black-striped sleeves. In *The Great Breeders and Their Methods*, Abram S. Hewitt described the colt as "big, burly, very vigorous and not over-refined."

Twenty Grand broke his maiden in his two-year-old debut on April 30, 1930, then bucked shins and was sidelined until July. He returned to finish second in an allowance event, then was sidelined again by minor ailments until September. Despite these setbacks, he was ranked among the leaders of the division at year's end. He defeated Equipoise in the Junior Champion and Kentucky Jockey Club Stakes, but lost to that colt on a muddy track in the Pimlico Futurity.

In 1931, during Twenty Grand's three-year-old season, many horsemen declared him the best on the American Turf since Man o' War. Although he lost to Mate in the Preakness (which at that time was run before the Kentucky Derby), his Kentucky Derby and Belmont wins proved him superior to his contemporaries. He also was victorious in the Wood, Dwyer, and Travers Stakes, plus the Saratoga Cup, Lawrence Realization, and Jockey Club Gold Cup. He returned at four, but after two starts, he was stopped by unsoundness and retired to stud at Greentree. However, due to fertility problems, he returned to race as a seven-year-old in 1935, but only managed one win in five starts and was subsequently retired again.

Sadly, Twenty Grand never was able to sire a foal; all efforts to correct his infertility proved futile. Eventually, he joined other Greentree pensioners Jolly Roger, Easter Hero, and Cherry Pie — a group

called the "Gashouse Gang" after the 1934 St. Louis Cardinals baseball team. He suffered a twisted intestine and died on March 2, 1948, joining Easter Hero and Cherry Pie in the Greentree cemetery.

Chapter 5 – Elmendorf, Normandy, and Clovelly Farms

The Elmendorf property has a long and distinguished history in the breeding of Thoroughbreds. Daniel H. Swigert in 1878 purchased 544 acres on the west side of Paris Pike, naming the farm Elmendorf. After a decade of breeding great horses, Swigert sold the farm to C. J. Enwright. Enwright's tenure was brief, and in 1897 James Ben Ali Haggin became the master of Elmendorf. Under Haggin's domain, Elmendorf grew to encompass some 10,000 acres. Haggin died in 1914, and the farm was fragmented into smaller tracts.

Joseph E. Widener purchased the core of Elmendorf in the early 1920s, and again the farm's size increased as Widener added adjacent tracts to bring the total acreage to more than 1,200. After Widener's death in 1943, the property again was divided into smaller tracts. Today, the farms Green Gates, Normandy, and Clovelly are situated on land once part of Elmendorf.

The 500-acre property which still carries the Elmendorf name was owned by Maxwell Gluck from 1952 until 1984, then by Jack Kent Cooke. Following Cooke's death in 1997, Elmendorf was sold to Louisville insurance magnate Dinwiddie Lampton Jr.

While James Ben Ali Haggin's champion Salvator was reportedly buried near the "Lion's Circle" intersection at Elmendorf (near the tall pillars of the Haggin mansion), his grave was never marked, nor were those of Haggin's other stars. The earliest markers are those of Fair Play and Mahubah, which date to

The columns are all that remain of James Ben Ali Haggin's mansion, Green Hills.

the period of Widener's ownership. These graves are located on what is today Normandy Farm, behind the main house. E. Barry Ryan purchased this tract in 1951, naming the farm for the French-style barn built there by Widener. Ryan's best Thoroughbreds also were interred in the plot graced by Fair Play's bronze statue.

Maxwell Gluck's champion Protagonist and stallions Speak John and Verbatim are buried on Lampton's property, in the shadow of the columns of Haggin's marble mansion, Green Hills. The columns are all that remain, the building having been razed by Widener in the late 1920s to avoid the heavy taxes levied on the mansion.

BONNIE BERYL

Bonnie Beryl was bred and raced by William Woodward. She was foaled at Claiborne in 1943, a daughter of Woodward's stallion Fighting Fox, himself a brother to Triple Crown winner Gallant Fox. Her dam was stakes winner Bonnie Maginn.

She compiled a record of four wins, three seconds, and one third in her ten starts as a two-year-old of 1945. Her victories included the Frizette and Autumn Days Stakes. At three, she beat the colts in a division

of the Jamaica Handicap, then lost to her own sex in the Acorn Stakes, the Coaching Club American Oaks, and the Gazelle Stakes. Taking on males again, she won the Empire City Stakes. She closed out her season with wins in the Delaware Oaks and Comely Handicap.

In her second career as a broodmare, Bonnie Beryl produced the stakes winners Nashville, Bug Brush, and Game Chance for Woodward. In January 1956, Barry Ryan bought her at the Keeneland mixed sale for $32,000; and she produced four foals at Normandy Farm. Monivea, a filly by Princequillo, was stakes-placed; and Fashion Critic, by Nashua, became a good producer herself. Bonnie Beryl apparently was struck by lightning and killed on May 17, 1963.

FAIR PLAY

In early issues of *The Blood-Horse*, Joe A. Estes penned a series entitled "Little Visits to the Studs." In his segment on Elmendorf, he wrote: "Fair Play stands on the hill and looks away to the north. The muscles are tense, the nostrils wide, the ears cocked forward, as if he hears sounds and sees sights which escape the flesh and blood beings passing that way. The hand that shaped him into bronze has made the cold metal apparently conscious that the ghosts of Virgil and *Glenelg, *Prince Charlie and Spendthrift are galloping up from the valley to give him greeting."

FAIR PLAY

CHESTNUT HORSE 1905·1929
CHAMPION SIRE
WHOSE SONS
AND DAUGHTERS
WON IN EXCESS OF
$2,700,000

HIS GRANDSONS
AND GRANDDAUGHTERS

The life-sized statue of Fair Play to which Estes refers was created by noted sculptor Laura Gardin Fraser and cost a reported $50,000. It stands on a base of pink marble, the matching headstones at its base marking the resting places of Fair Play and Mahubah. The statue's golden patina reflected the color of the great stallion, who died at Elmendorf on December 16, 1929.

August Belmont II bred Fair Play, who was foaled in 1905 at the Nursery Stud on Lexington's Georgetown Pike. He was by the Belmont Stakes-winning but ill-tempered Hastings, out of the mare Fairy Gold, who produced four other stakes winners besides Fair Play.

A good racehorse, Fair Play was nevertheless inferior to his contemporaries Colin and Celt. His best season was 1908 when, as a three-year-old, he numbered among his wins the Brooklyn Derby, the Coney Island Jockey Club Stakes, Lawrence Realization, First Special, and the Jerome Handicap. The following year, as a result of anti-gambling legislation's disruption of New York racing, Fair Play was shipped to England, where his sire's hot temper soon surfaced. Winless in his six starts abroad, he soon refused to train at all, and even while at stud could not be exercised on the grass.

Fair Play went to stud in 1910 and initially had limited opportunities. But when his first get reached the races, his quality as a sire became apparent: He sired eight stakes winners — forty-four percent of his foals — in his first two crops, and forty-seven stakes winners overall. Man o' War, indisputably his greatest son, blazed across the American turf in 1919 and 1920. Fair Play also sired Horse of the Year Chance Play and champion handicapper Mad Hatter, as well as Preakness Stakes winner Display and Belmont Stakes winner Chance Shot. Three times he was named America's leading sire, and he also was a three-time leading broodmare sire.

After Belmont's death in 1924, Joseph Widener acquired the twenty-year-old Fair Play for $100,000. The stallion served five seasons at Elmendorf before his death in 1929. *The Thoroughbred Record* reported:

> Fair Play is dead. The illustrious scion of a mighty race and one of the greatest progenitors this country has ever known answered the final call in his paddock at Elmendorf on Monday morning last shortly after eleven o'clock. Fair Play died as he lived: game to the core…And at Elmendorf he is buried. On a sloping emi-

A detail of a statue of Fair Play in the cemetery at Normandy Farm, which once was part of the vast Elmendorf property.

nence overlooking the training barn his grave was made and there space has been left for Mahubah, when her time comes, his mate in the production of the greatest of all great horses, Man o' War.[1]

FIRM POLICY

One of the best horses to carry the Normandy silks was Firm Policy, whom Barry Ryan bred, owned, and trained. In the words of Charles Hatton, she was "excelled only by that avid numismatist Cicada,"

Christopher Chenery's great filly. Hatton described Firm Policy for the *American Racing Manual* as "a mare of charming individuality. She is a dark bay by Princequillo, who breeds the St. Simon type of horse with remarkable regularity. Firm Policy is about 16 hands, closely coupled and balanced like a see-saw, the withers and croup nearly level. Her legs set on well under her and she has a round, fairly deep middle."

Firm Policy started just six times at two in 1961, tallying three wins, two seconds, and a third, for earnings of $36,490. She met Cicada twice, dropping a head decision in the Astarita and missing by a half-length in the Frizette Stakes. She rested at Normandy Farm before her three-year-old campaign.

Firm Policy began her sophomore year with easy victories in two allowance events before taking on the division leaders in the Mother Goose Stakes, where she again lost to Cicada by a length. In the Coaching Club American Oaks, she came within a nose of her rival, but both finished behind Darby Dan's filly Bramalea. Firm Policy then took the Monmouth Oaks (in which Cicada did not run) and a division of the Test Stakes. She had her first and only victory over Cicada that season in the Alabama Stakes on a muddy track at Saratoga. She finished third in the Beldame and the Spinster and off the board in the Gazelle Handicap.

Firm Policy started five times for four wins as a four-year-old, vanquishing Cicada one last time in the Top Flight Handicap. She sustained a minor injury in the New Castle Stakes and was sent back to the farm to join the broodmare band. Her best foal was the stakes-placed colt Senate Whip, but she was less successful as a producer than she had been as a racer. She died in 1985.

MAHUBAH

Mahubah raced only briefly, recording one win early in her three-year-old season. She was retired to stud in 1913 and was bred to Fair Play, who would sire each of her five foals. In addition to Man o' War, she produced the Jockey Club Gold Cup winner and sire My Play and the winners Masda and Playfellow. Masda went on to a successful career as a broodmare for the Whitney Stud, counting Assault and, more recently, Prove Out among her descendants.

Mahubah's death was reported in the October 17, 1931 issue of *The Thoroughbred Record*: "As the dam of

Man o' War Mahubah joined the immortals and as such her fame will endure as long as the traditions of the Turf survive."[2] She was interred next to Fair Play, in the shadow of the stallion's bronze likeness.

ORMONDA

Widener bought Ormonda while she was in training. A useful runner, she had won twelve of thirty-two races, and Widener thought she would make a good addition to the broodmare band at his recently acquired Elmendorf. The mare returned his confidence by becoming one of the most important producers of her day.

Ormonda's first foal was Orageuse, a 1922 daughter of Wrack and a winner at the track. Barren the following year, Ormanda, in 1924, foaled Osmand, a gelding who was one of the best sprinters of his generation. Next followed two fillies who never reached the races but who became good producers: Golden Melody, dam of stakes winners King Cole and National Anthem; and Dustwhirl, dam of Triple Crown winner Whirlaway as well as of stakes winners Reaping Reward and Feudal Lord. Ormonda's next two foals were the winners Alert and Robinson Crusoe. Her foals of 1931 and 1932 died as youngsters. Her 1933 foal, Brevity, was victorious in the Champagne Stakes and Florida Derby and was narrowly beaten in the 1936 Kentucky Derby. Her last three foals included a steeplechase stakes winner, Binder, by Sickle.

Ormonda was euthanized on January 8, 1944, at the advanced age of twenty-eight, and was given an honored place in the Elmendorf cemetery.

OSMAND

A chestnut son of Sweeper II and Ormonda, Osmand was described as a colt "of herculean proportions," whose size resulted in his being gelded before he began his racing career. At two, he won at first asking; and accumulated a record of six wins in seven starts. Among his victories were the Flash and National Stakes and the Eastern Shore and Nursery Handicaps. His only loss that season was a third in the Saratoga Special to his stablemate Chance Shot.

Osmand's first start at three was the Kentucky Derby, at a distance of ten furlongs — certainly beyond his optimum. But the gelding acquitted himself nobly, dropping a head decision to Whiskery. At Saratoga, he captured the Saranac Handicap as co-top weight. Later, at Belmont, he finished a close third in the Manhattan Handicap. His other wins that season included the Jerome and Capitol Handicaps.

At four, "He added to his renown and became an idol of race-goers by winning six out of eight races," wrote Neil Newman in the 1930 book *Famous Horses of the American Turf*. Osmand began the season by taking the Toboggan Handicap from Scapa Flow. His only two defeats that year followed, in the Metropolitan and the Memorial Day Handicaps. He then won the Carter and American Legion Handicaps and the Havre de Grace Cup. He capped his year with a win over Black Maria in the Laurel Stakes.

At five, Osmand won the Toboggan, Memorial Day, Carter, and Fall Highweight Handicaps — the latter under 140 pounds, in time just two-fifths of a second off the track record. Unsoundness stopped him after his sensational performance in the Fall Highweight.

Osmand returned to the races at six and seven, but scored only one win in those two seasons. He was retired to the life of a pensioner, and lived to the age of twenty-seven. He was laid to rest in 1951, not far from Ormonda.

QUICK PITCH

Quick Pitch, trained by Barry Ryan and owned by his brother, Fortune P. Ryan, was by Charlevoix, a son of Princequillo, and out of the winning mare The

Ghizeh, by Questionnaire. Charles Hatton of the *American Racing Manual* described him as a medium-sized pale chestnut with an attractive head; a deep girth; and good, straight hind legs. He noted that "Charlevoix' son has been described as an individual with a wild, white eye and a pugnacious disposition. He is intensely opinionated and on provocation will kick the shortening out of a cake."

Quick Pitch won the Brighton Beach, Bernard Baruch, Niagara, and Jockey Club Handicaps and the Fair Play Stakes before losing interest in flat racing. Switched to hurdles, he found his niche and went on to win his initial outing over fences at the age of six. He placed third in the New York Turf Writer's in his first stakes attempt. He won six of his seven starts as a seven-year-old and became the 1963 steeplechasing champion.

Quick Pitch's style was to go to the front immediately and dare anyone to catch him. He set a course record in a handicap event at two and one-sixteenth miles in the second start of his seven-year-old season. Next, he won the Bushwick Hurdle by an easy three lengths. He came home in front in the Holly Tree Handicap, then carried 166 pounds to victory in the Midsummer Handicap. In the Lovely Night Handicap, he sailed home eighteen lengths ahead of his closest pursuer in record time — carrying a staggering 170 pounds. In his final start, the Rouge Dragon Handicap, he carried a burden of 172 pounds, and won by sixteen lengths in record time — despite stumbling at the final fence.

Injured while preparing for his next race, Quick Pitch ended his career with a record of twenty-three wins in sixty-six starts. Over fences, he had won seven of nine. He enjoyed life as a pensioner at Normandy until his death in 1983 at the age of twenty-three. His memorial is a large, flat stone similar to surrounding markers, including the gravestone of Sickle.

SICKLE

Bred in England by Lord Derby, Sickle was by the emerging sire-of-sires Phalaris and out of Selene, who later produced Sickle's brother Pharamond II — also a successful sire in the United States — and the great Hyperion. A neat, medium-sized colt with lots of quality, Sickle enjoyed a successful two-year-old campaign, winning the Mersey, Prince of Wales' Stakes, and Boscawen Post Stakes. He placed second in the important Middle Park and July Stakes and third in the Champagne Stakes.

Sickle was winless in three starts as a three-year-old, although he did finish second (while giving nineteen pounds) in the Union Jack Stakes and third in the classic Two Thousand Guineas. He entered Lord Derby's stud as a four-year-old and was imported to America later that year by Joseph Widener. Sickle was to stand at Elmendorf for three seasons, with Widener having the option to purchase him.

In 1932, the final year of Widener's option, Sickle's first foal crop made their mark abroad. Widener promptly bought the stallion, and Sickle went on to lead the American sire list in 1936 and 1938. Among his best runners were the champions Stagehand, Star Pilot, and Gossip II. But it was his son Unbreakable who, through Polynesian and Native Dancer, continued his male line.

Sickle died unexpectedly on December 26, 1943, apparently from an enlarged spleen. He was buried near that other great progenitor, Fair Play.

STAGECRAFT

By Fair Play out of Franconia, by Sweep, Stagecraft was foaled in 1929. She was a good runner, winning three of her seven starts at age two, among them the Astoria Stakes and the Beldame Handicap. At three, she started only twice before being retired to the broodmare band at Elmendorf as the result of a wind affliction.

All of Stagecraft's foals were by Sickle. Her best was the three-year-old champion Stagehand, who defeated older rivals, including Seabiscuit and Pompoon, in the Santa Anita Handicap in track-record time. Stagehand's brother, Sceneshifter, was second in the Belmont and third in the Dwyer Stakes. (Unfortunately, neither achieved great success at stud.)

Stagecraft died suddenly on March 13, 1939, while in foal to Blenheim II. She was buried near her sire, her grave marked by a small headstone of pink marble.

CLOVELLY FARM

Robin Scully's Clovelly Farm has perhaps the largest Thoroughbred cemetery devoted exclusively to mares. Each of the sixteen flat stones lying not far from the Elkhorn Creek marks the grave of one of the outstanding mares Scully has owned or boarded for clients. Among them are Epsom Oaks winner Lupe II,

Regal Exception, and the New Zealand heroine Yahabeebe.

Scully purchased the 252-acre Eaton Ridge Farm on Hughes Lane near Lexington in 1965, and added it to a seventy-five-acre tract on Paris Pike that was known as Clovelly Farm. He augmented the Hughes Lane property by buying an additional 168 acres from Normandy Farm. All of the Hughes Lane property was at one time part of the Elmendorf empire, and buildings remain that date to the time of Widener's ownership. The farm's main residence was once the home of P. A. B. Widener III, and one barn is a variation of designer Horace Trumbauer's "circle barns:" an oval structure that includes stalls and a covered training track. The roof is adorned with ceramic animals — including a brilliant peacock — a hallmark of the French tradition. The hill overlooking the training barn was the original site of the graves of Fair Play and Mahubah; the graves later were removed to their present location.

Scully breeds to race but annually offers yearlings at the Saratoga sales. Those retained for the Scully racing stable are broken at the farm before being sent to Europe. Clovelly also boards mares for clients.

The Normandy barn dates to the Elmendorf era.

A picturesque drive winds among the sycamores and crosses a narrow bridge over Elkhorn Creek, leading to the farm's equine cemetery. The flat stones, not visible from the drive, are situated in a peaceful spot near the trees that line the creek.

CATERINA II

Timeform began its review of Caterina II's two-year-old performances with the comment, "There were few, if any, faster two-year-olds than Caterina in 1965." Indeed, the gray daughter of Princely Gift and Radiopye was a flier. Although she won just two races in her initial season, she showed her talent by finishing a game second by just a half length to the older Polyfoto in the Nunthorpe Stakes.

Scully bought Caterina II for 13,000 guineas at the December sales at Newmarket, at the close of the filly's two-year-old season. Caterina II went on to win two of her five starts at three, leading all the way in

the Stewards' Handicap and defeating July Cup winner Lucasland and her previous year's rival Polyfoto in the Nunthorpe Stakes.

Caterina II retired from racing to become a successful broodmare, producing eleven foals for Clovelly. Her first, the Warfare colt Mug Punter, became her first stakes winner. Caterina II's best offspring — stakes winners Ancient Regime, Olden, and Cricket Ball — resulted from matings to Olden Times. Ancient Regime, foaled in 1978, captured the Prix Morny and was named champion two-year-old filly in France and later produced stakes winners La Grande Epoque, Crack Regiment, and Rami. Olden won the Debutante at Churchill and Keeneland's Bewitch, and Cricket Ball was a multiple group winner in France and a stakes winner in the United States.

Caterina II died in 1989. Her daughter, Ancient Regime, died in 1998 and is the most recently interred in the Clovelly cemetery.

LUPE II

Racing for Mrs. Stanhope Joel, Lupe II captured the fillies' classic Oaks at three in 1970 and the Coronation Cup the following season. Upon her retirement, she proved an outstanding broodmare, with five of her ten foals becoming stakes winners.

At two, the daughter of Primera and Alcoa made just one start, winning a six-furlong maiden event. Timeform noted that Lupe II was "likely to go on to better things at 3 yrs." And she did, opening her season by winning the Cheshire Oaks, then the Epsom Oaks by four lengths. In her next race, the Yorkshire Oaks, she set the pace, was passed by Highest Hopes, but fought back gamely to win. She finished sixth in her final start of the season, France's Prix Vermeille.

Lupe II won both her starts at four: the Coronation Cup and Princess of Wales's Stakes. Timeform commented, "Lupe is an attractive filly and a most courageous one. She never knew when she was beaten."

Her five stakes-winning foals were Lascaux, Legend of France, Leonardo Da Vinci, L'Ile Du Reve, and Louveterie. (Louveterie has continued the line admirably, having already produced champions Loup Sauvage and Loup Solitaire.) Lupe II died at Clovelly in 1989.

REGAL EXCEPTION

Robin Scully purchased the classic-winning mare Rajput Princess in France in 1967, and mated her with the great European champion Ribot. The resulting filly was named Regal Exception. In just two starts as a two-year-old in 1971, Regal Exception finished third once. At three, she began by beating maidens but then ran poorly in the Prix Vanteaux at Longchamp. She did no better in her next start, placing fifth out of six.

Before her next engagement, in England's Oaks, Timeform stated that "Her breeding apart...Regal Exception had little to recommend her..." But she showed tremendous improvement in that race and finished second to Ginevra. Next, she ran in Ireland's Oaks. Wearing blinkers for the first time, she beat Arkadina and Pidget in an impressive showing.

Regal Exception was soundly beaten in her next race, the Prix Vermeille, but rebounded with a strong effort to finish fourth to San-San in the Prix de l'Arc de Triomphe. In a notable change of opinion, Timeform remarked, "She was a very fine staying filly in a year noted for the quality of its staying fillies."

Regal Exception joined the Clovelly broodmare band at age four and produced the stakes winners Twilight Hour, Sikorsky, and Orban as well as the stakes-placed Beyond Recall before her death in 1990.

Chapter 6 – Spendthrift Farm

Leslie Combs II developed Spendthrift Farm into one of the nation's foremost commercial breeding operations. Named for the great horse raced by Combs' great-grandfather, Daniel Swigert, the original 127-acre farm grew to encompass nearly 4,000 acres at its height. A pioneer in the area of stallion syndications, Combs purchased Nashua for a then-record of more than $1 million.

In addition to his success in the business of stallion syndication, Combs was a master at marketing yearlings for the annual summer sales at Keeneland. Spendthrift was the leading consignor there for fifteen consecutive years in the 1950s and early '60s, and again for two years in the early 1980s. The first yearlings to be sold for $100,000, $250,000, and $500,000 were from Spendthrift consignments.

Spendthrift Farm was incorporated in 1977 and went public in 1983. Combs and his son Brownell sold their interests in the farm in 1985, and Spendthrift later filed for bankruptcy. In 1994, the farm's remaining 636 acres were sold at auction in two tracts. The smaller tract, consisting of 140 acres, included the stallion complex and the main house.

Two Spendthrift equine cemeteries still exist, one near the stallion complex and one at the "Lion's Circle." An article by Jim Bolus which appeared in *Keeneland* magazine reported that other burial sites existed, but these have apparently been lost over the years. Some stones were moved to the Lion's Circle cemetery from other locations.

Nashua's bronze statue dominates the cemetery near the stallion complex, on the property that retains the Spendthrift name. Large memorials to Nashua,

The Lion's Circle marks the drive to the Green Hills mansion and used to be a part of the Elmendorf empire.

Gallant Man, and Raise a Native lie directly in front of the stallion barn once called the "Nashua Motel." Other stones lie to the right of that barn.

The second cemetery is located at the famous intersection called the Lion's Circle — named for the statuary that once marked the drive to the Green Hills mansion — on property once owned by Elmendorf. Combs added this land, which had been George D. Widener's Old Kenney Farm, to the Spendthrift empire in 1962. Widener's horses remained after the sale; many of them are buried in the cemetery at the Lion's Circle, as are a number of Spendthrift's great mares. Nashua's great rival, Swaps, also is buried there, although his headstone was later moved to the Kentucky Derby Museum in Louisville. Twenty-eight headstones lie within the hedges that mark the circle; five additional markers are situated outside, the hedges along a fence line.

THE LION'S CIRCLE

AFFECTIONATELY

Affectionately's obituary in the April 16, 1979 issue of *The Blood-Horse* noted that "Affectionately was a

Affectionately was a two-time champion.

queenly mare which was a champion runner and a major link in one of the most important producing families of modern American breeding." A daughter of Swaps and Searching (a stakes winner who earned more than $300,000), she came from the prolific family of the great La Troienne. Affectionately was bred by the partnership of Isidor Bieber and Hirsch Jacobs, and trained by the latter.

Named for her amenable disposition, Affectionately came out in January of her two-year-old season, winning her three-furlong debut. The 1962 edition of *American Race Horses* notes that "Her sweet disposition did not dilute her competitive spirit." Her two-year-old campaign did not end until October, by which time she had won nine of her thirteen starts. Among her triumphs were the Fashion, Polly Drummond, National Stallion, Astoria, Sorority, and Spinaway Stakes. Although she failed to capture any of the major fall races in her division, she had accomplished enough to be named champion two-year-old filly by the *Turf and Sport Digest* in the days before the Eclipse Awards put an end to multiple divisional champions.

The following season, Affectionately won just one stakes race. Her four-year-old campaign was more productive, with stakes victories in the Correction, Interborough, Las Flores, Sport Page, and Vosburgh Handicaps. She beat males in the latter two. At five, she had her best season since her two-year-old campaign, winning the Correction, Distaff, Toboggan, Top Flight, Liberty Belle, and Vagrancy Handicaps. She beat the boys in the Toboggan and carried 132 pounds to victory in the Liberty Belle. In one of her greatest performances, she carried 137 pounds — twenty-six more than the runner-up — home first in the Vagrancy. Again she received championship honors from the *Turf and Sport Digest*.

When Affectionately's career ended, she had won twenty-eight of her fifty-two starts and had earned $546,659. Noted racing writer Charles Hatton gave her this praise: "Affectionately is a lovely individual of the curvaceous sprinting type. The development of her hindquarters is conspicuous and she is balanced like a see-saw. Her deportment is all one could wish, as she is poised and placid in the paddock and on parade, though she is simply an explosion of sand at the start."

AFFECTIONATELY
1960 — 1979
SWAPS — SEARCHING

Affectionately's best produce was her first foal, Personality. A son of Hail to Reason, Personality won the 1970 Preakness and other major stakes to earn championship honors that year. None of her three later foals made a mark on the track or at stud. On March 31, 1979, she suffered an apparent heart attack and died at Spendthrift Farm.

EIGHT THIRTY

A son of the brilliantly fast Pilate, out of the High Time matron Dinner Time, the cleverly named Eight Thirty was described by noted racing writer John Hervey: "In color he is a chestnut, with two white front pasterns, has a fine, masculine head, an elegant neck, is symmetrical at all points, combining power with quality; his legs are of exceptionally good bone and chiseling."

Eight Thirty's racing career extended over four seasons, and in each he was among the best of his generation. Plagued by hind-leg soreness, he was nevertheless a model of consistency, being just three times unplaced while recording sixteen wins in twenty-seven starts. As a two-year-old of 1938, he was no match for El Chico, who handled him authoritatively in both the United States Hotel Stakes and the Saratoga Special. Eight Thirty's stakes wins that season included the Christiana and the Flash Stakes. He crossed the finish line first in the Albany Handicap, but was disqualified for interference. It was after the Albany that he sustained the hind-leg injury, striking himself during a training outing.

Eight Thirty's initial efforts as a three-year-old were disappointing. He rebounded to win the Diamond State Stakes, then headed for a sensational Saratoga meet, where he swept the Wilson, Travers, and Whitney Stakes and the Saratoga Handicap — defeating high-class older horses in three of the four. His three-year-old campaign ended when he was pulled up in distress after the Whitney.

In his four-year-old debut, Eight Thirty demonstrated his versatility, sprinting six furlongs to take the Toboggan Handicap in near-record time. He then added the Suburban Handicap before dropping the Brooklyn to Isolater. Another defeat in the Butler Handicap followed, but in his next start, the Massachusetts Handicap, Eight Thirty defeated Challedon in track-record time. He returned to Saratoga to take the Wilson Stakes a second time, but his troublesome hind leg stopped him once again after he finished third in the Saratoga Handicap.

At five, Eight Thirty made only two starts before his soreness sent him to stud, but both were brilliant efforts. In the Toboggan Handicap, he faced the good horse Roman under the burden of 129 pounds and won rather easily. In his final start, the Metropolitan Handicap, he carried 132 pounds — nine to thirty pounds more than each of his eight rivals — but again won convincingly.

Highly regarded as a stallion prospect, Eight Thirty for a time revived Rock Sand's male line in the United States. He sired forty-five stakes winners before he was

pensioned in 1958. His sons Sailor, Bolero, and Royal Coinage each sired notable horses, although the male line has not carried on to the present day. Eight Thirty's daughters were valued broodmares, producing top runners such as Belmont winner Jaipur, champion two-year-old filly Evening Out, Jester, Rare Treat, and Lady Be Good. He died of old age on April 7, 1965, and joined his dam Dinner Time in the Lion's Circle cemetery.

GOLD DIGGER

Gold Digger, foaled in 1962, was a daughter of the Spendthrift stallion Nashua and out of Sequence, a member of the famed Myrtlewood family. Gold Digger was a good race mare, but it was as a broodmare that she achieved her greatest success.

In her career, Gold Digger won ten races — among them two editions of the Gallorette Stakes and the Columbiana Handicap — and earned $127,255. Her second foal, by Raise a Native, was the good sprinter Mr. Prospector, who showed brilliant speed before suffering a career-ending injury. Put to stud in Florida, he met with immediate success and soon was moved to Claiborne Farm, where he led the American sire list

twice and sired more than 160 stakes winners before his death in 1999.

Gold Digger also was the dam of Kentucky Gold, a full brother to Mr. Prospector who brought a record $625,000 at the 1974 Keeneland summer sale; and the stakes winners Lillian Russell and Gold Standard. Pensioned in 1984, she was humanely destroyed on February 21, 1990, at the age of twenty, because of her declining condition. Her grave does not lie within the Lion's Circle itself but rather along a fence line that borders the intersection.

HIGH FLEET

High Fleet was foaled in 1933 at Widener's Pennsylvania nursery, Erdenheim Stud. She was by Jack High, out of the Man o' War mare Armada. A well-made, racy-looking chestnut, she raced but six times at two, recording two wins and placing third in the Schuylerville Stakes.

At three, High Fleet developed into a consistent, high-class filly. She began her season with front-running wins in allowance tests before tackling stakes company in the Acorn Stakes, where she finished a scant nose behind Blue Sheen after setting the pace.

The year-end review *American Race Horses* of 1936 called the Acorn "one of the most exciting two-horse duels that a pair of game fillies ever provided…Closely matched in speed, both were courageous, neither would yield." High Fleet gained her revenge in the

Gold Digger was a good race mare and a superlative producer.

Coaching Club American Oaks, defeating the pace-setting Blue Sheen with the benefit of a ten-pound weight advantage. High Fleet then added wins in the Blossom Time Handicap, Mary Dyer Handicap, New England Oaks, and Weybossett Handicap. In her last race of the season, the Potomac Handicap, she went up against colts and dropped a close decision to the late-flying Tatterdemalion, in perhaps the best effort of her career. Named the champion of her division, she then retired to her winter quarters.

High Fleet did not show the same dominance at four, although she did win the Catskill, Ritchie, and Baltimore Autumn Handicaps. The Ritchie Handicap, which she won by a neck from Wise Prince, was the final start of her career. In *American Race Horses*, John Hervey noted: "It was a brilliant adieu to the public on the part of the filly, placing a highly polished capstone on the edifice of her career. She retired perfectly sound after her thirty races, and not only was regarded as one of the fastest and most consistent, but most beautiful fillies of her time."

Retired to join Widener's broodmare band, High Fleet produced just four foals, among them the steeplechase stakes winner Fleettown and the stakes-placed Fleet Command. She died in 1952 and was interred not far from Armada.

ST. JAMES

One of the earliest graves at the Lion's Circle is that of George Widener's St. James. The son of Ambassador IV and Bobolink II was consigned by Arthur Hancock's Claiborne Farm to the 1922 Saratoga yearling sale, where Widener purchased him for $9,000.

St. James showed ability, if not durability, in his brief racing career. Second in his debut, the colt made his next start against stakes company in the United States Hotel Stakes. He won that six-furlong event, then added the Saratoga Special. The Grand Union Hotel Stakes saw him fail under 130 pounds, giving eighteen pounds to the eventual winner. Again assigned 130 for the Hopeful Stakes, he was fourth to Diogenes, who carried fifteen fewer pounds. He finally avenged himself in the Futurity Stakes, winning over Diogenes while again carrying 130 pounds.

St. James started just once as a three-year-old, defeating Zev in the Paumonok Handicap. He stood his first season at the Old Kenney Farm in 1925. His best offspring included Jamestown, Sailor Beware, Evening, Don Guzman, and Tatanne. Jamestown sired the good horse Johnstown, who, in turn, became the broodmare sire of Spendthrift's million-dollar stallion, Nashua.

St. James died in 1943 at the age of twenty-two from colic. Buried near him at the Lion's Circle are his son Jamestown and his daughters Tatanne and Evening.

STRAIGHT DEAL

Like Affectionately, Straight Deal was bred by the Bieber-Jacobs stable and trained by Hirsch Jacobs. She, too, was from La Troienne's family, her dam being No Fiddling, a granddaughter of that great matron. Her sire was Jacobs' star Hail to Reason, a brilliant two-year-old who became a top-class stallion.

Unlike Affectionately, however, Straight Deal was not a precocious two-year-old, winning just two races in her initial season. At three, she captured the Hollywood Oaks and the Ladies Handicap. Her improvement continued at four, and she won five stakes in 1966. It was at five, however, that she became a champion.

In 1967, Straight Deal won eight of her twenty-two

races, scoring in the Delaware, Top Flight, Vineland, Bed o' Roses, and Orchid Handicaps and in the Spinster Stakes. She carried top weight in each of her races against her own sex. She was third in the Whitney and Aqueduct Stakes against males, and was named champion handicap mare at year's end.

Straight Deal's career totals attest to her durability: ninety-nine starts, twenty-one wins, twenty-one seconds, and nine thirds. Her earnings of $733,020 ranked her second only to Cicada among fillies and mares.

Retired to stud after her five-year-old campaign,

Straight Deal produced the stakes winners Desiree, Reminiscing, and Belonging, daughters who have proven valuable broodmares. She was humanely destroyed at the age of twenty and was buried not far from Affectionately.

TURN-TO

Turn-to's racing career was one of short-lived brilliance. One of the better two-year-olds of 1953, he was sidelined early in his three-year-old year by a bowed tendon and retired to Claiborne. His stud career fulfilled the promise he had shown at the track.

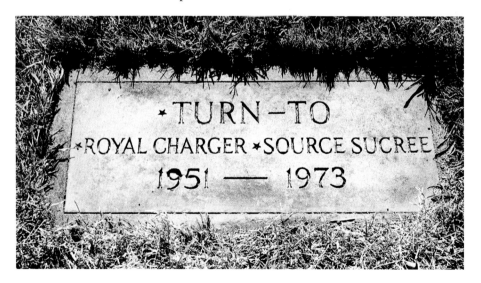

Claud Tanner imported Turn-to (carrying the name Source Royal) from Ireland as a yearling. Tanner died shortly after the colt's arrival, and Captain Harry F. Guggenheim bought the yearling at Keeneland's summer sale, soon changing his name to the nautically inspired Turn-to.

Turn-to won three of his five starts as a two-year-old, finishing second and third in his other two outings. He romped to a five-length win in a maiden event in his debut, then finished behind Porterhouse in the Saratoga Special. But Turn-to was awarded the victory, as Porterhouse's rider had struck Turn-to with his whip. His other stakes victory came in the Garden State Stakes.

Turn-to's initial outing as a three-year-old indicated that he would be a force to be reckoned with: He came home easily in a seven-furlong allowance event, then added another facile win at one and one-sixteenth miles. His first major race of the season was the Flamingo Stakes, which he won convincingly. Unfortunately, the Flamingo proved to be his final race, for he bowed a tendon shortly thereafter.

Turn-to enjoyed tremendous success at stud. He was moved from Claiborne to Spendthrift with the rest of

Guggenheim's horses in 1960. Among his sons were First Landing, the brilliant Hail to Reason, and Sir Gaylord, all of whom were successful stallions themselves. As a result, his male line continues to flourish today. Turn-to died on June 15, 1973, and was buried near his dam, Source Sucree, whom Guggenheim imported in 1953.

THE STALLION CEMETERY

CARO

Bred in Ireland, Caro raced primarily in France, and entered stud in that country before he was exported to the United States in 1977. He was by the crack sprinter Fortino out of the very stout mare Chambord, a daughter of St. Leger winner Chamossaire. Caro's own aptitude proved to lie somewhere between these two extremes. A very good two-year-old, he proved quite capable of staying the European classic distance of one and one-half miles as a three- and four-year-old.

At two, Caro won his four-and-one-half-furlong debut, and finished second in the 1969 Prix d'Arenberg and Prix Eclipse, and he looked the sort to improve the following season. As a three-year-old,

Caro proved that he was indeed a very good colt. His two victories came in the Prix d'Ispahan and in the classic Poule d'Essai des Poulains (by disqualification of Faraway Son). He finished a good third in the French Derby to Sassafras and Roll of Honour. Timeform's *Racehorses of 1970* noted that "Caro is a good sort of colt, lengthy and strong. He stays a mile and a half so well that the distance may not be the limit of his stamina, and he seems to act on any going. Not the least of his qualities is his gameness and consistency, and he should have another good season in the top class as a four-year-old."

As indeed he did. Caro won three of his five starts in 1971, and at year's end, he was ranked champion older horse in France. His victories came in his first three outings of the year, in the Prix d'Harcourt, Prix Ganay, and Prix Dollar. His only off-the-board finish was a respectable fourth in the Prix de l'Arc de Triomphe.

Retired to stud, Caro was an immediate success. Among his French-foaled runners were the champions Theia and Madelia and the French Derby winner Crystal Palace. His success continued after his move to Spendthrift. Among his best North American runners were the Canadian champion With Approval, champion turf horse Cozzene, and the Kentucky Derby-winning filly Winning Colors. Sons Crystal Palace and Cozzene have been successful at stud, with Crystal Palace becoming leading sire in France. Caro

Gallant Man was an outstanding racehorse and sire.

died at Spendthrift of an apparent heart attack, in 1989. He was twenty-two.

GALLANT MAN

Nicknamed "Mighty Man" by his handlers, the diminutive Gallant Man was living proof that good racehorses come in all shapes and sizes. As Charles Hatton wrote in his account of Gallant Man's 1957 campaign in the *American Racing Manual*, "Quality is not something to be gauged by either the standard or the tape. It is the size of the heart that matters."

The son of Prix de l'Arc de Triomphe winner Migoli and the crack mare Majideh topped out at just under 15.2 hands. Hatton called him "a lustrous bay with black points, a star and a magnificent head….His eyes …are large, gentle and expressive. He has deep, strong jowls with ample room at the throatlatch, a small muzzle, neatly turned ear and a stout neck…He has a well-developed shoulder and wither…flat knees, heavier bone than most horses of his size, rather rough fetlocks and tends to toe out, though not sharply. His middle is deep and round…with a strong, slightly arched loin and broad, flat hips…The hocks are a bit behind him, but are strong…"

In 1955, Ralph Lowe purchased Gallant Man as a yearling from the Aga Khan in a package deal. The colt was not regarded as the most promising of the lot, but he went on to outshine the others on the track. He was a bit of a slow starter at two, breaking his maiden in his third outing and then winning a pair of minor races.

Early in his sophomore season, however, Gallant Man's quality emerged — even surrounded as he was by rivals Bold Ruler, Round Table, and Gen. Duke. His seasonal debut, on January 3, was an allowance test at six furlongs. "Mighty Man" defeated Calumet's Gen. Duke, setting a new track record. He then scored his first stakes victory, in Hialeah's Hibiscus Stakes. In the Wood Memorial, he missed by just a nose to Bold Ruler after leading in the stretch. (Bold Ruler's winning time established a new track record for the one and one-eighth miles.)

As a result of his preliminary efforts, Gallant Man was highly regarded for the Kentucky Derby. He came within a nose of pulling it off, falling just short of catching Iron Liege. His rider, a young Bill Shoemaker, had misjudged the finish line, standing in the irons ever so briefly but likely costing his horse the

*GALLANT MAN
BAY HORSE, *MIGOLI—*MAJIDEH
1954 —— 1988
CLASSIC WINNER OF THE BELMONT STAKES AND $510,355.
SIRE OF MORE THAN 50 STAKES WINNERS
AND A LEADING BROODMARE SIRE

race. Gallant Man did not contest the Preakness, which went to Bold Ruler. His prep for the Belmont Stakes was a winning effort in the Peter Pan Handicap. He then took on Bold Ruler again in the Belmont, his cause aided by the entry of stablemate Bold Nero as a pacesetter. Bold Nero fulfilled his role with gusto, pushing the free-running Bold Ruler through suicidal fractions. Gallant Man came on late to score by eight lengths. His time of 2:26 3/5 set a record that stood for sixteen years, until it was demolished by Secretariat.

Continuing his winning ways, Gallant Man finished first in the Travers Stakes and the Nassau County Handicap, defeating good older horses in the latter in track-record time. His last win of the season was the Jockey Club Gold Cup. The Trenton Handicap, in which he finished second to Bold Ruler, was his last start of the year.

At four, Gallant Man started just five times, winning three races. He took the Metropolitan Mile from Bold Ruler despite carrying four pounds more than his rival. He then traveled to the West Coast to capture the Hollywood Gold Cup and the Sunset Handicaps, carrying 132 pounds in the latter. In his final race, the Sysonby Handicap, he finished fifth and pulled up lame. Combs had previously purchased a considerable interest in the colt, and Gallant Man retired to stud at Spendthrift with a record of fourteen wins in twenty-six starts and $510,355 in earnings.

In an article for *The Thoroughbred Record*, Timothy Capps summed up Gallant Man's career: "Packed into that tiny frame was the ability to go short, go long, go fast, carry tons of lead, and do it in championship style, year-end votes notwithstanding."[1] Although he never earned championship honors at the track, he was elected to the Racing Hall of Fame in 1987.

Gallant Man proved a successful sire, his fifty-one stakes winners including the champion Gallant Bloom, Gallant Romeo, Coraggioso, and My Gallant. His daughters produced the champions Lord Avie and Guilty Conscience. He was the longest-lived member of the great triumvirate from the 1954 crop: Bold Ruler, Round Table, and Gallant Man. He was euthanized on September 7, 1988, at the advanced age of thirty-four, and was buried near Spendthrift's other great sires, Nashua and Raise a Native.

MAJESTIC PRINCE

Majestic Prince was one of those exceptional Thoroughbreds whose racetrack performances exceeded already high expectations. The flashy chestnut was by the brilliant Raise a Native, and his dam was an unraced daughter of the early Spendthrift stallion Royal Charger. Charles Hatton described the colt as well muscled, with a short back and excellent quarters and good, straight hind legs. "He has a charming disposition, free of any meanness," Hatton wrote.

The handsome colt was consigned to the 1967 Keeneland summer yearling sale, where Frank McMahon, part owner of the dam, bought out Combs' interest in the colt for a then-record $250,000. Majestic Prince was sent to the California barn of trainer Johnny Longden, who in his riding career had piloted the great Count Fleet. Longden was patient with his expensive charge, bringing the colt out late in his two-year-old year to score maiden and allowance wins.

The following year, Majestic Prince encountered no serious competition on the West Coast. He scored successive wins in the Los Feliz, San Vicente, and San Jacinto Stakes and the Santa Anita Derby. His final prep for the Kentucky Derby was the Stepping Stone, in which he shaded Churchill's seven-furlong track record. Entering the Derby undefeated in seven starts, he found in that field a horse to test his courage, the East Coast star Arts and Letters; Majestic Prince won by a neck. Two weeks later, in the Preakness Stakes, Majestic Prince again led Arts and Letters at the wire, by a head. Following these two grueling races, Longden felt it best to rest the colt. McMahon overruled, and Majestic Prince met Arts and Letters for a third time in the Belmont Stakes. This time Arts and Letters proved strongest, winning by five and one-half lengths.

Majestic Prince then returned to the West Coast, where a series of physical ailments kept him away from the races throughout the summer and fall. He suffered another injury during training for his four-year-old campaign and was syndicated for $1.8 million and retired to stud at his birthplace.

Majestic Prince was moderately successful in his brief career at stud. His son Coastal won the Belmont over Spectacular Bid, avenging his sire's loss in that classic. His other stakes winners included Majestic Light and Sensitive Prince. His best representative at stud has turned out to be Majestic Light.

Majestic Prince collapsed in his stall on April 22, 1981, at the age of fifteen; an autopsy revealed a ruptured aorta. His stud career had ended prematurely, as had his racing career. But those who saw him flash across the American Turf will remember him as a bright spot in the annals of racing.

NASHUA

William Woodward Sr.'s breeding operation produced many high-class runners, but perhaps the best was the one he did not live to see race. Woodward died when Nashua was a yearling; and his son, William Woodward Jr., inherited his father's bloodstock. Foaled in 1952, the bay colt was a member of Nasrullah's first American crop, from Segula, a daughter of the Belmont winner Johnstown. Segula herself placed in the Coaching Club American Oaks.

Originally slated by the senior Woodward to race in England, Nashua was sent instead to Florida to be trained by James "Sunny Jim" Fitzsimmons, the dean of American trainers. Nashua was a big, sound colt, with something of Nasrullah's quirky temperament. In *American Race Horses* of 1955, Joe A. Estes wrote:

Nashua…was a playboy who found distraction in everything. He reared and snatched his handlers around in the walking ring. He was "fractious at the post." He played cat-and-mouse with opponents when he might have whaled the daylights out of them. He watched the infield and the stands. He shied from the strange objects which came out on the track to take pictures. He propped near the finish. Orders from jockeys he ignored, or, if the whip was laid on to the extent that he finally admitted having felt it, he was likely to respond by going sidewise. What he could have done in the way of being a racehorse, if he had put his mind to it, was never fully determined, because it never could be determined that he had put his mind to it.

Despite his idiosyncrasies, Nashua had an illustrious career. He was a champion at two, and the following year earned Horse of the Year and divisional championship honors. He raced with distinction at four although he was not voted a championship that year. He retired sound with twenty-two wins in thirty starts and was the second horse to win more than $1 million.

As a two-year-old, Nashua won the Grand Union Hotel, Hopeful, Juvenile, and Futurity Stakes. His only losses in eight starts that year were seconds in the Cherry Hill and Cowdin Stakes. At three, he accounted for the Preakness (in track-record time), the Belmont, Flamingo, and Dwyer Stakes; the Wood Memorial; Florida Derby; Arlington Classic; and Jockey Club Gold Cup. He defeated Swaps in a celebrated match race, evening the score with the rival who had handed him defeat in the Kentucky Derby. Swaps' performance in the match race was thought to have been hampered by a hoof injury, but the two never met again, so the question of which horse was superior remains a matter of conjecture.

William Woodward Jr. was killed in a tragic shooting late in Nashua's three-year-old year, suspending the colt's campaign. A syndicate headed by Leslie Combs II acquired Nashua by sealed bid for $1,251,200, making him the first horse to fetch a million dollars. Combs leased the horse from the syndicate for racing the following year, and "Mr. Fitz" continued in his role as trainer.

At four, Nashua won the Widener, Grey Lag, Camden, Monmouth, and Suburban Handicaps and a second renewal of the Jockey Club Gold Cup. In the last-named, he set a new American record for the two-mile trip. In the Camden and Monmouth Handicaps, he carried top weight of 129 pounds. He was unsuccessful in each attempt to carry 130 pounds and never shouldered more than that weight.

Nashua entered stud at Spendthrift in 1957. He became a highly successful sire, although he never led the list. His fillies were better than his colts and became sought-after matrons, producing more than 100 stakes winners, among them the superb stallion Mr. Prospector.

NASHUA
BAY HORSE. *NASRULLAH-SEGULA
1952 — 1982

HORSE OF THE YEAR
CHAMPION AT 2 AND 3
WINNER OF 22 RACES. $1,288,565.
INCLUDING THE PREAKNESS AND BELMONT STAKES
WORLDS FORMER LEADING MONEY WINNER
SIRE OF 77 STAKES WINNERS
AND THE EARNERS OF MORE THAN $17,000,000.

Nashua also became something of a tourist attraction, much as Man o' War had been. The modern, U-shaped stallion barn at Spendthrift was dubbed the "Nashua Motel," and the king of Spendthrift's stallions occupied the end stall on the left wing. He remained an active and fertile stallion through his twenty-ninth year. He was to serve a reduced book of mares at the age of thirty, but a rapid decline in his condition canceled those plans. He continued to decline and was euthanized on February 3, 1982. He was buried in front of the stallion barn, and his memorial is topped by Liza Todd's bronze sculpture depicting him with his groom, Clem Brooks.

The Thoroughbred Record's obituary commented: "In addition to his contributions to the breed, Nashua will be remembered for his personality by all who knew him. Nashua was revered as a race horse by the public who, if they could not get to the track, watched him on television. He never lost his magic through the years, as tourists and horsemen alike would go to Spendthrift to see the cantankerous champ and to listen to Clem Brooks, his groom of 25 years, faithfully recount Nashua's race record and exploits on the track."[2]

NEVER BEND

Foaled at Claiborne Farm on March 15, 1960, Never Bend was a member of the final crop of the brilliant but temperamental Nasrullah, out of the Kentucky Oaks winner Lalun. He possessed brilliant speed — although his stamina was suspect — and he showed an affinity for the turf. His death at the age of seventeen

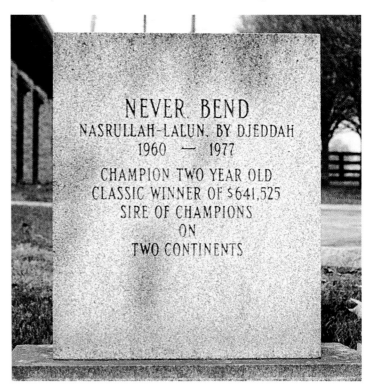

was a great loss for Spendthrift, as he had proved to be a top-class sire.

Never Bend flew home first in his two-year-old debut, a five-and-one-half-furlong maiden event, and gave a similar performance in his next outing at six furlongs. His speed got him in trouble in his stakes debut, as he engaged in an early speed duel and then was overtaken in the stretch to finish third. His stakes victories at two included the Cowdin, Champagne, and Futurity Stakes. He closed the season with seven wins from ten starts and was named champion of his division.

The colt's three-year-old season started off well enough, with wins in the Flamingo (in a wire-to-wire romp), Forerunner Purse, and Stepping Stone Purse. He finished second in the Kentucky Derby to Chateaugay and third in the Preakness to Candy Spots and Chateaugay. As a result of these defeats, his owner canceled the colt's proposed trip to Europe to try for the Epsom Derby. Never Bend then was sidelined with an ankle injury until the August Saratoga meeting. His only stakes win that fall came in the Yankee Handicap, but he finished second in the United Nations Handicap on turf to the good horse Mongo and second in the Woodward Stakes to the mighty Kelso. He was retired to stud at the end of his three-year-old campaign, with a record of thirteen wins from twenty-three starts.

John Sparkman, writing in *The Thoroughbred Record* series "Contemporary Stallions," described Never Bend as standing slightly over sixteen hands, with muscular shoulders, a short back, and outstanding quarters and gaskins. His main fault was his slightly sickle hocks. He sired sixty-one stakes winners, among them the European stars Mill Reef and Riverman, as well as J. O. Tobin. Mill Reef and Riverman have themselves both been outstanding stallions, carrying on Never Bend's male line with a host of top performers. Never Bend died of an apparent heart attack on January 11, 1977.

PRINCE JOHN

A member of Stoner Creek Stud's consignment to the Keeneland summer sales of 1955, Prince John was purchased for $14,300 by Maxwell Gluck. He was a chestnut son of the good stayer Princequillo and out of the unraced Count Fleet mare Not Afraid. Although not brimming with speed, his pedigree certainly was not lacking in the stamina department.

The big colt proved quite a good two-year-old. Although Prince John's only stakes victory came in the Garden State Stakes, he covered the one and one-sixteenth miles in an excellent 1:42 3/5. His other efforts that season included runner-up finishes in the Sanford Stakes, Washington Park Futurity, and Remsen Stakes. He closed out the year with a record of three wins and three seconds in nine starts, earning $212,818 for Gluck's Elmendorf Stable.

Sent to Florida to prepare for a spring assault on the classics, Prince John broke away from his groom at Hialeah in December and fractured a coffin bone while running loose. It was hoped for a time that he might return to the races, but instead he was retired to Elmendorf to serve the 1957 breeding season.

In "Contemporary Stallions," William G. Munn remarked that "Prince John…and his sons and daughters, would become the pillars of the Elmendorf empire. They would symbolize the new Elmendorf just as the famous columns of the Green Hills mansion symbolize the old."[3] Leslie Combs II and his partners purchased a majority interest in the stallion and moved him to Spendthrift for the 1962 season, and

Prince John remained there until his death.

Prince John sired fifty-five stakes winners, among them the champions Typecast, Stage Door Johnny, Silent Screen, and Protagonist. His offspring exhibited a wide range of aptitudes, from precocious sprinters to late-maturing stayers. He also was honored four times as leading broodmare sire. Among his daughters' produce were two-time Prix de l'Arc de Triomphe winner Alleged, Breeders' Cup Mile winner Cozzene, and Riverman — themselves important sires. His male line continues today, primarily through his son Speak John. Prince John fractured a foreleg in a paddock accident on January 29, 1979, and was euthanized.

RAISE A NATIVE

In just four starts — none at greater than five and one-half furlongs — Raise a Native showed such complete dominance of his contemporaries that many considered him one of the greatest two-year-olds of all time. The son of the once-beaten Native Dancer was the ninth foal of Raise You, a stakes winner and stakes producer. Raise a Native changed hands twice before reaching the races, being sold at Keeneland in 1961 as a weanling and then again at Saratoga the following August. His purchaser at Saratoga was Louis Wolfson's Harbor View Farm; the price, $39,000.

The colt, "muscled like a gladiator, with a coat like a sunburst," according to Charles Hatton, came out early at two. His first view of competition, if it can be called that, came on February 28, 1963, at Hialeah, where he coasted home by six lengths in a three-furlong dash. He reappeared on May 4, this time in a five-furlong allowance race, and again romped home, setting a track record for the distance. His nearest rival was some eight lengths behind. The Juvenile Stakes, again at five furlongs, was a virtual repeat of his previous effort, as he equaled his own track record. His final start came in the five-and-one-half-furlong Great American Stakes, in which the good colt Chieftain was expected to provide some actual competition. Raise a Native won "in hand," again setting a track record.

In preparation for the Sapling Stakes at Monmouth, Raise a Native suffered a bowed tendon and was retired. Still, he had accomplished enough to be named champion two-year-old in the Thoroughbred Racing Associations' poll that fall.

Raise a Native embarked on a long and illustrious career at stud at Spendthrift in 1964. He sired seventy-eight stakes winners, among them the champions Crowned Prince and Laomedonte. Perhaps his best colt was Alydar, whose misfortune it was to be foaled in the same year as Raise a Native's grandson, the Triple Crown champion Affirmed. Three of his sons became leaders of the general sire list; Raise a Native himself was the leading juvenile sire in 1973. Through his sons Alydar, Mr. Prospector, and Exclusive Native, his male line has continued to flourish at the top level of the sport. His daughters have proven valuable broodmares as well, with some 140 stakes winners to their credit.

Raise a Native was euthanized on July 28, 1988. He had been suffering from weakness in his hindquarters, which did not improve even with the suspension of breeding activities. He was buried in front of the Nashua Motel.

Chapter 7 – Idle Hour and Darby Dan Farms, and King Ranch

In 1906, Colonel E. R. Bradley purchased 336 acres on Old Frankfort Pike in Lexington, which had previously been a Standardbred farm called Ash Grove Farm. Already active in racing, Bradley hoped to breed a Kentucky Derby winner on his new property, which he renamed Idle Hour Farm. The farm grew to encompass nearly 1,500 acres on both sides of Old Frankfort Pike; a tunnel created under the road-

The statue of Black Toney presides over the cemetery at Darby Dan Farm.

way made it easier to move horses from one side of the farm to the other.

Critical to the development of Bradley's breeding program was his purchase of a colt by Peter Pan from William A. Prime. Prime had acquired the colt from the dispersal of James R. Keene's Castleton Stud, but was forced to sell because of a sudden reversal in fortunes. The colt, Black Toney, would become the stud's premier sire. Bradley would further strengthen his stud later by importing English mares, a practice similar to that at Castleton.

All of Bradley's horses had names beginning with 'B,' a tradition instituted to honor his first stakes winner, Bad News. The first Kentucky Derby winner bred at Idle Hour was Behave Yourself, who captured the 1921 renewal. Bradley later won Derbys with Bubbling Over, Brokers Tip, and Burgoo King. (In an ironic twist, his two best colts, Blue Larkspur and Bimelech, were beaten in that classic.)

Bradley, who listed his occupation as "gambler," experimented with various improvements for racehorses and riders. His most successful enterprise was the development of a safety helmet for jockeys; attempts to create corrective lenses for horses with poor vision and aerodynamic blinker hoods made less of a splash.

After Bradley's death in 1946, a partnership consisting of Ogden Phipps, Greentree Stud, and King Ranch acquired the Idle Hour horses. The farmland was divided and sold, with the portion on the south side of Old Frankfort Pike going to King Ranch. In 1957, John W. Galbreath expanded his Thoroughbred operation from its Ohio base by purchasing 616 acres on the north side of Old Frankfort Pike. This tract included the antebellum mansion and the stallion complex. He named the farm Darby Dan, and under his ownership the farm again rose to prominence. Since his death in 1988, the operation has continued, with Galbreath's grandson John Phillips purchasing the farm from the other Galbreath heirs in July 1997.

There are two equine cemeteries on the property. The first, beside the stallion barns and overlooking the stallion paddocks, is dominated by a statue of Black Toney. The second lies on a hill above the stallion barns and is the site of the graves of Bradley's Bubbling Over and Blossom Time as well as of Summer Tan and other Galbreath horses.

BLACK TONEY

Wrote Abram S. Hewitt in *Sire Lines*, "If by the strictest standards Black Toney came up short as a race horse, by the strictest standards he was a major success as a sire." In *The Great Breeders and Their Methods*, Hewitt added that the "Purchase of Black Toney…was perhaps the most important single event in the Bradley breeding operation."

Bred by James R. Keene's Castleton Stud, Black Toney's pedigree was a cross between the outstanding American strains of Domino and Ben Brush. Black Toney was by Peter Pan, a grandson of Domino, and out of the Ben Brush mare Belgravia. Foaled in 1911, he was a member of Castleton's penultimate crop.

In his four seasons on the track, Black Toney compiled a record of thirteen wins, eleven seconds, and seven thirds in forty starts. His only two stakes victories came in the Valuation Stakes and the Independence Day Handicap. He served one season at stud at five before briefly returning to the races at six. From his initial crop came the champion Miss Jemima; from his second, Black Servant. Among his other outstanding get were Black Gold, Bimelech, Balladier, Black Helen, and Black Maria. Although his male line has not continued, his influence is widely felt in American pedigrees through his daughters. Sons Bimelech and Black Servant and grandson Blue Larkspur also had an impact as broodmare sires.

As *The Thoroughbred Record* of September 24, 1938, reported:

> Another great patriarch of the turf has finished the course. Black Toney, full of years and honors, died in his paddock at Col. E. R. Bradley's

BAY MARE
FLOWER BOWL
1952 — 1968
WINNER LADIES HANDICAP, DELAWARE HANDICAP — $174,625.
DAM OF:
BOWL OF FLOWERS — 10 WINS AT 2 AND 3 — $398,504. VOTED
BEST 2 YEAR OLD FILLY & BEST 3 YEAR OLD FILLY OF HER YEARS.
GRAUSTARK — ONE OF THE BEST 2 YEAR OLDS & 3 YEAR OLDS OF
HIS YEARS; SIRE.

Idle Hour Farm here shortly after seven o'clock Monday morning, September 19. Seen a few minutes before by Olin Gentry, manager at Idle Hour, he was standing quietly by the fence, apparently as well as usual. Five minutes later he was dead. His heart had ceased to beat and he died apparently without pain or struggle of any kind. He was buried at Idle Hour by a statue erected in his honor some years ago.[1]

The statue — a bronze likeness by Joseph Krstolich — stands beside Black Toney's grave.

FLOWER BOWL

A daughter of the unraced Alibhai, Flower Bowl was out of Flower Bed, by Beau Pere. She raced for Isabel Dodge Sloane and scored in the Delaware and Ladies Handicaps. Charles Hatton described Flower Bowl as "a capital race mare in appearance, a tall, clipper-rigged bay…Propulsive power rose from every rippling muscle." In all, she won seven races and earned $174,625.

Flower Bowl retired to Mrs. Sloane's broodmare band in 1957. Her first offspring was the highly successful filly Bowl of Flowers, by Sailor, who was champion at two and three. Flower Bowl was sold to Winston Guest after the death of Mrs. Sloane. In 1962, Galbreath acquired Flower Bowl from Guest. Good as Bowl of Flowers was, Flower Bowl outdid herself with her first foal produced for Galbreath. A chestnut son of Ribot named Graustark, the colt performed brilliantly at two and three before a career-ending injury sent him to the breeding shed. There he proved equally successful and for years was a cornerstone of Darby Dan's stallion contingent.

Flower Bowl died on April 16, 1968, after foaling a full brother to Graustark. A bay named His Majesty, he, too, was an accomplished runner, though not in the same league as his older brother. At stud, however, he proved as good if not better. Flower Bowl was buried on the rise to the right of the stallion complex, near Bradley's great mare Blossom Time and the Derby winner Bubbling Over.

GRAUSTARK

Royally bred, Graustark was always regarded as something special. He was by the outstanding European champion and international sire Ribot and out of the stakes-winning mare Flower Bowl, who pre-

Graustark won all but one start during his brief racing career.

viously had produced the champion filly Bowl of Flowers. Graustark's racing career confirmed that early promise but ended much too soon. He was beaten but once, by a whisker, despite his having suffered a career-ending injury during that race. Wrote Edward L. Bowen in *The Blood-Horse*, "As always, he floated through his bright afternoons, the silent figure amid a crescendo of rejoicing. For here was a colt to touch the racing man's deep longing to behold greatness."

Although Ribot's runners were not generally known

for their precocity, Graustark proved a notable exception. His three starts as a juvenile included a victory in the Arch Ward Stakes. Wrote Charles Hatton in the 1966 *American Racing Manual*, "He started just three times and won each engagement with great éclat, none by less than six lengths." Unfortunately, Graustark's campaign was curtailed by a splint; and Buckpasser and Moccasin were ahead of him in the year-end rankings.

Graustark returned to racing as a three-year-old and showed his old brilliance, taking the Bahamas Stakes before moving to Keeneland for the Blue Grass Stakes, his final preparation for the Kentucky Derby. He suffered a gravel shortly before that event but seemed to be healing well. He began the race in the lead, but soon the upstart Abe's Hope began to challenge him. Graustark responded gamely but failed by the slimmest of margins. He had fractured a coffin bone during the race and was immediately retired.

Graustark's initial crop consisted of just three foals, owing to the lateness of the season when he was retired. It was not until his first full crop reached the races that his merit as a sire became evident. He went on to sire fifty-two stakes winners, including the champions Key to the Mint and Tempest Queen, and other talented performers such as Jim French, Proud Truth, Avatar, Caracolero, and Prove Out. Although several of his sons became successful sires, his male line today appears in danger of not continuing at the top levels. Still, his influence is evident in present-day pedigrees through his daughters.

At the age of twenty-five, Graustark suffered an injury to the same hoof that ended his racing days. Despite all efforts it failed to respond to treatment, and he developed laminitis. He was euthanized on August 21, 1988. His loss, coming just a short time after the death of Roberto, left a void in the stallion ranks at Darby Dan.

HIS MAJESTY

Flower Bowl's last foal, His Majesty, was a full brother to the famed Graustark and for much of his life, he lived in the shadow of his older sibling. Talented as he was, His Majesty was not in the same league as Graustark, but he went on to eclipse his sibling's accomplishments in the breeding shed, becoming America's leading sire in 1982.

His Majesty's racing career was plagued by various

infirmities, but he still managed to win five of his twenty-two starts, earning $99,430. His only stakes victory was in the Everglades Stakes at three, but he ran second in the Widener Handicap to another Darby Dan horse, Good Counsel, and placed in the Bahamas Stakes and the Seminole Handicap. He bowed a tendon at the age of five and was retired to stud.

His Majesty sired fifty-seven stakes winners, including Kentucky Derby and Preakness winner and champion Pleasant Colony, champion turf horse Tight Spot, Valiant Nature, Majesty's Prince, and Mehmet. Preakness and Belmont Stakes victor and champion Risen Star was produced from a His Majesty mare, as were the stakes winners Danehill, Dynaformer, and Wavering Girl, the last-named a champion in Canada. His Majesty was euthanized due to the infirmities of old age in 1995. He was twenty-seven. His grave lies near that of his brother, Graustark, and the other notable Darby Dan stallions.

RIBOT

At the conclusion of his career, Ribot was regarded as the world's best racehorse. He raced for three seasons and was unbeaten in sixteen starts. Sadly, his breeder, Federico Tesio, did not live to see him race. Instead, Ribot raced in the name of Tesio's widow and the Marchese Mario Incisa della Rochetta.

Ribot started three times as a two-year-old, racing exclusively in Italy. The only race he ever appeared in danger of losing was his final start that year, in the Gran Criterium. Reserved off the pace in very heavy going, he struggled to get up to win by a head from Gail.

The bay colt started four times in Italy as a three-year-old before he was sent to France to contest that country's premier event, the Prix de l'Arc de Triomphe. Ribot easily beat the other twenty-two entrants, leaving good runners such as Zarathustra, Rapace, and Hugh Lupus in his wake. He continued to dominate the following season, winning the King George VI and Queen Elizabeth Stakes in England as a four-year-old and capping his extraordinary career with a second facile win in the Arc.

The Thoroughbred Record's John Sparkman described the mature Ribot as "a big, strong, if not elegant, stallion…Standing a bit over 16 hands…Ribot's outstanding feature was the extraordinary depth and breadth of his chest and barrel. Perfectly correct in his forelegs, with plenty of bone, his hind legs were also well-placed, though some critics might have thought him comparatively weak in the gaskins. However, he was exceptionally strong in the back…loins, and quarters. Ribot's head was very wide in the forehead, with a flat profile and a particularly large, kind eye, and thick jowl."[2]

Ribot began his stud career in England, then returned to Italy. In 1961, John W. Galbreath leased him in a five-year arrangement. The stallion developed such a difficult temperament that he never returned to Europe for fear of the risk to his safety. Of his idiosyncrasies, Kent Hollingsworth wrote for *The Blood-Horse*, "For one thing Ribot cared nothing for other horses and was irritated by their very presence in nearby paddocks...Other stallions and all the Darby Dan yearlings had to be brought up before Ribot would deign to be taken to his paddock. One day, he peered over his high, solid-planked fence and noticed some cattle grazing on a hill three paddocks away; he tolerated this intrusion into his domain for a week or so, then began raising a fuss about it, and the cattle had to be moved to another field." Hollingsworth further recalled an incident in which Ribot refused to eat after a security camera was placed in his stall, necessitating its removal.

As he had been an extraordinary racehorse, Ribot also was an extraordinary sire. His sixty-six stakes winners included top-class performers in six countries. He was three times England's leading sire. Among his outstanding runners were the champions Molvedo, Arts and Letters, Tom Rolfe, Ragusa, Ribofilio, Romulus, and Alice Frey. His male line rests largely on the branches founded by his sons Tom Rolfe and His Majesty.

Ribot died at Darby Dan Farm on April 28, 1972, from a twisted intestine. He was buried behind the statue of the Idle Hour patriarch Black Toney.

Roberto won the Epsom Derby and later was a success at stud.

ROBERTO

Roberto was a medium-sized bay son of the brilliant Hail to Reason and the Nashua mare Bramalea. Bramalea won eight races, among them the Coaching Club American Oaks. Roberto's owner, John Galbreath, sent the colt to Ireland to be trained by Vincent O'Brien, a master of his craft.

Very highly regarded at two, Roberto won his three Irish outings most impressively, including a five-length score in the National Stakes. In his final race of the season, the Grand Criterium, he finished a somewhat disappointing fourth.

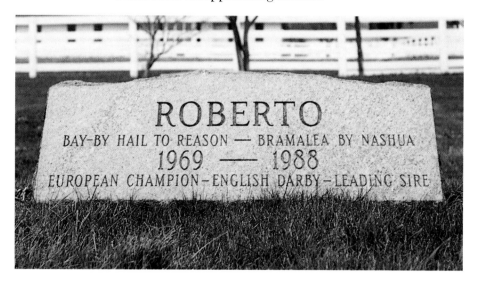

ROBERTO
BAY—BY HAIL TO REASON — BRAMALEA BY NASHUA
1969 — 1988
EUROPEAN CHAMPION—ENGLISH DARBY—LEADING SIRE

The following year, Roberto was pointed for the English classics. He won his seasonal debut, the Vauxhall Trial Stakes, at seven furlongs. Next, he fell a half-length shy of defeating High Top in the Two Thousand Guineas, in which his brilliant late run left the others adrift. Without High Top among the Derby contestants, Roberto started as the favorite. He won by a short head from Rheingold in a stirring stretch battle. Tom Forrest reported in *The Bloodstock Breeder's Review* that "Unwavering, thrusting his head out in grim determination, Roberto took all the relentless driving and answered it with superb courage. Breathtakingly locked together, the pair passed the post with barely a nostril separating them. But it was the nostril of Roberto which showed just ahead in the photo-finish print."

The climax of Roberto's season came in the Benson and Hedges Gold Cup, in which he met the undefeated champion Brigadier Gerard. In an astonishing performance, Roberto bested the Brigadier by three lengths and set a course record for the ten-and-one-half-furlong distance. Forrest commented, "Roberto will go down in living memory, not as the 1972 Derby winner, but as the only horse who ever beat Brigadier

Gerard." His final two starts of the season were less than brilliant, a second-place finish in the Prix Niel and a seventh in the Prix de l'Arc de Triomphe.

Roberto stayed in training at four, but did not return to his best form. His only stakes victory came in the Coronation Cup, against less-than-stellar opposition.

Back at Darby Dan Farm, Roberto was a marked success in his new career at stud. Among his best European runners were Sookera, Touching Wood, and At Talaq. His well-known American get included Brian's Time, Sunshine Forever, and Darby Creek Road. His sons Kris S. and Silver Hawk in the United States and Brian's Time in Japan have proven good stallions.

Roberto died on August 2, 1988, and was buried near Ribot and Black Toney.

KING RANCH

Robert J. Kleberg Jr. expanded his family's vast King Ranch empire to Kentucky in 1947 with the purchase of 680 acres on the south side of Old Frankfort Pike near Lexington. The property had been part of Idle Hour Farm. The Texas-based King Ranch was famous for its cattle and Quarter Horse breeding operations, and Kleberg used his knowledge of genetics to breed many outstanding Thoroughbreds — including Triple Crown winner Assault, Kentucky Derby and Belmont Stakes winner Middleground, Santa Anita Derby winner Ciencia, Coaching Club American Oaks winners Scattered and Resaca, and champions High Gun and Gallant Bloom.

Kleberg died in 1974 and his granddaughter, Helen Alexander, assumed management of the Kentucky farm. Among the best horses produced by King Ranch since that time was the champion two-year-old filly Althea, a daughter of the remarkable producer Courtly Dee. The cemetery at King Ranch has markers honoring the mares Igual, Bee Mac, Dotted Line, Gallant Bloom, Monade, and Green Finger. Althea and her dam Courtly Dee both died in 1995 and were buried at King Ranch, but their graves were moved to a lovely spot at Alexander's Middlebrook Farm, located just down the road from King Ranch. The King Ranch property on Old Frankfort Pike was sold in 1998 to Three Chimneys Farm.

ALTHEA

Althea was foaled at King Ranch in Kentucky in 1981, her dam having been purchased by a partnership which included Helen Alexander and her mother, Helen Groves, from Keeneland's November breeding stock sale the previous fall. Courtly Dee was already a proven producer, having foaled stakes winners Ali Oop, Princess Oola, and Native Courier. Althea was a member of the first crop of Calumet's young stallion Alydar. Retained for racing, Althea was sent to the California base of trainer D. Wayne Lukas. At two, she broke her maiden at first asking, then finished second in the Landaluce Stakes. Undaunted, Lukas sent Althea out against colts in the Hollywood Juvenile

ALTHEA
(1980)

ALYDAR   COURTLY DEE

Champion Two Year Old Filly
Arkansas Derby Winner

ALEXANDER, AYKROYD & GROVES
(OWNERS/BREEDERS)

Championship, and she left them ten lengths in arrears. Returned to competition against other fillies, she took the Del Mar Debutante, then again trounced the boys in the Del Mar Futurity.

Away from the races for six weeks, Althea returned with second-place finishes in the Anoakia and Oak Leaf Stakes. She rebounded to take the Hollywood Starlet before closing her campaign with a sixth-place finish in the Hollywood Futurity. Despite her late-season setbacks, Althea was voted champion two-year-old filly of 1983.

Althea began her three-year-old campaign in California, winning the Las Virgenes and Santa Susana Stakes. Venturing East to Oaklawn in Arkansas, she was second in the Fantasy Stakes, then defeated colts in the Arkansas Derby. Favored in the Kentucky Derby, Althea finished next-to-last in a twenty-horse field. She raced just once more, finishing sixth, and was retired to King Ranch.

Althea proved an illustrious producer, foaling Japanese champion two-year-old filly Yamanin Paradise and stakes winners Destiny Dance, Aurora, and Alyssum before her untimely death due to a paddock accident on April 15, 1995.

COURTLY DEE

Courtly Dee was an uninspiring runner, winning just four of her thirty-three starts and earning $19,426. She had, however, shown blazing speed, and possessed a good enough pedigree — by two-year-old champion Never Bend out of Tulle, by War Admiral — to be an attractive broodmare prospect. Lee Eaton claimed the mare for a paltry $15,000 and promptly retired her. Courtly Dee immediately justified Eaton's judgment. Her first foal was the stakes-winning Al Hattab colt Ali Oop, her second the stakes-winning turf campaigner Native Courier. Courtly Dee's next two foals, winners Vireo and Ragtime Knight, were by Darby Dan's stallion True Knight. The mare was returned to Al Hattab, and in 1978 produced the stakes-winning filly Princess Oola. Her 1979 filly by Sir Ivor did not race, and her 1980 filly by Seattle Slew, named Embellished, won just once. The Sir Ivor filly, Foreign Courier, and Embellished both became stakes producers.

Eaton sold Courtly Dee, in foal to Alydar, at Keeneland's 1980 November breeding stock sale. The mare was purchased for $900,000 by Alexander, Groves, and David Aykroyd. The resulting foal, Althea, was champion two-year-old filly of 1983.

Courtly Dee's next stakes winner was foaled in 1983, the colt Ketoh, by Exclusive Native. Her next three foals were the winners Maidee, Namaqua, and Karraar, followed by stakes winners Aishah and Aquilegia. Her 1990 colt, Press Card, was stakes-placed, and her 1991 Forty Niner colt, Twining, won the Peter Pan and Withers Stakes. Courtly Dee produced her last foal in 1992, a filly by Forty Niner. The mare then was pensioned, and died at age twenty-seven on August 16, 1995. She left behind her several promising daughters, but her finest daughter preceded her in death.

Chapter 8 – Calumet Farm

The white plank fences and red-trimmed white barns along Versailles Road in Lexington mark one of the most famous landmarks in Central Kentucky: Calumet Farm. The farm's great horses sleep under a blanket of bluegrass in a formal graveyard — the largest single Thoroughbred cemetery in the Lexington area — situated in a quiet spot toward the back of the property. The cemetery's centerpiece is a statue of Bull Lea on its white marble pedestal. On each side of the statue

A statue of Bull Lea overlooking the Calumet cemetery.

are markers honoring his greatest sons and daughters, and in front are the headstones of Calumet's Kentucky Derby winners. Other markers honor the mares who founded Calumet's most prolific families, and one is for Alydar, Calumet's greatest sire since Bull Lea. Henryk de Kwiatkowski, the farm's current owner, has remembered some of his own outstanding horses with markers as well.

William Monroe Wright, the founder of Calumet Baking Powder Company, purchased the 407-acre core of his Calumet Farm in 1924 as a Standardbred breeding farm. His ambition: to win the prestigious Hambletonian for trotters with a Calumet-bred. Sadly, when his dream came true, he was too ill to know of his triumph, and he died that same year, in 1931.

Wright's son, Warren Sr., inherited the farm. Warren preferred Thoroughbreds to Standardbreds, and under his guidance Calumet Farm became a perennial leader in that industry. By 1940, the farm comprised more than 1,100 acres, with facilities for stallions, mares, foals, and young horses in training.

Warren Wright Sr. died in 1950. His widow, Lucille, later remarried but continued to race and breed Thoroughbreds at Calumet. She died in 1982, after the death of her son, Warren Wright Jr. As a result, Calumet's ownership passed to Warren Jr.'s four children and to his widow, Bertha. None of the heirs were actively involved in the farm; son-in-law J. T. Lundy took over management duties. Under Lundy's leadership, Calumet enjoyed a resurgence for a time but then collapsed under a mountain of debt in 1991. The Polish-born de Kwiatkowski bought Calumet in a bankruptcy auction in March 1992.

De Kwiatkowski pledged to maintain the farm as it had always been kept. And so far, he has: The landmark white fences and barns still gleam amid lush green pastures dotted with grazing Thoroughbreds, preserving a part of Bluegrass history.

ALYDAR

In Alydar's obituary in *The Blood-Horse* of November 24, 1990, Edward L. Bowen wrote, "Part of his appeal was that a place in history was clearly perceivable even while his career was in progress. He was centrally identified with a return to glory of Calumet Farm, the all-conquering outfit of yesterday that staged a heartening comeback in the late 1970s…Alydar was a glistening link to a glistening

past. In his red blinkers and sporting Calumet's devil red and blue silks, he was the legend of Whirlaway returned to flesh and blood."

Foaled at Calumet in 1975, Alydar was by the Spendthrift stalwart Raise a Native and out of Sweet

Tooth, a great-granddaughter of the remarkable Calumet matron Blue Delight.

Alydar was a member of the same foal crop as Harbor View Farm's Affirmed, and the two chestnuts went on to treat racegoers to several thrilling displays of their breed's courage and will. The rivalry began early. Alydar made his racing debut in the Youthful Stakes, running against Affirmed. Affirmed won; Alydar closed well to finish fifth. In his next start, Alydar blasted past maidens by six and three-quarters lengths for his first victory. He evened the score with Affirmed by taking the Great American Stakes, then added the Tremont and the Sapling. He lost the next two, the Hopeful and the Futurity, to Affirmed, but got the better of his rival in the Champagne Stakes. Alydar closed out his season with a second to his old nemesis in the Laurel Futurity. The score stood: Affirmed 4, Alydar 2.

The spring saw the rivalry renewed with vigor, although Affirmed by this time had found his rival's measure and finished ahead on each occasion that they met. In preparation for the classics, Alydar had taken the Florida route to Kentucky. Along the way, he captured the Flamingo Stakes, Florida Derby, and Blue Grass Stakes. Affirmed, meanwhile, had prepared in California.

Affirmed won the Kentucky Derby, with Alydar a closing second. The Preakness saw the same result, except that Alydar got closer. In the Belmont, Alydar and Affirmed ran as a team down the long stretch with little to show between them. At the wire, it was Affirmed's head in front of Alydar's yet again. Alydar scored a Triple Crown of a different sort: He was the first horse to be second in all three races.

In the absence of Affirmed, Alydar scored lengthy victories in the Arlington Classic and the Whitney Stakes. The two rivals' final meeting came in the Travers, in which Affirmed crossed the line first but was disqualified in favor of Alydar. The final record: Affirmed ahead, seven to three.

After the Travers, a coffin bone fracture in his left front foot kept Alydar away from the races for the rest of the year. He returned at four to win twice in six attempts, with his only stakes win coming in the Nassau County Handicap. An ankle injury sent him to stud, with a record of fourteen wins in twenty-six starts and earnings of $957,195.

If Affirmed had been the superior on the track, it

was Alydar who stole the thunder in the breeding shed. He sired Horses of the Year Alysheba and Criminal Type, champions Easy Goer, Turkoman, and Althea, and seventy-two other stakes winners. He was America's leading sire in 1990, the year he fractured a hind leg in his stall at Calumet. Attempts to save him failed, and Calumet and the Thoroughbred industry lost a bright star. He was buried in the Calumet cemetery alongside the best of his antecedents.

ARMED

A bit of a slow starter, Armed was unraced at two and unremarkable at three. But, beginning with his four-year-old season, he raced with distinction through his ninth year. By the end of his career, he had made eighty-one starts, winning an incredible forty-one races and finishing in the money an additional thirty times. His earnings totaled $817,475.

An obstreperous temperament resulted in Armed's being gelded before he reached the races. Brought along patiently, he did not face the starter at two and for a time was used to pony the yearlings at the farm. He came out early in his three-year-old season, winning his debut by eight lengths on February 28, 1944,

in Florida. At season's end he had won three times in seven races. Commented Joe Palmer in *American Race Horses* of 1946, "He could have been considered useful, but no more."

However, Palmer continued, "Somewhere along

here Armed became a competitor, a horse that wanted to win." At four, he captured ten of fifteen starts. His first stakes win was a division of the Sheridan Handicap. Other stakes victories were the Washington Handicap and Pimlico Special. In the last-named, he won by four from a stellar field, leaving behind First Fiddle, Stymie, Gallorette, and Polynesian.

In 1946, he continued in the same vein, winning eleven of eighteen and being unplaced only once. His first major victory came in the Widener Handicap, where he gave nineteen pounds and beat Concordian. He also accounted for the Philadelphia Handicap, under 129 pounds; and the Dixie, Suburban, Sheridan, and Washington Park Handicaps; and the Whirlaway Stakes, each under 130 pounds. He was named champion handicapper and received some support for Horse of the Year honors.

Armed's record at six was comparable to that of the previous year. He won eleven of seventeen, and this time was not only champion handicap horse but also Horse of the Year. His wins included the Widener and Gulfstream Park Handicaps, as well as another renewal of the Washington Park Handicap and the Whirlaway Stakes.

Armed's last three seasons were less successful. He won just once in six starts at seven, three times from twelve starts at eight, and twice in six engagements at nine. He was retired at the age of nine after winning his final start on March 22, 1950. He died in 1964 at the age of twenty-three.

BEWITCH

A daughter of Calumet's top sire Bull Lea, Bewitch ranks as one of her owner-breeder's most outstanding race mares. Her dam was the good producer Potheen, who also was the dam of stakes winners Theen, Pot o' Luck, and Lot O Luck. An amenable filly, Bewitch exuded a certain charisma. Charles Hatton, writing for *The American Racing Manual*, noted, "There is something about her that allures and fascinates."

Bewitch raced for five seasons, scoring a total of twenty wins, ten seconds, and eleven thirds in her fifty-five starts. Her earnings of $462,605 eclipsed Gallorette's mark for earnings by a distaffer. She was at her best during her two and four-year-old seasons, in which she was named champion of her division.

Most remarkable was her two-year-old campaign. Bewitch won at first asking at Keeneland on April 10,

1947. She then added seven consecutive victories to her ledger, including the Debutante, Hyde Park, Pollyanna, and Arlington Lassie Stakes and the Washington Park Futurity. In the last-named, she handed her stablemate, Citation, his only defeat of the year. Troubled by an ankle problem late in the season, she came home first in the Matron Stakes — only to be disqualified — and then was third to Citation and Whirling Fox in the Futurity Stakes.

Leg problems limited Bewitch to just six races as a three-year-old, but she still managed to win four of the six. Her stakes wins came in the Ashland and Modesty Stakes and the Cleopatra and Artful Handicaps.

At four, Bewitch recorded four wins in thirteen trips to the post and finished second on four occasions. In every handicap, she carried more weight than her female rivals. In perhaps her best effort, the Beverly Handicap, she carried 125 pounds and got up to win by a neck from Stole, who carried 104. Her time of 1:34 2/5 for the mile was just two ticks off Coaltown's new world record.

Bewitch remained in training at five and six but won just one stakes event in each of those seasons. Sadly, Bewitch never produced a foal that raced. Her only named foal, a filly by Ponder named Quizzical, died at two. Bewitch was euthanized in 1963 due to the infirmities of old age.

BLUE DELIGHT

In *American Race Horses* of 1940, John Hervey wrote that "Blue Delight is a very big filly. A brown, with four white pasterns, she stood over 16 hands…and is of great scope and power, stands over a lot of ground, being somewhat long behind the saddle. Her rump is rather sloping, but she has a long, fine neck, clean head, and very racy look. Though possessed of tremendous speed, she is a long strider, her action suggesting the ability to go on, and it is to be hoped that we will see her back at the post next spring in good form."

Hervey was reviewing Blue Delight's two-year-old performances, in which she had accounted for the Joliet and Arlington Lassie Stakes before being sent to the sidelines by ankle trouble. She failed to recapture her two-year-old form the following season, but at four she returned to win four stakes: the Arlington Matron, Cinderella, Cleopatra, and Princess Pat Handicaps. A bowed tendon suffered in the spring of her five-year-old season sent her to owner John Marsch's stud.

(Throughout her career, she had carried the colors of Mrs. Marsch.)

Marsch dispersed his breeding operation in 1946, after breeding a single foal from the Blue Larkspur mare. Henry Knight bought Marsch's broodmares as a package and resold Blue Delight to Warren Wright.

At Calumet, Blue Delight compiled quite an amaz-

ing record. Five of her foals won stakes. The best one, Real Delight, was twice a champion and later was inducted into racing's Hall of Fame. (Real Delight produced the stakes-winning Plum Cake, who in turn produced Sweet Tooth, dam of Alydar as well as champion Our Mims and stakes winner Sugar and Spice.) Blue Delight's other stakes-winning offspring were Princess Turia (dam of Kentucky Derby winner Forward Pass), All Blue, Kentucky Pride, and Bubbley.

Blue Delight died in 1966 and was buried in the Calumet cemetery, which in later years would be the final resting place for many of her descendants.

BULL LEA

In 1930, Coldstream Stud owner Charles B. Shaffer imported Bull Dog, a full brother to Sir Gallahad III — a sire who had enjoyed remarkable success at Arthur Hancock's Claiborne Farm. Six years later, Coldstream consigned a brown son of Bull Dog, out of Rose Leaves, to the annual Saratoga yearling sale. Warren Wright bought the colt for $14,000 and named him Bull Lea.

The colt earned considerably more than his purchase price, amassing career winnings of $94,825 from ten wins in twenty-seven starts. At three, Bull Lea established two track records at Keeneland and won the Blue Grass Stakes and Autumn and Pimlico Handicaps. He raced just twice as a four-year-old, beginning with a narrow loss in the McLennan Memorial Handicap and then capturing the Widener Handicap. He then suffered a training injury; efforts to return him to the races were unsuccessful, and he entered stud at Calumet in 1940.

Remarked Abram S. Hewitt in *Sire Lines*, "Wright's seeming misfortune was, in fact, a lucky stroke, for in his first crop Bull Lea sired Calumet's champions Twilight Tear and Armed." Indeed, the stallion's offspring became the foundation of Calumet's racing stable and made it a perennial leader in the sport. Bull Lea himself was five times America's leading sire. He was the first stallion whose sons and daughters amassed more than $1 million in earnings in a single season. His best son was undoubtedly the great Citation. He also sired several remarkable fillies, among them champions Twilight Tear, Bewitch, Two Lea, and Real Delight.

Although Bull Lea's daughters were valuable matrons, none of his sons proved particularly success-

Bull Lea led the American sire list five times and among his best offspring were Citation, Twilight Tear, Bewitch, and Real Delight.

ful at stud. As a result, his influence in contemporary pedigrees is felt primarily through his daughters.

Sculptor Antonio da Costa spent February through May of 1958 at Calumet, creating a bronze likeness of Bull Lea. The approximately one-quarter life-size bronze statue, displayed on a pedestal of white marble, was unveiled that November.

Bull Lea died on June 16, 1964, and was buried near

his likeness. In later years, his greatest sons and daughters would be interred on either side of the statue.

CITATION

Citation's dam was the imported mare Hydroplane II, a daughter of the great Hyperion, out of the Oaks winner Toboggan. Hydroplane II's racing career was undistinguished, but she had every right — on pedigree alone — to become an outstanding broodmare.

Hydroplane II foaled a bay colt by Bull Lea at Calumet on April 11, 1945. Named Citation, he would become one of the greatest runners seen in America in the 20th Century, invoking comparisons to Man o' War. In *American Race Horses* of 1948, Joe Palmer described Calumet's champion: "Citation…is not particularly a striking horse, though this is not to be considered as any criticism of his appearance. He is a very smooth, very bloodlike dark bay, just over 16 hands, almost perfect in conformation, which means that no one feature stands out over another, and with a beautifully chiselled head. His expression is extremely intelligent…"

In his nine starts as a two-year-old, Citation lost just once, finishing second to stablemate Bewitch in the Washington Park Futurity. At three, he won an amazing nineteen out of twenty, including a walkover in the Pimlico Special. He had virtually no competition among his age group, strolling home in each of the Triple Crown events with consummate ease. Citation did not share the distance limitations of some of his sire's other offspring, as evidenced by his victory in the two-mile Jockey Club Gold Cup. He defeated talented older rivals in the spring, an amazing accomplishment for a colt not yet chronologically three years old.

As he prepared for the big western handicaps of 1949, Citation developed an osselet that kept him away from the races for the entire season. When he returned at five, he was not quite so invincible but still won twice and finished second seven times in his nine starts that year. His performances were always creditable, as he gave weight in many of his defeats. He finished second to Noor in the Santa Anita Handicap while carrying 132 pounds to Noor's 110. The margin was a length and a quarter, and he pushed Noor to a new track record. Similarly, in the San Juan Capistrano, Noor set a new world record to get a nose past Citation, who carried 130 pounds to Noor's 117.

Citation soon began to be bothered by a tendon, and he was never particularly sound in his final two seasons of racing.

Citation remained in training as a six-year-old with the objective of becoming racing's first millionaire. This he accomplished with three wins in seven starts. He went out on a high note, taking the Hollywood Gold Cup from Bewitch. He retired to stud with career totals of thirty-two wins from forty-five starts, for earnings of $1,085,760. In his final review of Citation for *American Race Horses* of 1951, Palmer wrote, "It was the ease with which he beat his horses, the frictionless effort of his action, the impossibility for the best horses of the year to bring him even to a challenge, the will to run which carried him to a mile and three-sixteenths in 1:59 4/5 in a walkover, which made him the greatest horse of his day. That after a year of absence bothered by osselets and tendon trouble, he was no longer unmatchable is not to his discredit."

Citation entered stud at Calumet for the 1952 season. He was an unremarkable sire, with just twelve of his 269 foals becoming stakes winners. His best included C. V. Whitney's champion filly Silver Spoon

and the Preakness winner Fabius.

At the time of Citation's death in 1970, no horse had matched his Triple Crown accomplishment. The greatest of his sire's sons, Citation was buried in front of Bull Lea's bronze statue.

EASY LASS

In 1933, Calumet Farm bought Slow and Easy with a foal at her side at Saratoga for $6,000. The mare was a daughter of the superb runner Colin and out of the imported mare Shyness, by His Majesty. Both the foal at Slow and Easy's side and the one she was carrying at the time became stakes winners. Easy Lass, by Blenheim II, was not one of her dam's stakes-winning offspring but became an illustrious producer.

In *The Thoroughbred Record* serial entitled "American Matriarchs," Bob Stokhaug described Easy Lass as "a glistening black mare with a beautiful white star just above her intelligent eyes."[1] The black filly showed some ability in a brief racing career, capturing her first three starts and giving the impression that she was destined for a distinguished racing career. In her stakes debut, she fell while at the post and finished eleventh. She made two more starts but failed to place. Fearing she had been injured more severely than first thought, she was sent home to Calumet.

Her first foal to reach the races was Coaltown, a son of Bull Lea and a contemporary of Citation, who early on was regarded as perhaps his superior. At three, Citation disproved this notion rather emphatically; but Coaltown won his share of stakes and did enough at four — with Citation on the injured list — to be voted Horse of the Year.

Her next foal was the filly Wistful. This daughter of Sun Again was champion at three and numbered the Coaching Club American Oaks among her victories. Easy Lass' third foal was Fanfare, a colt by Pensive. Although he was not in the same class as Coaltown and Wistful, Fanfare became the third stakes winner produced by his dam from as many living foals. Easy Lass' next foal, Rippling Rythm, a 1951 daughter of Bull Lea, went winless in four starts. In 1954, Easy Lass produced another Bull Lea filly, named Rosewood, who won nine races in three seasons, including the Black Helen, Misty Isle, and Suwannee River Handicaps. After Rosewood, Easy Lass had just two more foals in nine years: the winners Winter Park, by Alibhai; and Greenup, by Bull Lea. She was pensioned after being barren in 1963 and died in 1968.

Easy Lass' daughters carried on the family tradition. Wistful was the dam of Calumet's ill-fated star Gen. Duke, and Rosewood produced three stakes winners. Rippling Rythm was the granddam of English two-year-old champion Ribofilio. Easy Lass' sons, conversely, enjoyed little success at stud. Biggest disappointment was Coaltown, who eventually was sold to France after failing to sire anything of note.

PENSIVE

Imported by Arthur Hancock of Claiborne Farm, Penicuik II was a less-than-stellar race mare. She was a daughter of English champion Pennycomequick, a sterling broodmare who produced six stakes winners. At the time Penicuik II was imported, she was in foal to the great racehorse and sire Hyperion. Calumet's Warren Wright Sr. bought her, and her chestnut colt was foaled on February 5, 1941. He was named Pensive.

Pensive showed some promise during his two-year-old campaign but caused no one to wax poetic over his classic prospects. He won two of his five starts and twice finished third. His most prestigious win came in an allowance event over a nice field; his third-place finishes came in the Champagne and the Oden Bowie Stakes.

Pensive's first outing at three was on March 1, but he did not visit the winner's circle until two starts later, in a race at Tropical Park in Florida. Next, in Maryland, he beat older horses in the Rowe Memorial and finished second to the older horse Tola Rose in the Bowie Handicap. As he seemed to be improving, he was sent to Louisville for the Kentucky Derby. He closed strongly to win by four and one-half lengths. A week later, he romped home in the Preakness Stakes. However,

Pensive won the 1944 Kentucky Derby and Preakness Stakes for Calumet Farm.

Calumet's hopes for a second Triple Crown (Whirlaway had won in 1941.) were dashed when he finished second in the Belmont Stakes.

Pensive was winless in seven additional starts at three and then was retired as a result of tendon trouble. Wrote John Hervey in *American Race Horses* of 1944: "Pensive's 3-year-old campaign presents an interesting and not very well unraveled puzzle. For a time, he seemed to be quite ordinary. Then for a time he seemed to be the outstanding 3-year-old of the season. He ended by looking quite ordinary again, and one is left with the problem of deciding which aspect is really the most representative of the horse."

Pensive received few mares when he entered stud at Calumet, partly because of his on-again, off-again record and partly because Calumet already had Bull Lea and Whirlaway. Miss Rushin was the only one of Calumet's mares to produce a foal in Pensive's first crop, which totaled just six foals.

Miss Rushin's son, named Ponder, went on to win the 1949 Kentucky Derby. Pensive died just two weeks after that race, on May 19, from a twisted intestine. His grave lies in front of Bull Lea's statue, along with Calumet's other Kentucky Derby winners.

TIM TAM

David Dink wrote in *The Thoroughbred Record*'s 1982 obituary of Tim Tam: "The final week of July has not been kind to Calumet Farm. Following hard on the heels of the death of its owner, Mrs. Lucille Parker Wright Markey, comes news that Tim Tam, winner of the 1958 Kentucky Derby and Preakness Stakes, had to be put down the morning of July 30 at the farm."[2]

Tim Tam was foaled at Calumet in 1955, a son of Tom Fool and Calumet's champion Two Lea. He raced only once at two, finishing fourth. It was not until the following year that he showed his real ability.

Sent to Florida with the other Calumet runners, Tim Tam broke his maiden in his second start and followed that with an allowance win. After finishing third in his next two races, he scored eight consecutive victories, although his Flamingo Stakes win came by way of disqualification. His other stakes wins came in the Everglades and Fountain of Youth Stakes, Florida Derby, Derby Trial, the Kentucky Derby, and the Preakness.

After gritty victories in the Derby and Preakness, it looked as though Tim Tam would become Calumet's third Triple Crown winner — the first since Citation in 1948. However, Tim Tam finished second to Cavan in the Belmont after an erratic stretch run. He emerged from the race with a fractured sesamoid; whether he would have won had he not been injured remains a matter of conjecture.

Tim Tam retired to Calumet as a bright sire prospect but failed to have much impact. He sired just fourteen stakes winners, although one was the champion filly Tosmah. As a broodmare sire, he fared somewhat better. His daughters produced the Calumet champions Before Dawn and Davona Dale as well as the good runners and sires Known Fact and Tentam.

Tim Tam was pensioned in 1981 when weakness made it difficult for him to carry out his duties in the breeding shed. He suffered a heart attack on July 25, 1982, and was euthanized five days later.

TWILIGHT TEAR

Twilight Tear was a member of the Calumet stallion Bull Lea's initial crop. Her dam, the Blue Larkspur mare Lady Lark, was sold to Mereworth Farm before Twilight Tear raced. When the filly reached the races, she made her dam's purchase price of $1,700 look like a bargain. Her success also was a harbinger of things

to come for Bull Lea.

Twilight Tear won four of six starts at two, but her only stakes victory came in the Arlington Lassie. However, she was second to her stablemate Miss

Keeneland in the Selima Stakes. Twilight Tear shared divisional honors with stablemate Durazna, another daughter of Bull Lea.

Twilight Tear was better at three than she had been at two. *American Race Horses* described the sixteen-hand filly as "a rich wine colored bay…very distinctly a handsome filly…" She won fourteen of seventeen starts, with eleven consecutive victories. She dominated her own sex and also beat males and older rivals. Her stakes victories included the Pimlico Special, Acorn Stakes, and Coaching Club American Oaks. She was voted Horse of the Year as a result of her accomplishments.

Kept in training at four, Twilight Tear made just one start before being retired to join Calumet's broodmare band. She produced the stakes winners Bardstown, A Gleam, and Coiner; A Gleam was a good producer as well. Twilight Tear died from a post-foaling hemorrhage on March 8, 1954. Her obituary in *The Blood-Horse* noted that she was buried in front of the Calumet office, an area that for a time was reserved as the farm's cemetery. It is not known whether her remains were moved to the present cemetery.

TWO LEA

A bay daughter of Bull Lea and Two Bob, Two Lea became one of Calumet's outstanding runners before retiring to become one of its outstanding producers. By the time Two Lea was foaled in 1946, her sire's merits were well known. Her dam, acquired from the Whitney Stud, had won the Kentucky Oaks and already had produced the talented Bull Lea filly Twosy.

Two Lea's accomplishments were all the more remarkable given that she was plagued with bad feet. Early on, Joe Palmer noted in *American Race Horses* of 1952, "They worried a bit over the fact that she did not come with a spare set of feet." He further remarked, "She grew into a handsome filly, fine, feminine, and fast — but she always had to use the feet she was born with. They carried her with honor, if not with comfort."

Two Lea made just three starts at two, winning once in a maiden dash down the Widener chute at Belmont. She was not rushed at three, as Wistful was ably carrying the stable banner in the three-year-old filly division. Two Lea's first stakes win came in the Princess Doreen Stakes in June. Immediately thereafter, she suffered the only setback of her season, missing by a half-length to No Strings in the Modesty Stakes. She then annexed the Cleopatra Handicap and Artful Stakes and did not appear under silks again until December 29, when she took a six-furlong event in preparation for the rich winter stakes at Santa Anita. Two Lea's accomplishments were enough to garner her co-champion three-year-old filly honors with Wistful.

At four, Two Lea managed just five starts before being sidelined for nearly two years by her troublesome feet and ankles. She captured the Santa Margarita and Arcadia Handicaps and ran creditably to finish second and third to males in the Santa Anita Maturity and the Santa Anita Handicap. Even with just the five starts, she was named champion handicap mare of 1950.

Two Lea returned at six and took up where she left off, recording six wins and three seconds in eleven starts. Her stakes victories included the Vanity, San Mateo, and Ramona Handicaps and the Hollywood Gold Cup over males. At the close of her six-year-old campaign, she returned to Kentucky to join Calumet's burgeoning broodmare band.

Two Lea's produce record confirmed the class she had demonstrated on the track. Best of her foals was the three-year-old champion Tim Tam. She also was the dam of stakes winners On-and-On and Pied d'Or. Her daughter Mon Ange produced three stakes winners to add to the family's laurels. Two Lea was pensioned in 1966 and died in 1973 at the age of twenty-seven.

Two Lea, a champion for Calumet, produced Kentucky Derby winner Tim Tam for the revered farm.

Chapter 9 – Claiborne Farm

The stallion cemetery at Claiborne Farm draws many racing fans who come to pay their respects to Secretariat and the other greats who rest there.

The Hancock family's involvement with Thoroughbreds can be traced to the post-Civil War era, when Richard J. Hancock founded Ellerslie Stud in Virginia. The history of Claiborne Farm is slightly shorter. Richard's son, Arthur Boyd Hancock, took as a bride Nancy Clay, whose family owned Marchmont, a sizeable farm near Paris, Kentucky. Nancy inherited a portion of that property after the death of her parents in 1910. As Nancy's brother, Charlton Clay, retained the Marchmont name for his portion of the property, Arthur and Nancy settled on the name of Claiborne for their farm. Cattle, sheep, and tobacco were the original products of Claiborne; the Hancock family's Thoroughbred operations remained at Ellerslie. In fact, the first Thoroughbred mare at Claiborne was used to produce mules for farm work.

In 1915, Arthur B. Hancock began to develop the Kentucky property as a Thoroughbred farm. Claiborne's size has varied widely, growing from the original 1,300 acres to nearly 4,500 at its apex and shrinking back to today's size of about 2,000 acres. Claiborne eventually became the center of the Hancock family's Thoroughbred operations, and Ellerslie was sold in 1947.

Arthur B. "Bull" Hancock Jr. took over the farm's management duties in 1947 when his father became seriously ill. The senior Hancock had been a pioneer in assembling four or five partners to form stallion syndicates; such syndicates brought Sir Gallahad III and Blenheim II to America. Bull Hancock continued his father's practice of stallion syndication, and his notable imports included Nasrullah and Princequillo. He built the stallion roster at Claiborne into one of the finest in the nation.

After Bull Hancock died in 1972, his younger son, Seth, took over Claiborne's operation. Seth continued the family tradition of acquiring fine stallions, among them Secretariat and Mr. Prospector. Today, Claiborne continues to be home to some of the world's finest Thoroughbreds.

Claiborne has two equine cemeteries. The main cemetery lies just behind the farm office, and its entrance is flanked by pillars topped by crowing roosters. Here lie some of the greatest progenitors in history, their graves marked by simple headstones: Sir Gallahad III, Blenheim II, Nasrullah, Princequillo, Buckpasser, Hoist the Flag, Round Table, Secretariat, Mr. Prospector.

A second burial ground, often referred to as the Marchmont cemetery, was begun when the main cemetery neared capacity. Here, mares and stallions alike rest through the Bluegrass seasons: Moccasin, Numbered Account, and Tuerta among the mares; Sir Ivor, Forli, Ack Ack, and Easy Goer among the stallions. Off in one corner stands a memorial to the teaser stallion Boots, who performed his vital duties unheralded. Here, too, are the large granite stones that honor the memories of Sir Gallahad III and Marguerite, Gallant Fox's sire and dam. The markers once stood over their graves, on the hill above the stallion barn, but were moved to the new cemetery.

MAIN CEMETERY

BOLD RULER

A dark bay colt of the sterling vintage of 1954, Bold Ruler was foaled at Claiborne on April 6, the same day as his later rival Round Table. By Claiborne's champion sire Nasrullah and out of the hard-knocking Discovery mare Miss Disco, Bold Ruler raced with distinction for three seasons, then embarked on a stud career that outshone even that of his sire. His reign as a sire ended prematurely when he succumbed to cancer at the age of seventeen.

Charles Hatton penned this description of Mrs. Henry Carnegie Phipps' champion for *The American Racing Manual*: "In his sleek banker's brown coat, and in the lyrical quality of his action and his generosity, Bold Ruler somehow recalls artists' and racing journalists' descriptions of the popular Hindoo of the Dwyer dynasty. There is something distinctly 'old-fashioned' like a daguerreotype about him, as if he stepped from a Currier & Ives print into the vibrant present."

Bold Ruler was yet another of the superb performers

Bold Ruler was a Horse of the Year and influential sire.

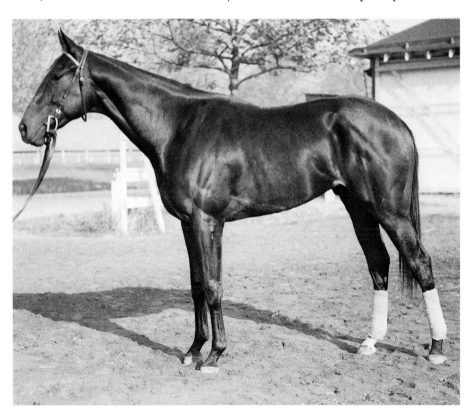

conditioned by "Sunny Jim" Fitzsimmons. Under the guidance of the master, the colt compiled a record of twenty-three wins from thirty-three starts and earned $764,204 for Mrs. Phipps' Wheatley Stable.

At two, Bold Ruler faced the starter ten times and won seven. He took the Youthful, Juvenile, and Futurity Stakes, demonstrating dazzling speed. However, Barbizon earned divisional-champion honors at year's end.

"Mr. Fitz" had Bold Ruler ready to begin his three-year-old season early. He made his first start on January 30 in the Bahamas Stakes. He gave Calumet's crack colt Gen. Duke twelve pounds and romped home a four-length winner. Gen. Duke got the better of him by a neck in the Everglades, again with a twelve-pound swing in the weights in his favor. Bold Ruler rebounded to win the Flamingo from his rival, setting a track record for the one and one-eighth-mile distance. The two met again in the Florida Derby, which Gen. Duke won in world-record time. Gen. Duke never raced again, and so the great rivalry came to a close.

Shipped north for the Wood Memorial, Bold Ruler won after a desperate struggle with Gallant Man. A tongue injury suffered as a yearling had left the colt with an extremely sensitive mouth, making it difficult for his jockey to rate him. That tactic failed miserably in the Kentucky Derby, when Bold Ruler fought jockey Eddie Arcaro's restraint and the colt had nothing left for the stretch. Arcaro allowed his colt to revert to his front-running style in the Preakness, and Bold Ruler defeated Derby winner Iron Liege. In the Belmont, Bold Ruler was pressed through rapid early fractions and then folded in the stretch while Gallant Man went on to set a record that would stand until Bold Ruler's son Secretariat set a new standard.

In the fall, Bold Ruler gave fans an incredible display of weight-carrying ability. He took the Vosburgh under 130 pounds, his time of 1:21 2/5 breaking a record that had stood for more than a half century. He went on to add the Queen's County Handicap under 133 and the Benjamin Franklin Handicap under 136. He closed out his campaign with a victory over Gallant Man and Round Table in the Trenton Handicap. He was named Horse of the Year as well as champion three-year-old.

At four, Bold Ruler won five of seven races and was voted champion sprinter. He won the Toboggan and the Stymie Handicaps carrying 133 pounds. His great-

est effort was the Suburban Handicap, which he won under 134 pounds while the runner-up carried but 109. His final victory came in the Monmouth Handicap. Recurring problems with his right front ankle sent him into retirement after a lackluster effort in the Brooklyn Handicap.

At stud, Bold Ruler's record was one of unparalleled success. He was America's leading sire eight times. He sired eighty-two stakes winners, among them the champions Gamely, Successor, Wajima, Bold Lad, Bold Bidder, Vitriolic, Bold Lad (Ire), Queen Empress, Lamb Chop, Queen of the Stage, and Secretariat.

William Robertson of *The Thoroughbred Record* wrote, "There are no adjectives adequate to describe Bold Ruler. In the case of his stud career in particular, it is best to let his record speak for itself...The cold, impassive figures literally scream that Bold Ruler was the most remarkable stallion of his era, if not of all time."[1] Although his sons were successful sires, it is mainly through the little-heralded Bold Reasoning that his male line continues today, through Seattle Slew. Bold Ruler's daughters proved outstanding broodmares, as well.

When the great stallion was sixteen, he developed a malignant growth in his nasal passages. The growth was surgically removed, and Bold Ruler underwent cobalt treatments at Auburn University in Alabama. The therapy was successful enough that he was able to cover mares the following season. In June 1971, he began to decline, and he was euthanized on July 12. He was buried among the other great progenitors who had contributed to Claiborne's fame.

BUCKPASSER

The Phipps family has had a long and productive association with Claiborne Farm. One of the many Phipps champions foaled at Claiborne was Buckpasser, who earned honors at two and three and raced with distinction at four. He was by Greentree's handicap star Tom Fool, out of the War Admiral mare Busanda, a granddaughter of La Troienne.

Writing for *The Thoroughbred Record*, William G. Munn described Buckpasser as "a 16.3 hands bay horse with beautiful balance and proportion. He had a beautiful, intelligent head and great hindquarters...In temperament, Buckpasser was unconcerned and poised at all times."[2] Unconcerned certainly described his attitude toward morning work, as the colt was notoriously reluctant to extend himself in training. Blinkers helped some, but the whip had no apparent effect on him. He generally found enough to get the job done at the races, though his last-minute rushes did nothing for the cardiac health of his connections and backers. When he retired, his record showed twenty-five wins in thirty-one starts, with earnings of $1,462,014. He was only once unplaced, in his first start.

The Phipps colt came to the races early at two, finishing fourth in his debut on May 13, 1965. He came right back to win, starting a streak that ran for eight races before he dropped a half-length decision to

Priceless Gem in the Futurity Stakes. He rebounded to close his season with a four-length triumph in the Champagne Stakes. His other stakes victories at two included the Sapling and Hopeful Stakes and the Arlington-Washington Futurity. He was named champion two-year-old colt, although he was somewhat overshadowed by Claiborne's two-year-old filly Moccasin, whose unbeaten status earned her honors as Horse of the Year.

Buckpasser's three-year-old campaign began well enough, with wins in the Everglades and Flamingo Stakes. His classic aspirations were dashed early in the season when he developed a quarter crack in his right front hoof. Kept away from the races until June, he returned to take an allowance race on Belmont Stakes day. After accounting for the Leonard Richards Stakes, he took the Arlington Classic, setting a world record of 1:32 3/5 for a mile. He continued to rack up triumph after triumph, adding the Chicagoan Stakes, Brooklyn Handicap, American Derby, Travers, Woodward, Lawrence Realization, and the Jockey Club Gold Cup. He was named Horse of the Year as well as champion three-year-old and champion handicap horse.

Buckpasser was plagued throughout his four-year-old season by the recurrent quarter crack and a troublesome ankle and made just six starts. He won the San Fernando Stakes and the Metropolitan Handicap under 130 pounds. His best performance came in the Suburban Handicap, in which, shouldering 133 pounds, he appeared beaten at the sixteenth pole but rallied to snatch victory at the wire. His attempt to emulate his sire by taking the Handicap Triple failed,

as he finished second under 136 pounds in the Brooklyn Handicap. He raced once on the turf, his connections planning a European foray, but finished an unimpressive third.

When Buckpasser retired to Claiborne, expectations of his abilities at stud ran high. As Timothy T. Capps noted in *The Thoroughbred Record*, "He had won over distances from five furlongs to two miles, beaten the best available to face him, and run as fast as was necessary to win, which was sometimes very fast indeed. He had triumphed on fast tracks and in the slop, and had overcome physical difficulties at three and four. His pedigree was impeccable, and he was as close to perfect in conformation as horses are likely to get."[3]

Buckpasser was a highly successful sire, if not a great one. His daughters were in general better than his sons, particularly in his early crops. Among his thirty-five stakes-winning offspring were the champions Numbered Account, Relaxing, La Prevoyante, L'Enjoleur, and Norcliffe. His daughters proved superb producers, and through them he has made a tremendous impact upon the breed. His male line continues rather tenuously, but he is currently represented by Silver Charm.

Buckpasser dropped dead from a heart attack on March 6, 1978, at the relatively young age of fifteen.

GALLANT FOX

Wrote Neil Newman in the 1930 edition of *Famous Horses of the American Turf*, "Since the retirement of Man o' War no horse has captured the imagination of the American public as has Gallant Fox…He swept like a meteor across the racing sky in 1930…He was more than a race-horse, he was an institution." The big bay raced for just two seasons but established himself as one of racing's legends as a three-year-old.

Marguerite, a daughter of the Ellerslie stallion Celt, foaled a blaze-faced bay colt by Sir Gallahad III on March 23, 1927, at Claiborne Farm. The colt was highly regarded from the first. In *Gallant Fox: A Memoir*, owner William Woodward recalled his first impressions: "He had the so-called 'look of eagles' and one could note a very fine skeleton in spite of his well covered frame. His well shaped legs, their cleanness, his very deep and beautifully placed shoulder, and his fork were to me his outstanding points. He was a bit high-headed, but foals are high-headed when they are taking notice, and this particular characteristic of taking notice he has carried all through his life except when he really had to set down and run for it."

Gallant Fox remained at Claiborne until after he was weaned and then was sent along with the other youngsters to Woodward's Belair Stud in Maryland. At two, he was placed under the tutelage of James "Sunny Jim" Fitzsimmons. Kent Hollingsworth noted in *The Great Ones*, "Gallant Fox was a big 2-year-old, ungainly, given to crowd-gazing in the post parade, and slow away from the gate." Further, he was not particularly enthusiastic about his morning works and had to be goaded into his best effort by relays of stable companions. Hollingsworth added, "Obviously Gallant Fox had a firmer grasp of the fundamentals of the game than did other horses — the purpose of racing is to beat others, if there is nothing out here to run down, why run?"

Gallant Fox started seven times at two, recording two wins, two seconds, and two thirds. His maiden victory came in the Flash Stakes, his third trip to the post. His other win came in the Junior Champion Stakes. He was put up for the year after that, in keeping with his owner's policy of saving something for the next season.

Gallant Fox's three-year-old campaign made racing men reminisce about Man o' War. The "Fox of Belair" made ten starts, won nine, and was second once. He opened his season with a facile score in the Wood Memorial Stakes. He next accounted for the Preakness, which in those days preceded the Kentucky Derby on the racing calendar. He followed with successive wins in the Kentucky Derby and the Belmont Stakes. Of the Belmont, Newman reported, "He strode to the front with the rise of the barrier. (Jockey Earl) Sande rated him in masterly fashion in front of his field. When Whichone made his challenge in the stretch he got to within a length of Gallant Fox, but Sande let out a wrap and maintained his advantage readily enough. As Whichone's last desperate effort failed, The Fox of Belair drew out to win by three lengths."

Gallant Fox continued his season with scores in the Dwyer Stakes and the Classic at Arlington. Given a respite until the Saratoga meeting, his next race was the Travers Stakes. On a muddy track, he and Whichone battled from the start. The two swung wide into the stretch, while rank outsider Jim Dandy came through on the rail to take the advantage. Whichone broke down but finished third; Gallant Fox was sec-

Gallant Fox won the 1930 Triple Crown.

ond. The colt rebounded from his loss to close his career with victories in the Saratoga Cup, Lawrence Realization, and Jockey Club Gold Cup. In the last-

named, only the maiden Yarn and The Fox's stablemate Frisius opposed him.

Gallant Fox became ill following the Gold Cup and was retired to stud. He returned to Claiborne by rail; Woodward noted that visitors came to see the great bay at each stop. Newman capped his report of the colt's three-year-old season with this description: "Gallant Fox is a horse of striking individuality. His most prominent trait is his marked curiosity. Nothing escapes his notice and as soon as he sees anything he wants to examine it — the examination complete he pays no more attention to it. He is possessed of an all-seeing eye which impresses one as his most prominent feature while he is being saddled."

Gallant Fox's first two foal crops were quite remarkable. Among his first was the Triple Crown winner Omaha, making Gallant Fox the only Triple Crown winner ever to sire another. His second crop was led by Horse of the Year Granville and the top stakes performer Flares. Although "The Fox" sired twenty stakes winners in all, his later crops did not match the quality of his first two, and he rapidly fell from favor with breeders. He died in 1954 at the age of twenty-seven and was buried on the hillside near his sire and dam.

HOIST THE FLAG

Hoist the Flag was a rare gem — a horse possessed of the extraordinary charisma that excites horsemen and racing fans alike. Both his racing and stud careers were cut short, but he made an impact in each realm. Foaled in 1968, he was a member of the first crop of three-year-old champion Tom Rolfe, out of the War Admiral mare Wavy Navy. Sold privately as a weanling, he was resold to Mrs. Stephen C. Clark at Saratoga the following year. His price, kept low by an injured eye, was a bargain $37,000.

Trainer Sidney Watters Jr. handled the colt patiently, choosing not to run Hoist the Flag until September of his two-year-old season. He won a maiden event by two and one-half lengths, then won by five in allowance company. His first taste of stakes competition came in the Cowdin, which he managed to win even after splitting rivals and bearing in down the stretch.

Sore shins reportedly were the cause of Hoist the Flag's rather erratic course in the Cowdin, but he soon raced again, rolling to a three-length victory in the Champagne Stakes. This time, his erratic performance got him disqualified and placed last. Despite these problems, voters were impressed enough to name Hoist the Flag the year's champion two-year old.

Hoist the Flag began his sophomore season with a fifteen-length romp in a Bowie allowance race, then flew home in the seven-furlong Bay Shore Stakes. He was next scheduled to contest the Gotham Stakes, but he took a bad step in a morning work and shattered a hind leg. As William H. Rudy wrote in *The Blood-Horse*, "Hoist the Flag's reputation will grow now, in retrospect, for no one will ever know how he would have reacted when hooked by another good colt and forced to battle nose and nose to the wire. His name will be added to those of Thingumabob, Hail to Reason, Raise a Native, Graustark, and all the others which were put out of action before they had a chance really to confirm greatness."

Veterinary surgeons repaired the colt's shattered leg with a plate and screws and a bone graft from his hip. The limb was placed in a cast, and Hoist the Flag was given a guarded prognosis. He proved a good patient and even learned how to lie down and get up with the cast on. Veterinary reports were "cautiously optimistic" when the cast was changed six weeks later. That fall, the colt had recovered well enough to be shipped to Claiborne Farm, ready to begin stud duties in the spring.

Hoist the Flag's stud career was as brilliant as his racing career and, sadly, as short-lived. He sired fifty-one stakes winners, among them two-time Prix de l'Arc de Triomphe winner Alleged and the champion two-year-old filly Sensational. Alleged himself has been a successful sire. Hoist the Flag's daughters provided him with honors as leading broodmare sire of 1987.

In March 1980, Hoist the Flag suffered a hairline fracture above his left knee. The fracture failed to heal with stall rest, necessitating surgery. Again he proved a good patient, but after the cast was removed he dislocated his left front ankle. He was euthanized and buried in the farm cemetery. His obituary in *The Thoroughbred Record* quoted farm manager John Sosby: "It was a gift that he lived as long as he did…He fought a tremendous battle, but everything finally fell apart for him and he just ran out of time. His courage and vitality took him as far as it could."[4]

MR. PROSPECTOR

June 1, 1999, was a sad day at Claiborne Farm. Twenty-nine-year-old Mr. Prospector was euthanized after suffering peritonitis, and he was buried in the final plot in the farm's main cemetery, alongside his contemporary, Secretariat. Mr. Prospector was one of the most successful sires ever to stand at Claiborne.

Mr. Prospector was bred by Leslie Combs II. Consigned to the 1971 Keeneland July yearling sale, he was purchased for a sale-topping $220,000 by Connecticut construction king A. I. Savin. The bay colt was the second foal from Combs' stakes-winning mare Gold Digger and was sired by the Spendthrift stallion Raise a Native.

Mr. Prospector did not reach the races until his three-year-old season. Trainer Jimmy Croll sent him out for his debut on February 6, 1973, at Hialeah. The colt won by twelve lengths in time just one second off the track record for six furlongs. He next started in a six-furlong allowance race and won by nearly six lengths. Kept out of the Hutcheson Stakes by a fever, he contested another allowance event at Gulfstream on the Florida Derby undercard, and smashed the track record for six furlongs, running the distance in an astounding 1:07 4/5. His margin of victory was nine and one-half lengths.

At this point, Mr. Prospector's potential seemed limitless, though he was as yet untried past six furlongs. Sent to Keeneland, he was third in his first attempt around two turns, in a one and one-sixteenth-mile allowance test. Mr. Prospector's next start was the Derby Trial at Churchill Downs. The colt finished second and emerged with a chipped pastern which kept him sidelined until his four-year-old season.

At four, Mr. Prospector started nine times and won four, including the Gravesend and Whirlaway Handicaps. He also was second in the Carter Handicap. In July, Savin's star suffered a fractured sesamoid in a morning workout and was retired to stud at his owner's Florida farm. His record showed seven wins from fourteen starts and earnings of $112,171.

Mr. Prospector became an immediate success at stud, and was moved to Claiborne Farm for the 1982 season. He was twice America's leading sire, and has twice been leading broodmare sire. At the time of his death, he was represented by 165 stakes winners (as of early December 1999, 168 stakes winners), including twenty champions. Among his best runners were Conquistador Cielo, Ravinella, Forty Niner, Rhythm, Machiavellian, Eillo, Tank's Prospect, and Kingmambo. His sons have been outstanding sires; his

daughters, top producers. David Schmitz of *The Blood-Horse* wrote: "Mr. Prospector attached his name to a breeding dynasty reminiscent of the one created by the brilliant, speed-producing stallion Domino a century ago. Domino's influence in racing and breeding lasted well into the 20th Century, and there's not a single doubt that Mr. Prospector's influence as a stallion and broodmare sire will endure at the highest levels well into the next century."

NASRULLAH

A son of Federico Tesio's great stallion Nearco, Nasrullah was produced by the Blenheim II mare Mumtaz Begum, she a daughter of the famous "Flying Filly," Mumtaz Mahal. In his racing career, Nasrullah demonstrated considerable ability along with an extremely difficult temperament. His stud career was one of marked success, although the temperament remained.

Nasrullah, who raced in England, made four starts at two and won twice, finishing second and third in his other attempts. He won the five-furlong Coventry

Stakes and the six-furlong Great Bradley Stakes. He also gave a good effort in his final race of the season, finishing a neck behind the smart filly Ribbon in the important Middle Park Stakes.

The following year, Abram S. Hewitt noted in *Sire Lines*, "His temperamental vagaries came into full flower." Nasrullah became reluctant to go to the post. He usually raced well enough until he took the lead, whereupon he would shorten stride and duck right or left as the mood struck him. Phil Bull's account of Nasrullah's performances at three in the Timeform publication *Best Horses of 1943* included photos with tart captions: "Nasrullah pretending to be a gentleman in the Derby parade," "Nasrullah condescends to pass the post in front in the Chatteris Stakes," and "Nasrullah impersonating a mule." Nevertheless, Bull was convinced of Nasrullah's inherent quality. The colt won three of his six starts as a three-year-old and finished third once. His wins came in the Chatteris, Cavenham, and Champion Stakes. He was third in the English Derby after he reached the front and then shortened stride and ducked to the right. Bull described him as having "a good head with small ears, a strong neck, well developed withers and excellent depth from withers to brisket; a fair shoulder and a fine, well ribbed-up body; plenty of muscle over the humerus, and full, well developed gaskins, strong straight hocks and pretty good legs generally. A high class, quality colt, possessing also range and size…None of his rivals of last season could beat him in appearance and none possessed a more delightful action or more space devouring stride when at full stretch."

Nasrullah began his stud career in England, then was purchased by Joseph McGrath and moved to Ireland. In 1949, a syndicate headed by A. B. Hancock Jr. bought him for a reported $370,000 and imported him to America. He proved as superior a sire as he had been perplexing as a racehorse. Ninety-four of his get — twenty-five percent of his foals — were stakes winners. He was England's leading sire in 1951 and America's leading sire five times. Among his outstanding offspring were Bold Ruler, Nashua, Noor, Never Say Die, Grey Sovereign, and Never Bend. His sons and grandsons carried on the male line with distinction.

Nasrullah died from a ruptured blood vessel on May 26, 1959. He was interred in the cemetery behind the

Nijinsky II won the 1970 English Triple Crown.

Claiborne Farm office. The mark he made upon the breed is indelible.

NIJINSKY II

Truly an international horse, Nijinsky II was bred in Canada; raced in England, Ireland, and France; and stood at stud in the United States. A son of the great Northern Dancer, he was much larger and coarser than the typical Northern Dancer offspring. Platinum magnate Charles Engelhard purchased him as a yearling and sent him to Irish trainer Vincent O'Brien.

At two, in 1969, Nijinsky II was unbeaten in his five starts. Only once tested, he was extended to beat Decies in the Beresford Stakes. His foray to England for the prestigious Dewhurst Stakes resulted in an easy victory, his rivals toiling in his wake. He appeared a prime classics prospect at season's end, although his stamina was somewhat suspect at the Derby distance of twelve furlongs.

Nijinsky II's prep for the Two Thousand Guineas was a romp in the seven-furlong Gladness Stakes. In the classic itself, he beat Yellow God impressively. His next engagement was the Derby, in which he faced the French challengers Gyr and Stintino. Although those two made a race of it, Nijinsky II strode clear to win by two and one-half lengths. He then returned to Ireland to add the Irish Sweeps Derby before tackling older rivals — including the previous year's Derby winner, Blakeney — in the King George VI and Queen Elizabeth Stakes. According to Timeform's

report, "Nijinsky, the only three-year-old in the field, treated his elders like so many selling platers, and was never more impressive in his life. He had the race won in a few strides about a furlong from home and took the lead travelling strongly on the bridle."

Nijinsky II suffered an attack of ringworm before his next race, the St. Leger, and started in the final classic with his coat still marred from its effects. Nonetheless, he came home a winner, becoming the first English Triple Crown winner since Bahram in 1935.

Sent to France for the Prix de l'Arc de Triomphe, Nijinsky II was unsettled in the preliminaries but made a tremendous attempt to catch French Derby winner Sassafras, failing by just a head. He started once more, in the Champion Stakes, but finished second.

Having been syndicated for a then-record $5.4 million, Nijinsky II returned to North America to enter stud at Claiborne. He was one of those rare horses whose accomplishments on the course were equaled by his accomplishments at stud. As a sire, he exceeded his own sire's greatness, with an incredible 155 stakes winners to his credit. He also is the only stallion to have sired a Kentucky Derby winner — Ferdinand — and an Epsom Derby winner — Shahrastani — in the same year. His sons have been successful stallions; his daughters, outstanding broodmares.

In 1992 at the age of twenty-five, Nijinsky II was euthanized due to declining health. He had suffered from laminitis for several years. He was the last of the Claiborne stallions syndicated by A. B. Hancock Jr. and his death marked the end of an era.

ROUND TABLE

In an article for *The Thoroughbred Record*, Munn wrote, "Fittingly, the horse named Round Table represents the most admirable and noble ideas that great sportsmen look for in a horse." He added, "A model of beautiful construction, Round Table's small frame (15.2 hands) was very difficult to fault. A bay, with only a small line of white about his left hind coronet, he seemed to have everything in the right place. However, if one is looking for something to criticize, one can point out his sickle hocks or his rather plain head, but little else."[5]

Round Table was among the most durable and versatile members of the stellar crop of 1954. Bred by Bull

Hancock, he initially raced in the Claiborne colors before Travis Kerr purchased a substantial interest in him early in the colt's three-year-old season. The son of Claiborne sire Princequillo and the fast mare Knight's Daughter raced for four seasons, earning championships in three. From sixty-six starts, he had forty-three wins, eight seconds, three thirds, with earnings of $1,749,869.

At two, Round Table won five of his ten starts, taking the Lafayette Stakes and Breeder's Futurity for

Claiborne. His three-year-old campaign began with two fairly dismal efforts in Florida, but he bounced back with a wire-to-wire allowance score. Sent to California, he was a close third in the Santa Anita Derby, then captured the Bay Meadows Derby before returning to Keeneland to take the Blue Grass Stakes. He was third in the Kentucky Derby to Iron Liege and Gallant Man but finished ahead of Bold Ruler. Leaving the remaining classics to Bold Ruler and Gallant Man, "Little Toughie," as Kerr referred to the colt, returned to California.

Round Table tackled older foes in the Californian Stakes, finishing second to Social Climber. To his ledger he added the Will Rogers Stakes, El Dorado Handicap, Hollywood Gold Cup, and Westerner Stakes on dirt as well as the American Derby and the United Nations Handicap on the turf. At Garden State, Round Table prepped for the Trenton Handicap with an easy eight-length allowance victory in the slop going one mile and seventy yards, but in the Trenton, eight days later, he appeared not to like the footing, rated good, and finished well-back in third to Bold Ruler and Gallant Man. He was named champion grass horse at year's end, with Bold Ruler annexing titles as champion three-year-old and Horse of the Year.

Round Table's 1958 campaign consisted of twenty starts in five states and Mexico. Noted Charles Hatton in *The American Racing Manual*, "Only a very comfortable shipper, an adaptable and even-tempered individual, and one of extraordinary inherent soundness could have withstood such vigorous campaigning." On his way to honors as champion handicap horse, champion grass horse, and Horse of the Year, Round Table racked up wins in the Santa Anita, Gulfstream Park, San Antonio, Arlington, Caliente, and Argonaut Handicaps, the Hawthorne Gold Cup, Santa Anita Maturity, Laurance Armour and Arch Ward Memorials, and the San Fernando Stakes. He won carrying 130 pounds or more on seven occasions.

At five, Round Table again raced to championships in the handicap and grass divisions. In what was for him a relatively light campaign, he won nine of his fourteen starts, among them the United Nations, Arlington, Washington Park, Manhattan, Stars and Stripes, Citation, and San Marcos Handicaps.

In late 1959, Round Table returned to Claiborne (Bull Hancock having retained an interest in the colt as a stallion) to begin his stud career the following spring. Commented Munn in *The Thoroughbred Record* series "Contemporary Stallions," "Round Table's stud career greatly resembled his racing career. He was a steady performer who consistently sired good horses."[6] Eighty-three of his foals (twenty-one percent) won stakes, including the champions Baldric, Targowice, Apalachee, Flirting Around, and He's a Smoothie as well as the top American runners Royal Glint and Drumtop. Round Table died on June 13, 1987, at the venerable age of thirty-three, and was laid to rest not far from his old rival, Bold Ruler.

SECRETARIAT

The chestnut colt with a white star and stripe and three stockings was foaled at Meadow Stud in Virginia on March 30, 1970 — fifty-three years and one day since the arrival of Man o' War at August Belmont's Nursery Stud in Lexington. Named Secretariat, the colt was the product of a mating from which great things were expected. His sire, Bold Ruler, had been a champion runner and had already led the sire list six times; his dam had produced the top-class colt Sir Gaylord.

Secretariat matured into a magnificent specimen,

standing over sixteen hands as a two-year-old and possessed of superb conformation. His chestnut coat and facial markings were similar to those of Man o' War, and from his earliest races he showed ability which led to comparisons between the two.

Wrote Edward L. Bowen in *The Blood-Horse*, "At two, Secretariat loved to charge around his field on the stretch turn, giving up ground on the outside, but recovering it and more through his own theorem: At any distance, the vastly superior horse will run as fast as he needs to to squash all opposition."

Secretariat finished fourth in his debut but came home first in his other starts at two, although he was disqualified from his Champagne Stakes victory. He had already accounted for the Sanford and Hopeful Stakes at Saratoga and the Futurity at Belmont. Following the Champagne, he added the Laurel Futurity and the Garden State Stakes to close out his season. So impressed were the voters for year-end honors that they named Secretariat Horse of the Year as well as champion two-year-old.

But it was Secretariat's three-year-old campaign that ranked him among the greatest sports heroes and made him a household name. He had already been syndicated as a stallion for more than $6 million, a move necessitated by the death of Meadow Stud owner Christopher Chenery. Trainer Lucien Laurin selected the New York route to the Triple Crown for his chestnut charge, and Secretariat obliged with easy scores in the Bay Shore and the Gotham Stakes. The colt equaled the track record in the latter, and racing writer Charles Hatton noted that "it took an outrider and two lead ponies" to pull him up.

His time for a mile and one-quarter, pulling up, was 1:59 2/5.

His final race before the Kentucky Derby was the Wood Memorial Stakes, in which he met West Coast star Sham. In a shocker, Secretariat finished a lackluster third behind stablemate Angle Light and Sham. It was later reported that he had raced with an abscess on his lip, which rider Ron Turcotte believed made him reluctant to pick up the bit.

Suddenly the invincible red horse appeared mortal — another brilliant Bold Ruler who failed to train on at three. The Triple Crown appeared increasingly elusive. Citation, who died the year Secretariat was foaled, was the last to capture the crown. As Bowen noted, "A patina not polished into the crown by its winning eventually was exuded in its aloofness. Indeed, the dearth of winners prompted some talk that it could never be won again under its present format…And then came Secretariat."

Secretariat silenced the doubters with a gradual move from last to first in the Kentucky Derby, setting a track record of 1:59 2/5 that still stands. Sham also ran a sub-two minute mile and one-quarter to finish two and one-half lengths in Secretariat's wake. Last early in the Preakness, he rolled past his rivals on the first turn, then maintained a two-and-one-half-length margin over Sham to the wire. Denied the Preakness record by a timer malfunction, he is generally conceded to have run in record time, as *Daily Racing Form* clockers caught him in 1:53 2/5, a time that was confirmed by television-replay technology.

That left only the Belmont's testing one-and-one-half miles between Secretariat and the first Triple Crown in a quarter of a century. "Big Red," as fans had taken to calling him, appeared on the covers of *Time*, *Newsweek*, and *Sports Illustrated*. Surprisingly, he went to the front immediately, with Sham in close attendance. The fractional times were incredible — :23 3/5, :46 1/5, 1:09 4/5, 1:34 1/5, and 1:59 — faster than those that had cooked his sire in 1957. Sham was through after three-quarters, but the big red horse rolled on to a thirty-one-length victory in 2:24, which remains the standard today.

To his list of victories Secretariat added the Arlington Invitational and the Marlboro Cup on dirt and the Man o' War Stakes and the Canadian International on turf. He suffered two defeats, in the Whitney and Woodward Stakes. In the Marlboro Cup, he defeated a stellar field of older rivals plus Onion, winner of the Whitney, in world-record time. In the Man o' War, he raced top grass-runner Tentam into submission with a course-record-setting performance.

All too soon, it was over. Big Red paraded before his fans one last time at Aqueduct and then was off to Claiborne Farm, where he occupied the stall that had once been Bold Ruler's. He was unable to match the high expectations held for him there, but he was far from a failure. His fifty-seven stakes winners included Horse of the Year Lady's Secret and the three-year-old champion Risen Star as well as General Assembly, Terlingua, and Tinners Way. His sons have not been particularly successful, but his daughters have become sought-after matrons. Through them, Secretariat's impact on the breed seems secure, for they have produced the top sires Storm Cat, Gone West, and A.P. Indy as well as Chief's Crown and Sword Dance.

Like Man o' War, Secretariat's popularity never waned, and he thrived on the attention. Wrote Don Clippinger in *The Thoroughbred Record*, "People would show up each day in Paris, Kentucky, to see the big horse, to be photographed beside him, to show their children the horse of a lifetime."[7] In September of

1989, he developed laminitis; and at 11:45 a.m. on October 4, the great red horse's life was ended. He was buried in his entirety across from Round Table and Swale.

Edward L. Bowen closed his obituary of Secretariat with these words: "Secretariat, of course, did not actu-ally defy Nature; he was not her rival, but her gift…He had moved us to tears before, and now he has again."

SIR GALLAHAD III

Bred in France by Jefferson Davis Cohn, Sir Gallahad was by the excellent runner and sire Teddy out of the remarkable mare Plucky Liege. A partner-ship headed by A. B. Hancock Sr. purchased him for a reported $125,000 in 1925. Installed at Claiborne, the bay horse now known as Sir Gallahad III was an instant success in his new land and helped to cement Claiborne's stature among the elite farms of the Bluegrass.

In *Famous Horses of the American Turf*, Neil Newman described Sir Gallahad III as "a solid bay, with plenty of size and scope." He had been quite a good racehorse, capturing the French classic Poule d'Essai des Poulains and placing in the French Derby (or Prix du Jockey-Club). He raced for three seasons, winning twelve races from his twenty-five starts. Best at around a mile, he nevertheless won twice at one and one-quarter miles. He was precocious enough to win five of seven starts at two.

Sir Gallahad III sailed for America aboard the

Sir Gallahad III was a major acquisition for Claiborne.

Minnetonka, then completed his journey to Kentucky by rail. Noted Abram S. Hewitt in *The Great Breeders and Their Methods,* "The advent of Sir Gallahad III at Claiborne was perhaps the most decisive single event in its long ascent to the top as a stud farm."

Leading sire on four occasions, the stallion in his first crop produced the Triple Crown winner Gallant Fox. His fifty-six stakes winners also included Vagrancy, Tintagel, Foxbrough, Gallahadion, and High Quest. He was even more successful as a brood-mare sire and led that sire list twelve times. His daughters produced 152 stakes winners, including Gallorette, Johnstown, Rare Perfume, and Revoked. Today, his influence is carried into modern pedigrees primarily through his daughters. His male line has not continued.

Sir Gallahad III was a favorite at Claiborne, not only because of his success but also because of his kind disposition. Frank Jennings of *The Thoroughbred Record* wrote in the stallion's obituary that "He was a favorite of all the hands at Claiborne because of his tractable and affectionate nature. He liked having his tongue pulled and if a groom or anyone else he recognized came around him he would loll his tongue out, hoping

for a friendly pat or playful tug…May his bones rest in peace. May his spirit live forever."[8] He lived to the advanced age of twenty-nine, dying peacefully in his paddock the evening of July 8, 1949.

A distinguished group lies in the Marchmont cemetery.

MARCHMONT CEMETERY

ACK ACK

Bred by Captain Harry F. Guggenheim and foaled at Spendthrift Farm, Ack Ack was by Alsab's grandson Battle Joined and out of the unraced Turn-to mare

Fast Turn. Fast Turn was a daughter of the Coaching Club American Oaks winner Cherokee Rose, from the family of Joseph Widener's Nipisiquit.

Ack Ack raced for Guggenheim for three seasons

Ack Ack was a handicap star who as a sire continued the Domino line.

and two starts. Unfortunately, Guggenheim, who died in January 1971, did not live to see the colt reach the pinnacle of his racing career. The Forked Lightning Ranch of E. E. Fogelson and his wife, actress Greer Garson, bought the horse following his owner's death.

Ack Ack started just three times as a two-year-old. He proved himself a high-class colt at three, winning seven of his eleven starts. His stakes victories included a track-record-setting performance in the Derby Trial, but he did not contest the classics. His other stakes wins came in the Bahamas Stakes, Arlington Classic, and Withers Stakes.

The following season, the bay colt faced the starter just five times and emerged victorious from four, although his Los Angeles Handicap came by way of disqualification. He also accounted for the Autumn Days Handicap. Charlie Whittingham had taken over training duties from Frank Bonsal.

At five, Ack Ack won the San Carlos for Guggenheim and an additional six stakes for his new owners. In the Santa Anita Handicap, Ack Ack toted 130 pounds to victory over Cougar II. The Hollywood Gold Cup was his final race and one of his finest, as he won under the burden of 134 pounds. Illness prevented any further racing, but at year's end he was remembered by the voters and named champion sprinter, champion handicap male, and Horse of the Year. Charles Hatton wrote that "Ack Ack was indeed a terror, terribly fast and terribly competitive. He could be rated, but (jockey Bill) Shoemaker has light hands and it would be unthinkable to fight him needlessly, and chance doing strange things to his psyche. Usually the little rider 'let 'im roll.' When he was presented with a target, he came with a rattle…so fast that he sometimes neglected to change his legs, but he ran straight and was the last to tire. He neither wore nor needed blinkers, and riding him must have been a pleasure, involving only tying on securely."

Ack Ack's stud career revived the tenuously surviving male line of Domino. His fifty-four stakes winners included the talented yet quirky Broad Brush as well as Youth, Ack's Secret, and Caline. He died in December 1990, having been pensioned in July of that year.

DAMASCUS

Bred and raced by William Woodward's daughter, Edith Woodward Bancroft, Damascus carried the famous Woodward colors to further glories. Foaled in 1964 at Jonabell Farm, Damascus was by Horse of the Year Sword Dancer. His dam was an unraced daughter of My Babu, from the same family as Colonel E. R. Bradley's Bubbling Over.

Damascus was lightly raced at two, winning three of his four engagements, including the Remsen Stakes. At three, he compiled a sterling record of twelve wins, three seconds, and a third from sixteen starts, defeating the best older horses and dominating his age group. Charles Hatton wrote, "He danced all the dances and ran all the distances from a mile to two miles. Never did we see him spit out the bit…and he was confronted with such defiant tasks as carrying top weight of 128 pounds in the Dwyer, giving Ring Twice and Straight Deal actual weight in the Aqueduct, and running smooth-shod in unaccustomed going in the grassy Laurel International. Fort Marcy won the money that day, but Damascus won the crowd's heart."

After opening his sophomore campaign with a facile allowance score, Damascus took Aqueduct's Bay Shore, then was outdueled in the Gotham by the brilliant Dr. Fager. His final Derby prep was a six-length romp in the Wood Memorial.

Favored for the Kentucky Derby, Damascus was undone by the crowds and atmosphere and could do no better than third behind Proud Clarion and Barbs Delight. The Preakness was a different matter, with Damascus home first in front of In Reality and Proud Clarion, and he took the Belmont from Cool Reception. After adding the Leonard Richards Stakes, he finished a nose behind the older horse Exceedingly in the William du Pont Jr. Handicap, while giving weight. He bounced back to take the Dwyer Stakes and the American Derby, the latter in track-record time.

In the historic Travers at Saratoga, Damascus gave an astounding performance, coming from fifteen lengths back to roll home twenty-two lengths in front, equaling the track record. Another victory followed, in the Aqueduct Handicap. He next met Buckpasser and Dr. Fager in the Woodward, winning by ten lengths. Hatton called his action "long and low as a southern hound." Damascus added the Jockey Club Gold Cup, then fell a nose short of eventual grass champion Fort Marcy in the Washington, D.C., International at Laurel. This closed his campaign, and he was named champion three-year-old, champion handicap horse, and Horse of the Year.

Mrs. Bancroft's colt returned to race at four, with Hatton commenting that he "proved a first-class handicapper...though he stood in the shadow of his old rival Dr. Fager." Nevertheless, he won half of his twelve starts and added $332,975 to his bankroll to bring the total at year's end to $1,176,781. His stakes wins at four included the Brooklyn Handicap, in which he defeated Dr. Fager, as well as the Aqueduct and San Fernando Stakes. He bowed a tendon in the Jockey Club Gold Cup and was retired.

Damascus had been remarkably consistent in his three seasons of racing, winning twenty-one of his thirty-two starts, with seven seconds and three thirds. His only off-the-board finish was in the Jockey Club Gold Cup, when he bowed a tendon. Remarked Hatton, "At a glance, Damascus is a demure little horse who goes quietly on parade and handles himself with decorum at the gate. But in the heat of conflict, when his blood is up, he has iron resolution."

Damascus stood his entire career at stud at Claiborne and sired seventy-one stakes winners. Among his best performers were Private Account, Time for a Change, Desert Wine, Highland Blade, and Judger. His sons Private Account, Time for a Change, and Timeless Moment in particular proved to be good stallions. To date, his daughters have produced more than 100 stakes winners. Damascus lived to the venerable age of thirty-one, and died peacefully in his paddock at Claiborne in 1995. Mary Fleming Simon of *The Thoroughbred Times* wrote, "Like a bygone era, Damascus represented something now irretrievably lost to us. His was a closing chapter of great on-track sport — a pre-off-track betting, presimulcasting period wherein vast numbers of fans actually showed up at the track to watch their heroes in live action…Until last week, Damascus stood as a living symbol of a time when racing was golden."[9]

MARGUERITE

Bred by A. B. Hancock and E. F. Simms, Marguerite was by Hancock's stallion Celt and out of the imported mare Fairy Ray. She was foaled on April 24, 1920, at Hancock's Ellerslie Stud in Virginia. William Woodward purchased her as a yearling.

The chestnut filly made only one start, as a two-year-old. Although she was highly regarded, she showed nothing in the race and emerged with a strained muscle. Fast workouts to prepare her for rac-

ing the following season brought about a recurrence of her injury. Marguerite was retired as a three-year-old.

Marguerite's first foal, a bay colt by Wrack, was born in 1925. Named Petee-Wrack, he showed promise at two, and at three became one of the leading performers of his day. Among his wins were the Travers Stakes and the Suburban and Metropolitan

Handicaps. Marguerite's second foal, also by Wrack, was a filly named Anastasia; she made little mark at the races or as a broodmare.

In 1926, Marguerite was among the first mares bred to the newly imported Sir Gallahad III. The result of this mating was a blaze-faced bay who became known as Gallant Fox, the best runner of his day. So successful was the match that all of Marguerite's subsequent offspring were by Sir Gallahad III. After failing to produce a foal for four years, Marguerite foaled Marigal in 1932. The filly showed little at the races but proved a decent producer, foaling the stakes winners Uncle Seaweed, Lone Eagle, and My Emma.

Next came Lucky Pledge, the best runner of Marguerite's fillies. A winner at two, at three Lucky Pledge was second in the Pimlico Oaks. She failed to produce anything of note following her retirement. In 1935 and 1936, Marguerite foaled full brothers to Gallant Fox. First came Fighting Fox, a very good colt who won the Grand Union Hotel Stakes, Wood Memorial, and Massachusetts Handicap, earning more than $100,000. Her 1936 colt, Foxbrough, raced in both England and the United States. Foxbrough was the best of his division at two in

England, winning the Hopeful and Middle Park Stakes. After he returned to the U.S., he added the Butler and Yonkers Handicaps.

In 1938, Marguerite foaled Marguery, who did not race but became the link that has carried Marguerite's name into modern pedigrees. The dam of stakes winners Whirling Fox and Marullah, Marguery also produced Russ-Marie. Russ-Marie's stakes-winning daughter Margarethen continued the female line, with present-day representatives including Trillion, Triptych, Margravine, and Generous.

Maraschino, foaled in 1938, was Marguerite's last foal. Maraschino produced the stakes winners Reinzi and The Senator; her daughters produced the crack steeplechaser Amber Diver and stakes winners Ballet Rose, Amber Stone, and Bruce South.

Marguerite died on October 27, 1945, of old age. She was buried on the hill above the stallion barn, and a large granite marker was placed over her grave. When the sire of her three great sons died four years later, he, too, was buried on the hill and a similar marker placed. Both markers were later moved to the Marchmont cemetery, although the horses' remains were not disturbed.

MOCCASIN

Wrote Charles Hatton in *The American Racing Manual*, "Thoroughbreds who complete a campaign undefeated, even two-year-olds, run very few to the acre, as they say in the Blue Grass. During 1965, Moccasin joined Tremont, Colin, Regret, Morvich, Dice and others whose introductory seasons found them running up perfect scores."

By Nasrullah's son Nantallah and out of the imported mare Rough Shod II, Moccasin was foaled at Claiborne. She was a full sister to the talented colts Ridan and Lt. Stevens.

Possessed of an amenable disposition, Moccasin was a large chestnut with a blaze and three white stockings. She stood sixteen hands as a two-year-old. She faced the starter eight times at two without a setback. Along the way she accounted for the Spinaway, Matron, Alcibiades, Selima, and Gardenia Stakes. Named champion two-year-old filly, she also was honored as Horse of the Year by the voters for the Thoroughbred Racing Associations and *Turf and Sport Digest*.

Her career continued for two more seasons, but Moccasin failed to exhibit the invincibility she had displayed at two, winning just three races in her remaining thirteen starts. She did win a division of the Test Stakes at three and the Phoenix Handicap at four before joining the Claiborne broodmare band with earnings of $388,075.

Moccasin's record as a producer was as sensational as her two-year-old season had been. She produced nine foals, of whom seven won stakes. Perhaps the best was Apalachee, a son of Round Table, who won four of his five starts and was England's champion two-year-old in 1973. He has also been a successful sire, though his fillies have been rather better than his colts. Belted Earl, Moccasin's 1978 colt by Damascus, was champion older horse in Ireland. Her other stakes winners were Nantequos, Indian, Brahms, Flippers, and Scuff. The latter two, both fillies, also foaled stakes winners.

Moccasin was pensioned in 1983 and died three years later of old age. She was the first to be interred in the Marchmont cemetery and the first of Claiborne's great mares to be so honored.

NUMBERED ACCOUNT

Bred and raced by Ogden Phipps, Numbered Account was a member of the initial crop of Phipps' champion Buckpasser and was descended in the female line from Colonel E. R. Bradley's great matron La Troienne. Her dam, Intriguing, won twice and placed in three stakes and was a half-sister to four stakes winners.

Charles Hatton noted of Intriguing's daughter, "A filly of imposing size and substance from foalhood, Numbered Account always was rather eye-catching. Additionally, she was and is sound, and has a disposition like Mary's lamb. Indeed, her handlers found her deportment at breaking time so cooperative and ingratiating, some wondered if she had the competitive spirit which is the prerequisite of a mettlesome, high class racemare."

Numbered Account wasted no time in answering the doubters, compiling a record of eight wins in her first season's ten starts. Her earnings of $446,594 set a record for a juvenile filly. She scored by ten lengths in her debut, then took the Fashion Stakes to become the first stakes winner for her sire. Numbered Account added Saratoga's Schuylerville Stakes before finishing third in the Adirondack at the same venue. She bounced back with consecutive wins in the Matron, Frizette, Selima, and Gardenia Stakes. Indisputably the champion of her division, she closed her campaign with a fourth against males in the Garden State Stakes.

At three, Numbered Account was hampered by a splint but took the Test and Spinster Stakes and was awarded victory in the Matchmaker Stakes via disqualification. In the Spinster, she equaled Keeneland's track record for a mile and one-eighth. Kept in training for an additional season, she won just once before being retired. Her record stood at twenty-two starts, fourteen wins, and earnings of $607,048.

Wrote David Schmitz in *The Blood-Horse*, "It's hard to say whether...Numbered Account accomplished more on the racetrack or in the breeding shed." She certainly proved an outstanding broodmare, producing the stakes winners Private Account (by Damascus) and Dance Number (by Northern Dancer). Private Account won the Gulfstream Park Handicap and the Widener Handicap before becoming a successful sire at Claiborne. Dance Number won the Beldame Stakes and produced champion two-year-old colt Rhythm and stakes winner Get Lucky. Numbered Account's daughters Confidentiality and Secret Asset also have produced stakes winners.

Numbered Account died at age twenty-seven on August 3, 1996.

SIR IVOR

For $42,000, Raymond Guest purchased a yearling colt by Sir Gaylord out of the Mr. Trouble mare Attica at the Keeneland July yearling sale in 1966. The colt went on to win stakes in Ireland, England, France, and the United States before retiring to a stud career in which he was perennially ranked among the leading sires.

Sir Ivor was sent to Ireland to be trained by Vincent O'Brien. He started four times at two, winning all but his first attempt. He took the Probationers' Stakes and National Stakes in Ireland before being sent to France for the prestigious Grand Criterium, where he scored a decisive victory over the filly Pola Bella and Timmy My Boy. Timeform noted that "Sir Ivor couldn't have been more impressive and he is an exciting prospect for the classics."

Sir Ivor wintered in Italy and returned to England to win his preparatory race for the Two Thousand Guineas. In the one-mile classic itself, he faced the highly regarded Petingo. Reserved early well behind the leaders by Lester Piggott, Sir Ivor produced his run when asked and won easily. In *The British Racehorse*, John Hislop commented that "Mr. Guest's colt glided by the opposition like a Rolls Royce passing mowing machines." With Petingo not among those in the Derby field, Connaught appeared the main threat to

The American-bred Sir Ivor won the Epsom Derby.

the Ambassador to Ireland's runner. Again held up until the last possible moment, Sir Ivor passed Connaught to win going clear. According to *The British Racehorse*, "Sir Ivor was undoubtedly the best looking colt in the field and is every bit as good as he looks. He has plenty of substance, excellent limbs, scope, power and quality; also that mark of the really great racehorse, blinding acceleration and the class which makes distance immaterial."

Unfortunately, Sir Ivor proceeded to lose his next four races. After a shocking second in the Irish Sweeps Derby, he was third behind the top older horses Royal Palace and Taj Dewan in the Eclipse Stakes. After a respite from racing, he was second in his prep for France's Arc. He was second again in the Arc itself, to the top-class colt Vaguely Noble. He closed his career on a winning note, taking the Washington, D.C., International from Fort Marcy and Czar Alexander. He retired with eight wins in thirteen starts. He was England's champion three-year-old colt and Horse of the Year for 1968.

Sir Ivor stood two seasons at his owner's Irish stud before moving to Claiborne Farm. He sired ninety-one stakes winners in twenty-four crops, among them the Prix de l'Arc de Triomphe winner Ivanjica and the champions Bates Motel, Ivor's Image, Malinowski, Cloonlara, and Godetia. Although his sons made little impact at stud in the U.S. and Europe, Sir Tristram became a sire sensation in Australia and New Zealand. Sir Ivor's daughters proved outstanding broodmares and have assured the continuance of Sir Ivor's influence in Northern Hemisphere pedigrees.

Pensioned from stud duties in 1991, Sir Ivor was euthanized on November 10, 1995. He was thirty.

TOM ROLFE

Owned by Raymond Guest, Tom Rolfe was by the great European champion Ribot, out of Pocahontas. Pocahontas had previously produced the good colt Chieftain and came from the family of Nipisiquit (Ack Ack's dam also descends from this mare.). Tom Rolfe stood just 15.2 hands and proved again that small stature is no deterrent to racing class.

As a two-year-old of 1964, Tom Rolfe started ten times and won three. His only stakes victory was in the Cowdin, a race that his half-brother Chieftain also had won. That was his final start at two, and the colt spent the winter in the temperate clime of

Camden, South Carolina.

Tom Rolfe duly won his three-year-old debut, an allowance race. He was third in the Bay Shore Stakes, then won his remaining three starts prior to the Kentucky Derby, including the Chesapeake Stakes. Finishing behind Lucky Debonair and Dapper Dan in the Derby, he gained his revenge in the Preakness, coming home a neck in front of Dapper Dan. He completed the classics with a narrow loss to Hail to All in the Belmont.

Tom Rolfe fared even better in the Midwest, winning four stakes at Arlington: the Citation Handicap, Chicagoan Stakes, Arlington Classic, and American Derby. He closed out his season by shipping to France to contest Europe's premier event, the Prix de l'Arc de Triomphe. The colt's sixth-place finish was quite commendable, considering that he had never raced clockwise over an undulating surface.

At home, Tom Rolfe was named champion three-year-old. He was described in Charles Hatton's year-end review as "a charming specimen physically, a true bay like his illustrious sire, neither having any conspicuous markings. He is a hard type, all bone, sinew and animation. He can be a bit of a puller…and was always more than willing. Like many other short coupled, pony built individuals, Tom Rolfe is clever and always 'in cadence' as the French say."

Tom Rolfe was syndicated at the close of his sophomore season, but terms of the agreement permitted him to race through his four-year-old year. Hampered by a quarter crack, he was unable to make his first start at four until July. He won just two stakes events, the Aqueduct and the Salvator Mile Handicaps. He closed his career with sixteen victories in thirty-two starts, for earnings of $671,297.

Tom Rolfe was an immediate success at stud, his first crop including the champions Hoist the Flag, Run the Gantlet, and Droll Role. In all, he sired forty-nine stakes winners, his other notable performers including London Company, Bowl Game, and French Colonial. Today, his male line continues primarily through Hoist the Flag. Tom Rolfe was euthanized in 1989 at the age of twenty-seven and was buried in the Marchmont cemetery.

Part Three: Resting Places of Other Notables

Chapter 10 – Other Runners Remembered

rominent New York real estate magnate Walter J. Salmon founded Mereworth Farm in 1919 as a racing stable and breeding farm. Encompassing more than 700 acres, Mereworth comprised facilities for stallions as well as for mares, foals, and yearlings. Early Mereworth-breds included the Preakness winners Display and Dr. Freeland; the Grand National Steeplechase winner Battleship; and Annapolis, Free For All, and Swivel.

The racing stable was discontinued in 1933, and the focus of the Mereworth operation shifted to the production of yearlings for sale. The best horse Salmon bred was Discovery, a son of Mereworth stallion Display. Discovery was purchased by Alfred Vanderbilt, and became a Horse of the Year and successful sire.

Walter Salmon died in 1953; and his son, Walter Jr., assumed the farm's management duties. During his tenure, Mereworth ceased to stand stallions and took up racing once again, keeping some fillies to run and eventually to join its broodmare band. All told, Mereworth has bred more than 140 stakes winners, including Cathy Baby, Waltz Fan, Pacific Princess, and Palace Music. Today the farm is in the hands of Susan Donaldson, daughter of Walter Salmon Jr.

Mereworth's equine cemetery lies along a fence line between two barns, with the horses being buried in their entirety. The headstones trace the history of the farm, from Ariel, Display, and Snowflake to Cathy Baby and Waltz Fan.

ARIEL

Ariel was a son of the very fast horse Eternal, and his granddam was a full sister to "The Black Whirlwind," Domino. He was bred and raced by the Rancocas Stable of Harry F. Sinclair. His brief racing career consisted of just nine starts at two and a single outing at three, but he showed he had inherited the blazing speed of which his pedigree was chock-full.

After breaking his maiden in his second attempt, Ariel captured the 1927 Youthful Stakes, then added the Saratoga Special in wire-to-wire fashion. In the Hopeful Stakes, he failed to finish in the frame. His final start at two came in the Remsen Handicap, in which he finished second despite being impeded.

Ariel's first three-year-old effort, the Kingston Handicap, which he took from older rivals, was his final race. He retired with six wins from ten starts and earnings of $31,230. In 1930, Adolphe Pons bought Ariel from the Sinclair dispersal, and the horse entered stud at Greenwich Stud on Georgetown Pike. Walter Salmon acquired a half-interest in the stallion in 1936 and moved him to Mereworth, where the horse remained until his death.

In a 1936 article, *The Blood-Horse* described Ariel as "compact, heavily muscled, with a grand masculine head." Speed he possessed; and speed he transmitted. He was well-known as a sire of precocious two-year-olds. His thirty-three stakes winners included Maerial, Airflame, Chicuelo, High Breeze, and Swiv.

Ariel died on March 31, 1950, at the age of twenty-five, as a result of nasal hemorrhages. He was buried not far from Display and other Mereworth notables, his grave marked by a headstone with a bronze plaque.

DISPLAY

Earning the sobriquet "The Iron Horse," Display raced 103 times over six seasons. He won twenty-three races, was second twenty-five times, and third twenty-seven times. At his retirement in 1930, his earnings of $256,506 placed him fourth on the list of leading money-earners. A 1954 article in *The Blood-*

Horse stated that "Display (Fair Play—*Cicuta, by *Nassovian) was the most troublesome and most successful runner bred by Mr. Salmon. Along with an iron constitution, he had a virtually inexhaustible energy and capacity for mischief. The starting point, behind the old tape barrier, was his favorite scene for demonstrating to the world that the domestication of the horse was not quite complete. But once in action, despite the energy used up in wild rebellion, he frequently proved himself one

of the most powerful runners of his time."

Display faced the starter nineteen times at two and won seven times, including the Niagara Stakes in Canada. At three, he won both the Preakness Stakes and the Latonia Championship, and was second in the Cincinnati and American Derbies, the Champlain and Pierrepont Handicaps, and the Saratoga Cup. He was third in six added-money events, including the Travers.

At four, Display added the Washington, Champlain, Ontario Jockey Club, and Baltimore Handicaps and the Pimlico and Toronto Cups. He beat a stellar field in the Washington Handicap, leaving in his wake the crack mare Black Maria as well as top runners Mars and Crusader. At five, he again took the Toronto Autumn Cup and set a track record in the Hawthorne Gold Cup. He won just one stakes event at six, the Baltimore Handicap.

A bruised foot interrupted Display's preparations at seven, and he was bred to a few mares while recovering that spring at Mereworth. On his return to the track, he started four times, managed but one finish in the frame, and was permanently retired.

Display's temperament, always on the difficult side, continued to be a problem at the farm. *The Blood-Horse* remarked that "the fire which raged on the racetrack...was never quite quenched. His stall was padded part of the way up, so the tattoo he beat on it would not harm him. He was not allowed to run as the other stallions did, because he would undertake to kick the planks out of the fence after the first hour or so. He wore a muzzle in his stall to prevent him ripping at his flanks. He was not mean or vicious; he was a Fair Play plus."

Display's first season at stud produced his best offspring: Discovery, who, like his sire, made a name for himself as "The Iron Horse." Although Display sired ten additional stakes winners, none was in Discovery's league. Display died of an apparent heart attack on August 23, 1944. *The Blood-Horse* commented that the stallion "was an outstanding manifestation both of the valor and the headlong impetuosity associated with the tribe of Fair Play."

LADY LARK

Mannie Gray, Lady Lark's fourth dam, was "not only the dam of Domino, but a group of other foals through which she ranks as ancestress of a veritable army of turf stars," John Hervey wrote in *American Race Horses*. Among Mannie Gray's foals was Mannie Himyar, Domino's full sister.

Mated with the stallion Adam, Mannie Himyar produced the filly Adana. Sent to France as a yearling and stakes-placed herself, Adana foaled three stakes winners in France before being repatriated. Back in America, she produced four more stakes winners: Nedana, the speedy Ariel, Celidon, and Ladana. Ladana showed a good deal of ability at the races, winning the Clover Stakes and the Adirondack, Pocahontas, and Flying Fairy Handicaps.

Lady Lark was Ladana's first foal, by Colonel Bradley's fine runner and sire Blue Larkspur. The filly showed little at the track, winning just one of her five starts. She produced her first foal in 1939, a filly by Chance Play named Chance Lark. Chance Lark eventually won seven races from her fifty-two starts over four seasons. In 1940, Lady Lark produced a colt by Bostonian; the following year, she foaled a filly by Bull Lea. When her Bull Lea filly was weaned, Lady Lark was culled from the Calumet broodmare band. Walter J. Salmon's Mereworth Farm bought her for $1,700, in foal to Sun Teddy.

Lady Lark proved a fortuitous acquisition, as her Bull Lea filly went on to race for Calumet as Twilight Tear and was one of the top performers of her day. The foal Lady Lark was carrying at the time of her sale, the filly Sun Lady, also became a stakes winner.

Mereworth was breeding to sell, and so Twilight Tear and Sun Lady's accomplishments enhanced the market value of Lady Lark's subsequent offspring. Each of her next four foals was a winner; but only War Rings, by War Admiral, was of stakes class.

In 1949, Lady Lark was again mated with Bull Lea. The resulting 1950 filly, a full sister to Twilight Tear, sold for $60,000 at Keeneland, at that time a record price for a yearling filly. Named Perfection, she, too, became a stakes winner.

Twilight Tear and Perfection themselves went on to produce stakes winners. Lady Lark produced her last foal in 1957. She died in 1959 and was buried at Mereworth.

SUNGLOW

A chestnut colt by Sun Again out of the Mad Hatter mare Rosern, Sunglow was foaled at Mereworth Farm on April 23, 1947. Although his dam had only placed at two, she was a half-sister to the great Gainsborough. Sold as a yearling for $8,000, Sunglow raced for Isabel Dodge Sloane's Brookmeade Stable, winning nine of his forty-five starts and earning $168,275.

Sunglow showed promise at two, winning only once but finishing third in the Champagne and Kentucky Jockey Club Stakes. He showed improvement at three, winning the Chesapeake Stakes as well as the Saranac and Discovery Handicaps. In the Discovery, he broke Whirlaway's nine-furlong track record. At four, he won the Widener Handicap before being sidelined by injury. Away from the races throughout his five-year-old season, he returned at six to win divisions of both the Turf Cup and Boardwalk Handicaps and was third in the Washington, D.C., International.

After one last start, Sunglow returned to Mereworth to enter stud in 1954 and was bred to just a few mares in his initial season. Sword Dancer was a member of his 1956 crop, and his exploits at three, culminating in Horse of the Year honors, led to his sire's syndication.

Unfortunately, Sunglow never sired another foal that approached Sword Dancer's class and, in fact, sired only five other stakes winners. Despite his rather dismal record in the stud, Sunglow's male line continues through Sword Dancer's son, Damascus. Sunglow, the last stallion to stand at Mereworth, died of an apparent heart attack on June 5, 1964.

THE STALLION STATION

New Yorker L. P. Doherty's initial exposure to racing came at Belmont Park, where he watched the mighty Equipoise race. Bitten by the bug that infects all Thoroughbred-lovers, Doherty came to Kentucky after World War II and got a job as the manager of

Spendthrift Farm. After holding a series of farm-management positions, he decided to establish his own venture, and in May 1953 he purchased forty-seven and a half acres on Russell Cave Pike outside Lexington. Previously the Grant Dorland farm, it became a stallion operation, which Doherty called The Stallion Station. The first residents were the former Elmendorf stallions Roman and Bolero.

Under Harold Snowden's management, The Stallion Station amassed a contingent of stallions with fees ranging from inexpensive to moderate. Snowden purchased Doherty's interest in the farm in 1984, then traded the Russell Cave property for a larger tract on Greenwich Pike. (William du Pont III's Pillar Stud took over the Russell Cave Road site.) Today the former Stallion Station is part of 505 Farm.

The Stallion Station's equine cemetery lies behind the old stallion complex amid a small grove of trees. Large headstones mark the resting places of Roman and Sassafras; the other eighteen graves have flat headstones. Kentucky Derby winner Tomy Lee and fellow stallions Bolero, Royal Coinage, and Bupers, as well as the mares Zonta and Ludham, are some of the horses buried there.

DEVIL DIVER

Racing for the Greentree Stable of Mrs. Payne Whitney, Devil Diver was among the best of his generation at two; a tremendous disappointment at three; and again among the best at four, five, and six. Hampered throughout his career by a troublesome right front hoof, he retired with a record of twenty-two wins, twelve seconds, and three thirds from forty-

Devil Diver was a two-time champion.

seven starts, for earnings of $261,064. He was named champion handicap male for 1943 and 1944.

Devil Diver's sire was the Greentree stallion St. Germans, a son of Swynford who had previously gotten Greentree's smashing Twenty Grand as well as the Kentucky Derby and Preakness winner Bold Venture. Foaled on March 11, 1939, Devil Diver was out of the stakes-placed mare Dabchick. In the 1944 edition of *American Race Horses*, Joe Palmer described him as "a very impressive horse, a little above middle size, muscled with extraordinary strength, with straight hind legs, finely modeled shoulders and stout forearms, and

the air and carriage associated with the Thoroughbred at his best."

Highly regarded at two, Devil Diver won the Sanford and the Hopeful Stakes and the Breeder's Futurity. He was second in the Futurity Stakes, the Remsen Handicap, and the Pimlico Futurity.

At three, Devil Diver's only stakes win came in his initial outing, in which he defeated Whirlaway in Keeneland's Phoenix Handicap. After dismal performances in the Kentucky Derby and the Preakness, he was sidelined by his ailing hoof but returned to finish second in the Vosburgh Handicap and third in the Jerome in the fall. Noted John Hervey, "He closed the season very decidedly under a cloud. If anyone had then ventured to predict that he would prove one of the stars of 1943, there would have been little support for that prognostication among the experts."

Devil Diver rallied to enjoy quite a successful four-year-old season, winning four of nine starts in an abbreviated campaign. He took the six-furlong Toboggan Handicap, the one-mile Metropolitan, the seven-furlong Carter, and the one-and-one-quarter-mile Brooklyn Handicap. He made his final start of the year in the Stars and Stripes Handicap, finishing unplaced. Once again, he was shelved because of his right front hoof.

In his return to the track at five, Devil Diver won the Paumonok Handicap, then took the Toboggan under 134 pounds. He went on to win his second Metropolitan Handicap under another 134-pound burden. His hoof troubles flared up again on the morning of the Brooklyn Handicap, necessitating his withdrawal. He returned to win the American Legion Handicap under 136, then took the Whitney from Princequillo and Bolingbroke. Unplaced in the Saratoga Handicap, he added the Wilson Stakes and the Manhattan Handicap. Although the latter's one-and-one-half-mile distance was probably beyond his normal scope, the early part of the race was run at a virtual snail's pace, enabling him to sprint home. (Joe Palmer noted that Greyhound had trotted a half mile as fast as they had run the opening half that day.) The horse closed out his season with successive losses in the Jockey Club Gold Cup, Gallant Fox Handicap, and Pimlico Special.

The original intention had been to retire Devil Diver to stud in 1945, but instead he was rested and returned to training. He made just five starts at six,

winning three and finishing second twice. He opened his campaign with a second win in the Paumonok Handicap and then dropped the Toboggan to Apache. Next, he took his third consecutive Metropolitan Handicap by four lengths under 129 pounds. He won the Suburban but then lost to Stymie in the Brooklyn. With his hoof bothering him again, he was retired.

Devil Diver began his stud career at his birthplace, Greentree Farm, but later was moved to The Stallion Station. He met with limited success, siring just eighteen stakes winners, including The Diver, Lotowhite, Anchors Aweigh, and Devilkin. He fractured his left hind leg in a paddock accident on November 16, 1961, and was euthanized.

ROMAN

Roman was sired by the good middle-distance horse Sir Gallahad III and was out of Buckup, a daughter of the English Cup horse Buchan. The colt's proclivities ran to the pure speed demonstrated by Ultimus, the sire of his second dam. Bred and raced by Joseph E. Widener, Roman retired sound after racing for three seasons, with a record of eighteen wins in forty starts and earnings of $56,060.

In *American Race Horses*, John Hervey described Roman as "a good-sized, powerful horse, rich dark bay in color, with a head much like his sire's, and of the same expression about the eyes." The colt won six of his nine starts as a two-year-old, including the Lafayette Stakes at Keeneland, Churchill's Bashford Manor Stakes, and Arlington's Hyde Park Stakes.

The three-year-old Roman proved no match for the best of his division, particularly when tried over middle distances, but was a useful sprinter and won stakes at a mile. Among his wins were the Chicago and Jerome Handicaps and the Laurel Stakes. He finished second to Bimelech in the Blue Grass Stakes at Keeneland and ran well for a mile in the Kentucky Derby before faltering.

Brought out again at four, Roman managed to win in just four of thirteen trips to the post. In the fall, he ran what was perhaps the best race of his career in the six-furlong Fall Highweight Handicap. Assigned the burden of 140 pounds, he was reserved behind the leaders early, then battled Speed to Spare in the stretch. He emerged the victor by a length, his time of 1:10 equaling the track record.

Initially leased to Harrie Scott for stud purposes, Roman moved to Elmendorf in 1950 and remained there after Maxwell Gluck purchased the farm. L. P. Doherty managed Roman during the stallion's tenure at Elmendorf and moved him to The Stallion Station in 1953.

Remarked Abram S. Hewitt in *Sire Lines*, "Roman was one of those rare horses, which — like Black

Toney, High Time, Bull Dog, Pilate, and Bull Lea was considerably better at stud than he had been on the race course." Perennially among the nation's leading sires — especially as a sire of two-year-olds — he got fifty-four stakes winners, including the Preakness winner Hasty Road, Romanita, Roman Patrol, Times Roman, and Roman Line. Broodmare sire of eighty-five stakes winners, he led that list in 1965. Although his male line has not continued, extinguishing that of Sir Gallahad, Roman's name is still found in pedigrees through his daughters, who produced good sires such as Chieftain, Tom Rolfe, and Proudest Roman.

Roman died on August 26, 1960, at the age of twenty-three, apparently of a ruptured small intestine. One of the first stallions to stand at The Stallion Station, he was the first to be buried in the plot behind the stallion barns.

ROYAL SERENADE

Bred in Ireland by Hilltown Stud, Royal Serenade was among the speedy Royal Charger's first foal crop. Royal Serenade's unraced dam, Pasquinade, was by the Two Thousand Guineas winner Pasch, out of Fur Tor, herself second in the One Thousand Guineas. In 1949, Mrs. Geoffrey Kohn bought the attractive chestnut colt as a yearling for around $6,700.

At two, Royal Serenade showed something of his sire's brilliant speed, winning five of his seven starts, all at five furlongs. While members of his female line had shown some staying ability, Royal Charger's son was expected to have some stamina limitations, although *The Bloodstock Breeders' Review* commented that "he is a delightful colt to ride...He can be dropped out and is content to do the jockey's bidding without making any fuss. That kind can sometimes get a distance beyond their natural capacity."

Royal Serenade was unplaced in the Two Thousand Guineas and thereafter competed primarily at sprint distances, although he did win the Jersey Stakes at something over seven furlongs. His only other stakes victory was in the five-furlong Nunthorpe Stakes.

Canadian G. M. Bell bought Royal Serenade before the colt's four-year-old campaign for $20,580. Bell raced him in England in 1952, and the horse won the Cork and Orrery, King George, and a second Nunthorpe Stakes. Royal Serenade closed out the year with a third in the July Cup after a bad start. He was named England's champion sprinter.

Sent to California to prepare for his 1953 campaign, Royal Serenade raced in the U.S. in the name of Alberta Ranches, Inc. He began, rather inauspiciously, with defeats in two six-furlong handicaps before taking two allowance races at the same distance.

In the one-and-one-sixteenth-mile Inglewood Handicap, Royal Serenade finished second to Pet Bully. After winning an overnight handicap at the same distance with a front-running performance, he took the American Handicap in similar style.

Royal Serenade was assigned but 113 pounds for the rich Gold Cup — fifteen fewer pounds than high-weighted Royal Vale. Noted Joe Estes, "*Royal Serenade made the race look like a gift. He was in front all the way, Longden never even showing him the whip." In what was to be his final start, the colt was fourth in the San Diego Handicap, emerging with a hind leg injury. A subsequent injury sent him to stud. His record showed sixteen wins from thirty-one starts, with seven seconds and a third.

Royal Serenade began his stud career in California and moved to The Stallion Station in 1955. His twenty-six stakes winners included Gay Serenade, Golden Joey, and Royal Smoke. He was euthanized at the age of twenty-seven on March 27, 1975, the same day the farm lost twenty-nine-year-old Bolero.

SASSAFRAS

French-bred Sassafras was by the Ascot Gold Cup and Grand Prix de Saint-Cloud winner Sheshoon, out of the mare Ruta, who was descended from one of France's premier Thoroughbred families. Sassafras, foaled in 1967, was a contemporary of the great Nijinsky II. He evolved from a rather uninspiring two-year-old to the best of his year in France at three and the conqueror of Nijinsky II in the Prix de l'Arc de Triomphe.

Sassafras started just four times at two, winning in his initial outing on August 5, at Vichy. In his next race, Longchamp's Prix des Chenes, he could do no better than fourth; and he finished fifth in the Prix Eclipse at Saint-Cloud. In his final appearance of the season, on November 9 at Bordeaux, he ran second to The Beauty King in the Grand Criterium de Bordeaux. The Handicap Optional ranked him well below the best of the French two-year-olds.

At three, the attractive bay colt opened with a second in the Prix LaGrange. He then scored successive victories in the Prix Androcles and the Prix La Force. In May, he came out for Longchamp's Prix Lupin, facing the top class colts Stintino and Dragoon. He finished third to that pair but had behind him the well-regarded colts Caro and Faraway Son.

While the French colts Stintino and Gyr journeyed to Epsom to tackle Nijinsky II in the Derby, Sassafras remained in France to contest that country's equivalent, the Prix du Jockey-Club, on June 7. Reserved early, he came on late to win by three parts of a length.

Sassafras did not reappear on a racecourse until September 13, for the Prix Royal-Oak. Hallez bested him easily but was disqualified, making Sassafras the victor. Next, in the Arc, he took on a fine field, including Nijinsky II, Blakeney, Miss Dan, Gyr, and Stintino. Reserved not far off the early pace, he bested Miss Dan in the straight and then held off a late charge by Nijinsky II to win by a head. The victory helped garner the colt champion three-year-old honors in France.

The Arc also was Sassafras' last race, and he entered stud in Ireland the following year. He stood only one season in Ireland before being imported to the U.S. to stand at William du Pont III's Pillar Stud. Among his

fifty-six stakes winners were Marmolada, Glenaris, and Henri la Balafre. His son Saros proved a useful sire in California, getting millionaire Fran's Valentine, among others.

Sassafras was euthanized on December 7, 1988, due to a pituitary tumor that caused breathing problems. A large headstone, similar to Roman's, marks his grave.

JONABELL FARM

In an article for *Keeneland* magazine, Arnold Kirkpatrick referred to Jonabell Farm founder John A. Bell III as "a man whose prescience and ultimate knowledge of racing have made him a leader in the Thoroughbred business." Bell turned an unimproved tract of land into a thriving, full-service operation.

Although he had ridden as a youngster on his father's farm outside Pittsburgh, Bell was not exposed to Thoroughbred racing until his college years, when his father turned to Thoroughbreds after an unsuccessful venture in raising crossbred hunters. After the younger Bell returned from World War II and served a stint assisting veterinarian Art Davidson in Lexington, he began breaking yearlings at a leased facility on Georgetown Road in Kentucky. In 1948, he leased a portion of Hamburg Place and called it Jonabell Farm. Bell stood a couple of stallions, boarded mares for clients, and maintained his father's bloodstock. Among Jonabell's first foals was Battlefield, George D. Widener's champion two-year-old.

Bell bought the current Jonabell Farm, located on Bowman's Mill Road, in 1954. He added to the original 254-acre tract to bring the farm's total acreage to about 800. Jonabell stands stallions (including the Triple Crown winner Affirmed); boards mares; and prepares, sells, and breaks yearlings. Prominent runners with connections to Jonabell include Battlefield, the Epsom Derby winner Never Say Die, Horse of the Year Damascus, Epitome, and Green Forest.

Jonabell's equine cemetery lies along the driveway that leads to the farm office. The stallion Vigors is buried at a curve in the drive, and along the straight stretch nearer the office are buried such prominent Thoroughbreds as Cicada, Dark Discovery, Stellar Role, and Kerala.

CICADA

Christopher Chenery's Meadow Stable raced a number of descendants of Hildene, including the champion Cicada. Her sire was the Meadow homebred Bryan G., and her dam was Hildene's daughter Satsuma. Foaled on May 7, 1959, at Claiborne Farm, Cicada went on to become a champion at two, three, and four. She retired as the leading female money-winner.

Cicada's delicate appearance belied her strength and soundness. She withstood three rigorous campaigns before being sidelined by a stifle injury. Her temperament was deceiving as well: She was sweet-natured in the barn and fiercely competitive on the track. "If anything, she was competitive to a fault," noted Charles Hatton, "so that she lost a few races she might otherwise have won by dragging her rider to the pace leaving the gate."

At two, Cicada faced the starter sixteen times, beginning February 23, 1961, with a win in a three-furlong maiden dash and concluding October 21 with a winning effort in the Gardenia Stakes. In between, she won the Blue Hen, National Stallion, Schuylerville, Spinaway, Matron, Astarita, and Frizette Stakes. Her record earned her honors as champion of her division.

At three, Cicada had another arduous campaign of seventeen starts, of which she won eight. Again she started her season in February, with an allowance victory. She took on the boys in the Florida Derby and though defeated was not disgraced. She set a pressured pace, then battled Ridan gamely to the wire, coming up just a nose short. Returned to competition among fillies, she scored in the Kentucky Oaks, Acorn, and Mother Goose Stakes. She competed against males one more time that season, in the Travers, but finished last after bumping Military Plume at the start.

The Chenery filly returned to take the Beldame and the Jersey Belle Stakes, but her final two efforts were subpar fourth- and fifth-place finishes, respectively, in the Vineland and Ladies' Handicaps. Despite her late-season losses, she had done enough to garner another championship.

The Columbiana Handicap on February 13, 1963, was Cicada's four-year-old season opener. Top-weighted, she won rather easily. She next was fifth in the Black Helen Handicap, and was second in the Suwanee River while having not the best of trips. At Aqueduct she took the Distaff Handicap, then was away for five weeks.

On her return, Cicada was third in the Top Flight Handicap, then won the Vagrancy. Tried on turf, she

annexed the Sheepshead Bay Handicap, giving the runner-up nineteen pounds. The Delaware Handicap, in which she finished second, proved to be her final race of the season, as she shortly thereafter injured a stifle and was retired.

Sent to the court of her former stablemate, Sir Gaylord, Cicada failed to conceive and returned to training. She was permanently retired after finishing fourth in her single start as a five-year-old.

Cicada never achieved the success as a broodmare that she had enjoyed on the track. She started off well

enough, producing first the Sir Gaylord colt Cicada's Pride in 1966, then Conversation Piece and Bold Flip (both by Bold Ruler). Plagued by problems, she produced only three more foals before her death. Of her six foals, only Cicada's Pride won a stakes race. She died hours after giving birth to a filly by Bailjumper at Jonabell in 1981.

SUMATRA

Charles T. Wilson Jr. bought Sumatra's dam, the Aboukir II mare Sunda Strait, from a sale in Pomona, California, for $7,500. Sunda Strait finished her racing career in Wilson's name, winning six of her forty-five starts and earning $31,334. She then joined her owner's small band of broodmares at Jonabell Farm.

Sumatra was Sunda Strait's second foal and was by the Nashua stallion Groton. Carrying the Wilson colors, Sumatra made thirteen starts in three seasons, recording five wins and five seconds. Her best season was at three, when she won a division of the 1972 Santa Ysabel Stakes from Foreseer as well as Pimlico's Flirtation Stakes. In California, she had been second to champion Susan's Girl in the Pasadena Stakes. Noted *The Thoroughbred Record*, "Sumatra had proven herself to be a fast, game, consistent filly...who stayed a mile well, but was extremely effective over six furlongs in good company."[1]

At the close of Sumatra's racing career, she joined the other Wilson broodmares at Jonabell. Her first foal was the One for All filly One Sum, who won several stakes for Wilson and earned $394,737. Her second foal, Starsum, by Pia Star, was winless in four starts.

In 1977, Sumatra was bred to Elmendorf's Verbatim. The resulting colt, named Summing, became the most accomplished of his dam's foals, winning the 1981 Belmont Stakes at the height of his career. He also won the Pegasus Handicap, Pennsylvania Derby, and Hill Prince Stakes for his breeder.

Returned to One for All the next two seasons, Sumatra produced the stakes-winning fillies Twosome and Some for All. In all, she produced eighteen foals for Wilson before she died from foaling complications on February 4, 1995.

VIGORS

A nearly white son of the French imports Grey Dawn II and Relifordie, Vigors went from "big, green, and lazy" at two to "White Lightning of the West" at five. Bred and raced by W. R. Hawn, the roan colt was foaled and raised at Jonabell and later returned there to stand at stud.

Vigors ran but once at two and at three won just two races. He did not gain his initial stakes victory until his third season. At that time, he was regarded primarily as a turf specialist; both of his stakes wins came on the grass, in the Rolling Green and Hollywood Invitational Handicaps.

Vigors continued to improve the following year and also showed that he was not strictly a turf performer by winning several major races on the main track.

Vigors' first start at five was the San Marcos Handicap, which ordinarily was a turf event but had been moved to the main track due to the sodden condition of Santa Anita's turf course. The colt closed with a rush to win by four and one-half lengths in near track-record time. He ran on dirt in his next outing, the San Antonio Stakes, again coming from far back to win by seven over the millionaire Ancient Title, breaking Bug Brush's track record for the distance.

The track for the Santa Anita Handicap was muddy, but Hawn's horse still scored his third consecutive victory. Vigors' next race was to be the San Juan

Capistrano on the grass, but a throat infection kept him away from the races until June. He returned to competition in the Bel Air Handicap, and he had little trouble obtaining his fourth consecutive victory.

The Hollywood Gold Cup proved to be "White Lightning's" final start. He ran well but was unlucky enough to miss by a neck and a head after being carried wide. An ankle injury sent him to the sidelines and eventually to stud.

Vigors sired several notable performers, among them the champion Air de Cour, Hodges Bay, Lovlier Linda, and Royal Mountain Inn. Vigors was euthanized on September 27, 1994. The stallion had been in poor health for several months after a severe bout of colic.

STONER CREEK STUD

Austrian immigrant John D. Hertz was an American success story, rising from modest beginnings to become one of America's leading industrialists. He met his wife, the former Frances Kesner, at the racetrack, and bought his first Thoroughbreds in 1921.

Hertz's first good ones were champions Anita Peabody and Reigh Count, who took the first two places in Belmont's Futurity Stakes in 1927. Reigh Count went on to become the best colt of his year at three, winning the Kentucky Derby. The stallion retired to Hertz's Leona Farm in Illinois.

In 1938, Hertz purchased an unimproved tract of land that adjoined Arthur Hancock's Claiborne Farm. Through the property ran the picturesque Stoner Creek, from which the farm took its name. In 1940, Reigh Count moved to Stoner Creek after a brief stint at Claiborne, and the Triple Crown winner Count Fleet was among his first crop raised at Hertz's Kentucky farm.

In later years, after the deaths of John and Frances Hertz, Stoner Creek Stud became the Standardbred nursery of Norman Woolworth.

The Stoner Creek cemetery honors both Thoroughbreds and Standardbreds. Triple Crown winner Count Fleet's memorial holds a place of honor near the front, along with a similar marker for the great trotter Nevele Pride and an obelisk in memory of Meadow Skipper. Toward the rear of the cemetery, near one of the farm's beautiful stone walls, is a tribute to Count Fleet's sire and dam, who are buried elsewhere on the farm.

COUNT FLEET

In a racing career that lasted just over one calendar year, Count Fleet proved himself to be the most dominant runner seen on the American Turf since Man o' War. Although his career ended before he could be tested against older rivals, his superiority over his contemporaries was unquestionable.

Count Fleet's sire, Reigh Count, won both the Kentucky Derby and England's Coronation Cup. Count Fleet's dam, Quickly, did not possess such illustrious credentials, having never won a stakes, but had shown ability and durability by winning thirty-two races over six seasons.

Count Fleet first appeared in Hertz's yellow-and-black colors on June 1, 1942. As Abram S. Hewitt wrote in *Sire Lines*, "Like many good colts that stay well and continue developing, Count Fleet was not overwhelming in his first efforts." It was not until the colt's third start that he achieved his first victory, taking a five-and-one-half-furlong event at Aqueduct. Next, facing other winners, he ran the same distance in 1:05 4/5, just three-fifths of a second off the track record. He scored his first stakes victory on July 22 in the Wakefield Stakes.

Sent to Chicago to take on Occupation in the Washington Park Futurity, Count Fleet missed by a neck. Given a month's respite, he reappeared at Aqueduct to take an allowance event and a similar contest at Belmont.

Prepping for Belmont's Futurity Stakes, Count Fleet worked the six-furlong distance four days prior in an eye-popping 1:08 1/5. In the Futurity itself, the Count could do no better than third, his tremendous effort earlier in the week apparently having taken its toll.

Just one week later, Count Fleet took the Champagne Stakes by six lengths in track-record time of 1:34 4/5, then trounced Occupation in the Pimlico Futurity. His final start of the season was a facile score in the Walden Stakes. John Hervey closed his remarks on Count Fleet in *American Race Horses* of 1942 with the following: "His *tout ensemble* is racy, striking and

Stoner Creek Stud pays tribute to Thoroughbreds and Standardbreds.

indicative of both speed and staying power. In action he is equally striking. He runs with a high head, his stride is slashing, he rises high off the ground in his air-flight, has strong finishing capacity and goes at his work with utmost resolution. There is every indica-

Count Fleet, the 1943 Triple Crown winner.

tion that, like his sire, he should develop into a great staying three-year-old…"

Count Fleet began his brief three-year-old season on April 13, winning an allowance event easily on a sloppy track. Next, in the Wood Memorial, he again won handily in a time just two-fifths off the track record.

The Hertz colt was heavily favored for the Kentucky Derby and romped home three lengths in front of Blue Swords. Remarked Hervey, "The field behind them seemed utterly demoralized…Seldom, indeed, in a classic race, did one behold so many colts so badly beaten."

In the Preakness, the colt faced just three opponents. Wrote Hervey, "Count Fleet shot to the front like a skyrocket when the get-off came, and thereafter his flying form, steadily increasing the distance between him and his ineffectual pursuers, drew farther and farther off from them." At the finish, it was Count Fleet by eight over Blue Swords, in a time just two-fifths off the Preakness record.

Between the Preakness and the Belmont, Count Fleet won the Withers Stakes. Only Fairy Manhurst and Deseronto, who between them had won but three races, faced him in the Belmont. He again led from the start and widened throughout, winning by twenty-five lengths.

Count Fleet struck his left front ankle during the Belmont. The injury initially looked minor but did not respond well to treatment, and the colt was retired with a record of sixteen wins from twenty-one starts.

Count Fleet proved a successful, if not great, stallion. He led the sire list in 1951 and sired thirty-nine stakes winners. Among his best offspring were Horses of the Year Counterpoint and One Count, champion Kiss Me Kate, and Kentucky Derby winner Count Turf. Pensioned in 1965, Count Fleet died at age thirty-three on December 3, 1973.

HAGYARD FARM

Dr. Charles E. Hagyard's grandfather, Edward T. Hagyard, was one of Lexington's first veterinarians, starting a practice there in 1876. Charles's father also graduated from veterinary college and set up in practice with his father and brother.

Charles Hagyard was born in Montana in 1902, while his father was resident veterinarian for Marcus Daly's Bitter Root Stud. After Daly's death, the Hagyards returned to Lexington. Charles followed in

his father's footsteps and graduated from vet school in 1924, joining his father's Lexington practice. Dr. Charlie, as he was fondly known, pioneered the practices of examining mares and certifying them to be in foal; he became the area's first specialist in equine reproduction.

Hagyard also enjoyed breeding and raising horses and purchased 175 acres on Paris Pike in 1928. Further acquisitions increased the farm's size to its present 336 acres. Hagyard Farm also boarded horses, and among the boarders were the horses of the Bieber-Jacobs partnership. In the mid-1970s, the Société Aland of Alec Head and Roland de Chambure also began boarding mares at the farm.

Hagyard Farm's equine cemetery is located at the first crossroads of the main drive. Simple headstones mark the graves of the Bieber-Jacobs stars Stymie and Hail to Reason as well as the Société Aland mares Dancing Maid, Gold River, and Pistol Packer.

HAIL TO REASON

Bred by the partnership of Isidor Bieber and Hirsch Jacobs, Hail to Reason was foaled at Hagyard Farm on April 19, 1958. His sire, Turn-to, had been brilliant at

two but bowed a tendon early in his three-year-old season. His dam, Nothirdchance, had won a division of the Acorn Stakes in 1951.

Standing well over sixteen hands as a two-year-old, Hail to Reason began his racing career three months before his actual birthday. In his debut at Santa Anita on January 21, he beat just two horses in a three-furlong dash. He scored his first win in his sixth start, setting a track record for five furlongs.

The Youthful Stakes on May 11 was Hail to Reason's first stakes triumph. He then lost the Juvenile to Iron Rail and Globemaster and came home fifth in Monmouth's Tyro Stakes after breaking poorly.

The Jacobs color-bearer continued to show improvement, winning the Tremont and the Great American Stakes, the Sanford at Saratoga, and the Sapling Stakes at Monmouth. Hail to Reason emerged from a sixth-place finish in the Saratoga Special with sore shins but recovered well enough to contest the Hopeful just ten days later. Here he scored a decisive victory, coming home ten lengths in front and lowering the track record as well.

Hail to Reason's final race was a triumph in Atlantic City's World's Playground Stakes. On September 18, working toward his engagement in the Champagne Stakes, Hail to Reason fractured both sesamoids in his left front leg. He recovered, then returned to his birthplace to begin his stud career in the spring. Hail to Reason received champion two-year-old male honors.

Wrote John P. Sparkman in *The Thoroughbred Record* serial "Contemporary Stallions," "At stud, he became one of the most powerful influences for soundness, stamina, and class seen in postwar America."[2] Hail to Reason was an immediate and sustained success in his new sphere. His first crop included Horse of the Year Personality, Belmont Stakes winner Hail to All, and champion Straight Deal. In all, he sired winners of each of America's classics as well as the Epsom Derby winner Roberto. Hail to Reason sired forty-three stakes winners, and was named leading sire in 1970.

Several of Hail to Reason's sons have continued his male line, and his daughters were valued broodmares. The stallion became ill in the fall of 1975 and never recovered. He was euthanized on February 24, 1976.

STYMIE

Stymie's story is not one of a regally bred youngster who goes on to fame and fortune at the races and in

Stymie worked his way to the top.

the stud. Rather, it is of a colt of modest lineage who began at the bottom and worked his way to the top of the earning charts.

Stymie was bred by Robert Kleberg's King Ranch (although a delay in completing the transfer of the paperwork caused his breeder to be listed as Max

Hirsch). He was by Equipoise's son Equestrian, who had little to recommend him as a stallion other than his paternity, as he had won only two races. Stymie's dam, Stop Watch, had accomplished even less, not even placing in four attempts. Both his sire and dam descended in male line from the brilliant Domino, and each carried the blood of Man o' War.

Neither was Stymie exceptional in appearance. In *American Race Horses* of 1945, Joe Palmer wrote, "Stymie is not particularly striking. His head is cleanly cut and has a good deal of character, though the crooked blaze down his face gives him an irresponsi-

ble, rowdy look. He is of moderate size, with strong but not thick hindquarters. His back is of medium length. He is fairly narrow in front. His cannons are neither short nor long. Point by point he is not remarkable, but he is perfectly balanced…"

Stymie's first races did little to encourage any thoughts of later success, for he finished well beaten in claiming races. In his third start, Hirsch Jacobs claimed him for $1,500; the colt thereafter raced in the name of Jacobs' wife, Ethel. Showing some improvement, Stymie finished second in each of his next five outings, still running for a claiming tag. He continued winless until his fourteenth start, when he finally got that elusive maiden victory. At the end of his freshman season, he had won four races in twenty-eight starts.

The three-year-old Stymie continued in much the same vein, although he kept markedly better company. He won three of his twenty-nine starts and placed in several stakes, including a second in the Wood Memorial and thirds in the Flamingo Stakes and the Pimlico Cup. The latter was the final race in his second arduous campaign, and he was given a well-earned rest. He returned at four much improved.

The high-headed chestnut began his third season

with a second in an allowance contest, then took a handicap easily under top weight of 119 pounds. His next race saw him garner his first stakes win, in the Grey Lag Handicap. After seconds in the Suburban and Queens County Handicaps, he took advantage of a sixteen-pound swing in the weights to take the Brooklyn from Devil Diver. Over the course of the season, he won the Butler Handicap, Saratoga Cup, Westchester and Riggs Handicaps, and the two-and-one-half-mile Pimlico Cup. He was named champion handicap male for the year.

At five, Stymie won eight of twenty starts, including the Grey Lag Handicap (equaling the track record) as well as the Whitney Stakes and the Edgemere, Manhattan, New York, and Gallant Fox Handicaps. He also won the Saratoga Cup in a walkover.

Stymie's six-year-old season began rather unremarkably, with a fifth-place finish in a six-furlong overnight handicap and a fourth behind Assault in the Grey Lag. However, he bounced right back to win the one-mile Metropolitan Handicap. Among his other stakes victories that year were the Questionnaire and Sussex Handicaps; the Gold Cup; and the Massachusetts, Aqueduct, and Gallant Fox

Handicaps. The last named purse brought Stymie's earnings to a world-record $816,060.

In 1948, the Bieber-Jacobs horse won four of eleven starts, taking a second Metropolitan Handicap as well as the Aqueduct and Sussex Handicaps. In the Sussex, Stymie broke his own track record for the one-and-one-quarter-mile distance. His final start was the Monmouth Handicap, in which he finished fourth. He pulled up obviously lame and was found to have suffered a fractured sesamoid.

Stymie bred ten mares in the spring of 1949 and then returned to training. He failed to win in five starts but was second in the New York Handicap. He was permanently retired with thirty-five wins from 131 starts, with record earnings of $918,485.

The stallion began and ended his stud career in Kentucky at Hagyard Farm, with a six-year interlude in California at Sunnyslope Farm. He sired twelve stakes winners, including Rare Treat, Joe Jones, and Paper Tiger. He died of a heart attack on June 24, 1962.

BOSQUE BONITA

The Bosque Bonita property, which today is encompassed by William Farish's Lane's End, is one of the

oldest Thoroughbred farms in Woodford County. In a small grove of sycamores not far from the main residence is a memorial to the ill-fated Bally Ache and the headstone of Bally Ache's dam, Celestial Blue.

Dating to the time of R. A. Alexander's Woodburn Stud and Jacob Harper's Nantura Farm, Bosque Bonita ("beautiful woodland") was given its name by General Abe Buford, who stood Longfellow's sire Leamington and later Leamington's son Enquirer.

After Buford went bankrupt, forcing the farm's sale, noted trainer and breeder John H. Morris acquired Bosque Bonita. Morris died in 1948, and the property has changed hands several times since. Robert A. Alexander III owned the farm in the early 1960s, when Bally Ache was retired due to a severe ankle injury.

BALLY ACHE

On April 23, 1957, Celestial Blue foaled a colt by Ballydam at Twin Oak Farm near Walton, Kentucky. Celestial Blue had won eight times in fifty-eight starts over four seasons. Ballydam had won stakes in England at two, and at three in the United States. He continued to race through his eight-year-old year although plagued throughout his career by bad feet.

Bally Ache was a member of his first foal crop.

Sold as a yearling to Leonard Fruchtman, Bally Ache broke his maiden in his second try, taking a division of the Hialeah Juvenile Stakes. In his next start, he set a five-furlong track record at Jamaica. Clearly, he had inherited some of his sire's abundant speed. He next annexed the Comely Stakes, then was beaten by Vital Force in the Cherry Hill.

Bally Ache won Belmont's Juvenile Stakes, then added the Mayflower Stakes at Suffolk. He was third in the Tremont after tossing his rider and running off before the start, but returned to beat Tremont winner Vital Force in the Great American Stakes, his last win of the season.

At three, Bally Ache proved that he was not merely a good sprinter. Beginning on January 20, 1960, at Hialeah, Bally Ache won the Hibiscus, Bahamas, and Flamingo Stakes. At Gulfstream he added the Florida Derby. His final prep for the Kentucky Derby was Churchill's Stepping Stone Purse, in which he defeated Venetian Way. Venetian Way turned the tables in the Derby itself, winning by three-and-one-half lengths, with Bally Ache second.

A syndicate, whose members included Robert Alexander III, bought Bally Ache before the Preakness. In the race, the colt took an uncontested lead and romped home an easy winner. He then won the Jersey Derby over Tompion but was kept out of the Belmont by an ankle injury.

Bally Ache returned to the track in September. He won two exhibition events, then finished third in the United Nations Handicap. Next, to prep for the Hawthorne Gold Cup, he ran in the Gold Cup Prep Handicap. Unfortunately, the colt had dislocated his ankle and ruptured ligaments. His leg was placed in a cast and he was flown to Lexington on October 23, with veterinarians in constant attendance.

Bosque Bonita threw a party to welcome the gallant colt to his new home. Sadly, Bally Ache lived just five more days, dying on October 28 from an intestinal infection. Joe A. Estes wrote in *American Race Horses*, "A modest headstone was erected over the grave at Bosque Bonita. The inscription could well have repeated the lines from a stone a few miles away, marking the resting place of one of Bally Ache's ancestors. It was beyond question that Bally Ache, like Domino, was 'one of the gamest and most generous of horses.' "

NORTH RIDGE FARM

Construction magnate Franklin Groves purchased his first Thoroughbred in 1975, bidding a then world-record $715,000 for a chestnut colt by Raise a Native. Along with wife Carolyn and partner Ann Trimble, Groves continued to invest in the highest-quality bloodstock available, spending large sums to acquire the most desirable individuals.

In 1978, Groves purchased the 207-acre core of North Ridge Farm near Lexington, which had previously been the property of long-time breeder Thomas Piatt. Groves added further acreage to bring the total to more than 1,000 acres on both sides of Spurr Road and extending past the interstate to the north.

North Ridge enjoyed considerable success as a commercial breeding operation, earning an Eclipse Award as the nation's leading breeder in 1989. Among the North Ridge-breds running that year were the champions Blushing John and Blushing Katy and eleven other stakes winners.

Financial problems in the family's construction firm led to the sale of North Ridge to Kenneth T. Jones Jr. in 1990. The farm has since been split into smaller tracts; Hill 'n' Dale now occupies a portion on the south side of Spurr Road, while Breckinridge Farm is on the north side.

Breckinridge Farm has one Thoroughbred memorial, a monument to the great race mare Desert Vixen.

DESERT VIXEN

In his "Profiles of Best Horses" for the 1974 edition of the *American Racing Manual*, Charles Hatton wrote that "A petite, vivacious dark bay or brown filly called Desert Vixen burst on the scene with great éclat in 1973. She was among the most admirable, and extensively admired three-year-olds of her sex developed in years. We should think no one will deny she deserved the fans' adulation."

Bred by Muriel Vanderbilt Adams, Desert Vixen was by the crack miler In Reality out of the stakes-winning Moslem Chief mare Desert Trial. Harry T. Mangurian Jr. purchased Desert Vixen from the 1971 Adams dispersal for $40,000.

At two, Desert Vixen won just once in five starts, but at three, she showed great improvement, winning nine of her eleven starts. Mangurian's filly got her first stakes win when she captured a division of Monmouth's Post-Deb Stakes. She also won the

Monmouth and Delaware Oaks, a division of the Test and the Alabama at Saratoga, and the Gazelle and Beldame. In the Beldame, she won by eight and one-half lengths and equaled the track record for nine furlongs. Her accomplishments earned her the Eclipse Award as champion three-year-old filly.

Desert Vixen's progress as a four-year-old was hampered by a respiratory ailment, and she did not start until May. In her first five starts, she showed little of the brilliance of her fall races, winning only once. She returned to form in the fall and ran off with the Maskette, Beldame, and Matchmaker. After a narrow loss in Keeneland's Spinster Stakes, she took on Dahlia in the Washington, D.C., International. In her first race on grass — and her first try at one and one-half miles — she set a leisurely pace and just missed to the strong-finishing Admetus, holding the place spot safe from Dahlia. She earned her second Eclipse Award that year.

Again beset by various problems, Desert Vixen made just one start at five, finishing unplaced. She was retired with thirteen wins in twenty-eight starts and earnings of $421,538.

After producing a filly by What a Pleasure, Desert Vixen was sold in a dispersal of Mangurian's breeding stock to Franklin Groves for $700,000. Her first foal for Groves was a Roberto colt that fetched $360,000 at the summer sales. The colt went on to win a graded stakes in Europe as Real Shadai before going to stud in Japan. Desert Vixen produced just two more foals, colts by Damascus and Northern Dancer.

On September 8, 1982, Desert Vixen underwent surgery for a twisted intestine. She then foundered and developed peritonitis. She was euthanized on September 25 and was buried between two foaling barns.

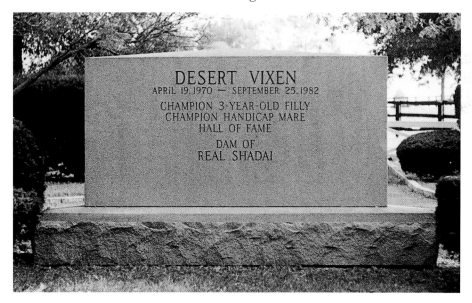

Chapter 11 – Kentucky Horse Park

Horseman John R. Gaines conceived the Kentucky Horse Park, located north of Lexington, as an educational attraction devoted to equines. The Park hosts horse-related events of all types, gives tourists a taste of the workings of a typical horse farm, and is home to numerous equine associations. It opened its doors in 1978, and the World Three-Day Event Championship was held on the grounds in the Park's inaugural season.

Once part of the Standardbred nursery Walnut Hall Farm, the Park's approximately 1,000 acres are criss-crossed with classic white plank fencing. Near the entrance stands Herbert Haseltine's magnificent statue of Man o' War, which was moved from its original site on Huffman Mill Road in 1977.

The original site of Man o' War's grave — as well as those of War Admiral, War Relic, and other Faraway Farm notables — was a small park that had once been part of Faraway Farm, where Man o' War stood during his long stud career. The cemetery was situated in a circle of trees, with the statue surrounded by a moat, similar to its setting today. Although the decision to move the statue was controversial, advocates thought that the Kentucky Horse Park site would allow more visitors to enjoy it and also would offer better protection from vandalism.

Over the years, other Thoroughbreds have been buried at the Park. Hall of Fame steeplechaser Jay Trump lies in the infield of the steeplechase course, the annual site of Lexington's High Hope meeting. Near the Big Barn is another graveyard, in which horses of any breed can be buried for a fee. Among those are the Thoroughbred mares Allez France and Sefa's Beauty. Finally, multiple Horse of the Year Forego is buried outside the barn called the Hall of Champions, where he lived for much of his retirement.

ALLEZ FRANCE

At the close of her four-year-old season, Allez France earned nothing but praise from Phil Bull in *Racehorses of 1974*:

> Allez France is an exceptional filly in every important respect. On the score of ability she is without doubt one of the best fillies to have raced in Europe in the past thirty years or so, worthy of comparison with those brilliant race-mares Sun Chariot, Coronation V, and Petite Etoile. In looks Allez France is one of the most

beautiful fillies we have seen, a magnificent, imposing individual, perfect in conformation. Her pedigree too is impeccable…Moreover, Allez France has an equable temperament, a quality lacking in the make-up of many tip-top fillies.

Bred in Kentucky, Allez France was a daughter of the great Sea-Bird and out of Priceless Gem, a stakes-winning daughter of Hail to Reason. Daniel Wildenstein of France purchased the bay filly as a weanling for $190,000.

Allez France ran twice at two, winning both and being acclaimed on that basis as one of Europe's best fillies. At three, Wildenstein's filly won just three of her seven races, but her wins came in the Poule d'Essai des Pouliches, the Prix de Diane, and the Prix Vermeille. Perhaps her best race was the Prix de l'Arc de Triomphe, in which she gave a tremendous performance to finish second to Rheingold.

Allez France's four-year-old season marked the pinnacle of her career. She was undefeated in five starts, at year's end being ranked the best horse in France. She opened her season with a win in the Prix d'Harcourt, then added the Prix Ganay, the Prix d'Ispahan, the Prix Foy, and the Arc, which she won by a head over Comtesse de Loir.

Kept in training for a fourth season, Allez France was not invincible as she had been at four. She won a second renewal of the Prix Ganay as well as the Prix Dollar and the Prix Foy. In the Arc, she finished fifth, emerging with a cut on her hind leg and missing a hind plate. After a second to Rose Bowl in England's Champion Stakes, she traveled to America and ran in the National Thoroughbred Championship on dirt, finishing last — a disappointing end to an illustrious career. Injured in that race, she remained in the U.S. as a broodmare.

Allez France produced just five foals, including the stakes winner Action Française. She was euthanized after being injured in a paddock accident on December 10, 1989, at Lane's End Farm. She was buried at the Kentucky Horse Park near the Big Barn.

FOREGO

Forego was a member of the stellar 1970 crop, which also produced Triple Crown winner Secretariat, Mr. Prospector, Allez France, Desert Vixen, and Dahlia. Forego proved his greatness in the handicap ranks, where he gave weight and a beating to the best in the nation over a four-year span.

Bred by Martha Gerry, Forego was by the Argentinian champion Forli, out of Lady Golconda. He was foaled and raised at Claiborne Farm. All told, Forego won thirty-four of fifty-seven starts, earned $1,938,957, and garnered eight Eclipse Awards.

Sent to the track under the tutelage of Sherrill Ward, the huge bay was unraced at two due to his tremendous size. He had been gelded because of a notoriously bad temperament. He began his three-year-old campaign in January at Hialeah, where he finished fourth in a maiden event. Forego broke his maiden later that month at Hialeah. Before leaving Florida, he ran second in the Hutcheson Stakes and Florida Derby. Forego next finished fourth behind Secretariat in the Kentucky Derby, then followed with a third-place finish in the Withers. Ward kept him in allowance company until the fall, when he was second in the Jerome Handicap, and the giant bay scored his first stakes victory in November in the Roamer Handicap. He closed his three-year-old season with a win in the Discovery Handicap.

At four, Forego started his campaign in Florida and reeled off victories in the Donn, Gulfstream Park, and Widener Handicaps before heading north to New York. After taking the Carter Handicap, he was asked to shoulder 134 pounds in the Met Mile, and finished second to Arbees Boy. Assigned 132 pounds for the Nassau County Handicap, he went under by a half-length to Timeless Moment. With his burden reduced to 129 pounds for the Brooklyn Handicap, Forego won, giving the runner-up fifteen pounds. Forego closed the year with wins in the Woodward Stakes, Vosburgh Handicap, and Jockey Club Gold Cup. He earned his first Eclipse Awards as champion older male, sprinter, and Horse of the Year.

At five in 1975, Forego scored in the Seminole and Widener Handicaps in Florida, then returned to New York to take the Carter Handicap, carrying 134 pounds. Forego finished third under 136 pounds in the Metropolitan, but carried 132 pounds home first in the Brooklyn, setting a track record for the ten furlongs. He then won the Suburban under an impost of 134 pounds. Consecutive losses to the top three-year-old Wajima followed, though the younger colt had the benefit of nineteen- and ten-pound weight concessions. The Woodward, under weight-for-age conditions, saw Forego defeat Wajima by one and three-quarters lengths. Again the big gelding earned Horse of the Year and champion older horse honors.

In 1976, Forego was trained by Frank Whiteley to his third consecutive Horse of the Year and champion older male titles. Bypassing Florida this time, Forego made his seasonal debut by winning a New York allowance test. He followed with scores in the Metropolitan and Nassau County Handicaps, under 130 and 132 pounds, respectively. He missed by a nose in the Suburban to Foolish Pleasure while conceding nine pounds, then took the Brooklyn under 134. Forego next won his third Woodward (under 135

pounds) and closed his campaign with a stunning come-from-behind run to nail three-year-old Honest Pleasure at the wire in the Marlboro Cup. Forego carried a staggering 137 pounds in the Marlboro — eighteen pounds more than Honest Pleasure. It was one of the most brilliant efforts of his career, accomplished on a wet surface not particularly to his liking.

Forego returned at seven for another brilliant campaign, winning the Metropolitan and Nassau County Handicaps again, and a fourth Woodward. Again the gallant gelding was the season's champion older horse, but Horse of the Year went to Triple Crown winner

Forego was one of the era's great handicap horses.

ing a hind leg in a paddock accident.

Edward L. Bowen, writing in *The Blood-Horse*, described the great gelding as "a Thoroughbred and an athlete, possessed of the fire for battle but also an intelligence to fight wisely, and he stands in the company of those which have lent distinction to handicap racing for the last 90 years or so. He stands with Exterminator, and Discovery, and Tom Fool, and Kelso, and the others which have taken up their heavy tasks and won against other more lightly burdened."

JAY TRUMP

Since 1977, the Kentucky Horse Park has served as the site of the High Hope Steeplechase. One of the meeting's featured events is the three-mile timber race, named in honor of Jay Trump.

When Jay Trump was euthanized as a result of a twisted intestine on August 24, 1988, he was buried in the infield at the finish line of the steeplechase course. Since his retirement, he had lived at his owner's Meshewa Farm near Cincinnati, Ohio.

Jay Trump was foaled in 1957, the result of a convenient mating between the mare Be Trump and Tonga Prince, a colt recovering from an injury at the farm

Seattle Slew. Forego started twice at eight before finally being sent into retirement by troublesome ankles. He was pensioned at John Ward's farm near Keeneland, but was moved to the Kentucky Horse Park in 1981. There he lived out his retirement in the Hall of Champions, dying in 1997, at the age of twenty-seven after fractur-

where the mare lived. The mare's aversion to vans led to her being mated with the handsome Tonga Prince, who — despite having been sired by Polynesian — had little to recommend him other than his proximity.

Jay Trump began his racing career at the Charles Town and Shenandoah tracks in West Virginia. Running in cheap claiming company, the big bay colt showed little; although he improved enough to finish second in his final start for owner-breeder Jay Sensenich. Crompton "Tommy" Smith had been scouting for a steeplechase prospect for Mary Stephenson, liked the bay, and bought him for $2,000.

Jay Trump took readily to jumping and hunted successfully when ridden by hunt staff at the head of the field. He made his hunt-meeting debut in a three-mile ladies' race at Warrenton, Virginia, but was well beaten by the only other starter. The gelding made amends his next time out, winning a three-and-one-half-mile race at Upperville, Virginia, with Tommy Smith in the irons. After two more wins, he capped his season with a win in the Radnor Hunt Cup in Pennsylvania.

In 1963, Jay Trump recorded his first victory in the prestigious Maryland Hunt Cup, a four-mile race over testing timber fences. The next year, Jay Trump took a second straight Maryland Hunt Cup. He was then shipped to England to begin preparations for the Grand National, held in March 1965.

Former steeplechase jockey Fred Winter took over Jay Trump's training in England. The gelding made five starts in England before the Grand National, winning the Autumn Trial at Sandown, the Brocas

JAY TRUMP BG 1957 - 1988
TONGA PRINCE - BE TRUMP BY BERNBOROUGH
THE GRAND NATIONAL, AINTREE ENGLAND 1965
FIRST AMERICAN BRED, OWNED AND
RIDDEN WINNER
MARYLAND HUNT CUP 1963, 1964, 1966
HALL OF FAME STEEPLCHASER 1971
BRED BY JAY SENSENICH, WEST VIRGINIA
OWNED BY MARY C. STEPHENSON LEBLOND, CINCINNATI, OHIO
RIDDEN BY CROMPTON (TOMMY) SMITH, VIRGINIA
TRAINED BY H. ROBERTSON FENWICK,
D. MICHAEL SMITHWICK, MARYLAND AND FRED WINTERS, ENGLAND
BRED FOR BY SERENA STEPHENSON MOLLOY, CINCINNATI, OHIO

Steeplechase, and the Harwell Amateur Rider's Handicap Steeplechase. In addition, he was second in the King George VI Steeplechase.

In his final outing before the Grand National, Jay Trump gave his admirers pause by finishing fifth in the Royal Porcelain Handicap. Despite his recent loss, Mrs. Stephenson's runner was highly regarded for the Grand National, although Freddie went off the favorite in the field of forty-seven.

Reserved on the inside in the early going, Jay Trump raced into contention coming to the infamous Becher's Brook for the second time. After the twenty-sixth of thirty rugged fences, Jay Trump had only Freddie to beat. They cleared the last fence together but had a quarter-mile left to run. Freddie put forth a strong challenge but Jay Trump fought bravely, coming home a length to the good to become just the second American-bred and -owned winner of the Grand National. Tommy Smith became the first American rider to win the prestigious event.

Jay Trump next traveled to France to contest Auteuil's Grand Steeplechase de Paris, another four-mile race but over fences much different from Aintree's stiff hedges. The gallant bay was third in a tremendous effort. He returned to America a hero.

Jay Trump was kept in training in 1966, a third Maryland Hunt Cup his objective. He won just one of his three prep races, finishing second in the Butler Grand National a week before the Maryland Hunt Cup. Jay Trump won the event by eight lengths, closing a remarkable career on a high note. He then retired to a life of well-deserved leisure, following the hounds with his owner aboard.

MAN O' WAR

"Heroic" aptly describes Herbert Haseltine's one and one-quarter life-sized statue of Man o' War. Commissioned by Samuel Riddle in 1938, the statue took ten years to complete, its progress delayed by war-related metal shortages. Cast in eight pieces, it was unveiled at Faraway Farm nearly a year after the great horse's death.

Perhaps nothing smaller would have captured the essence of the subject. As Abram S. Hewitt wrote of his first encounter with Man o' War, "He radiated majesty, energy, and power — a veritable Alexander — awaiting the moment for new worlds to conquer."

Man o' War was foaled on March 29, 1917, at Major

August Belmont's Nursery Stud on Georgetown Pike outside Lexington. He was by the fiery Fair Play, a good runner who had begun to show even greater prowess at stud. His dam, Mahubah, was a winning daughter of the English Triple Crown winner Rock Sand.

As a result of World War I, Major Belmont decided to sell his 1917 crop as yearlings. The youngsters were shipped to the Saratoga sale, where Louis Feustel purchased the tall, gangly chestnut for Samuel D. Riddle for $5,000, the seventh-highest price of the sale.

Man o' War's early race preparations were largely uneventful, except for a brief but serious illness when he spiked a temperature of 106. In his first start, on June 6, 1919, at Belmont Park, he went off the overwhelming favorite and won easily from other maidens. He then added the Keene Memorial and the Youthful, Hudson, Tremont, and United States Hotel Stakes, all in easy fashion.

In Saratoga's Sanford Memorial, Man o' War faced the good colt Golden Broom, who had bested the red colt in a yearling trial. After a straggling start, Man o' War gained a good position on the rail. But when Golden Broom packed it in ahead of him, Man o' War was trapped by Upset and Donnacona to his outside.

His rider, John Loftus, checked him and switched the colt to the outside, but Upset's rider had taken full advantage and had his colt in full flight. Man o' War came charging when he finally reached the clear but fell a half-length shy at the wire. It would be the only race he would ever lose.

Man o' War closed out his two-year-old campaign with easy victories in the Grand Union Hotel,

Hopeful, and Futurity Stakes. Of the last-named, *The Thoroughbred Record* reported, "Few Futurity winners have been given the ovation that came to Man o' War when Loftus jogged him back to the scales. The handsome chestnut looked fit and ready to do it all over again, while great cheers went up for him and the band paid its compliment to a good horse."[1]

Man o' War's stall at Faraway Farm.

Man o' War reappeared at three in the Preakness Stakes, his owner having eschewed the Kentucky Derby on the grounds that one and one-quarter miles on the first weekend of May was too much to ask of a young three-year-old. The bright chestnut made short work of the Preakness, winning over Upset and Wildair. In his next outing, he set an American record for the mile in the Withers Stakes.

Only Donnacona opposed the Riddle colt in the Belmont; and despite leaving him far behind, Man o' War set an American record for the one and three-eighths miles. In the Stuyvesant Handicap, he again had only one opponent and won as he pleased, carrying 135 pounds to his rival's 103.

The colt John P. Grier faced the Riddle colorbearer in the Dwyer Stakes, and he would go down in history as the only horse to bring Man o' War to a drive. The two raced as a team for much of the one and one-eighth miles, and at one point John P. Grier edged ahead. For the only time in his career, Man o' War felt the sting of his rider's whip. He came away to win by a length and a half, again setting an American record.

Man o' War then took the Miller and Travers Stakes, Lawrence Realization (by 100 lengths), Jockey

Club Stakes, and the Potomac Handicap. His final outing was a match race against the older Sir Barton, in which Man o' War was victorious over a rival not at his best.

Not wishing to risk his colt in the handicaps the following season, Riddle retired his great chestnut. Man o' War's final appearance under silks came in a parade at the Kentucky Association track in Lexington.

Man o' War stood his initial season in 1921 at Elizabeth Daingerfield's Hinata Farm, as Riddle did not own a stud. During that year, Riddle bought a part of Mt. Brilliant Farm; and Man o' War moved to his new home in May 1922. Will Harbut became Man o' War's groom in 1930 and shared the fame of his great red charge.

At stud, Man o' War sired sixty-four stakes winners from 380 named foals. He was America's leading sire in 1926, and the best of his stakes winners included the Triple Crown winner War Admiral, American Flag, Bateau, Crusader, Annapolis, Battleship, and Scapa Flow. He also ranked perennially among the leading broodmare sires. Although his male line remains extant, continued to the present day through his son War Relic, it is primarily through his daughters

The entrance to Faraway Farm, where Man o' War stood at stud.

that he has exerted his tremendous influence.

In retirement, "Big Red" attracted throngs of visitors from all over the world. Man o' War would pose majestically while Harbut recited the great horse's accomplishments. Retired from stud duties in 1943, he still posed for visitors until May of his thirtieth year, when his health began to deteriorate.

He died on November 1, 1947, after a gradual decline. His death, though not unexpected, brought sadness to racing fans as well as to those whose knowledge of racing was limited to the great horse's name. Some 2,000 mourners attended his funeral service on November 4, and a crane lowered his casket to its prepared spot under the base for Haseltine's not-yet-completed sculpture.

Joe A. Estes, editor of *The Blood-Horse*, closed his obituary of "Big Red" with the following:

> (O)ver the world the scattered millions of princes and paupers who have once gone out to Faraway to see him will remember the look in his eye, the ceremonial dignity with which he held himself for their inspection. They will remember that it was hard to tell whether his coat was red or yellow, and that there were faint little spots here and there, and a wen near his shoulder, and that some of them patted him on the neck. They will remember the patient and eloquent recital of his worshipful groom. Truly he was a memorable horse. Almost from the beginning he touched the imagination of men, and they saw different things in him. But one thing they will all remember, that he brought an exaltation into their hearts.

WAR ADMIRAL

Wrote John Hervey in *American Race Horses* of 1937, "War Admiral, while in appearance so unlike him, has, in his manner of racing, been more nearly the counterpart of Man o' War than any other of his sons. Of them all he alone has possessed that imperious, masterful, irresistible, whirlwind way…"

A small brown colt, standing just slightly over 15.2 hands at maturity, War Admiral bore a considerable resemblance to his dam, the tiny Sweep mare Brushup. But he proved on the racetrack that he had inherited a good deal from his sire as well.

Foaled on May 2, 1934, at Faraway Farm, War Admiral was broken and received his early preparation at his owner's Glen Riddle Farm in Maryland. He began his racing career on April 25, 1936, at Havre de Grace, winning a four-and-one-half-furlong maiden event by a neck. He won his next start, then placed in both the National Stallion and the Great American Stakes. Sidelined for ten weeks by a virus, War Admiral gained his first stakes victory on his return, in the Eastern Shore Handicap. He closed his season with a second in the Richard Johnson Handicap.

At three, the Admiral again kicked off his campaign at

Havre de Grace, winning an allowance event easily, then adding the Chesapeake Stakes. The colt's next objective was the Kentucky Derby; owner Samuel Riddle had departed from his longstanding policy of bypassing that event. War Admiral broke quickly from his rail post position and sailed along in front to win by daylight over Pompoon. Pompoon nearly gained revenge in the Preakness a week later, cutting the corner on the turn for home as War Admiral swung wide and battling gamely down the stretch to miss by just a head.

In the Belmont, War Admiral dashed to the front after a stumbling start and won by three lengths from Sceneshifter, equaling the American record of 2:28 3/5 for one and one-half miles in the process. He had, however, grabbed a quarter at the start, as reported by Hervey: "Every time his foot struck the track it had caused blood to spurt from the wound and the under side of his body was dyed with it. That under such circumstances, he should have run the record-making race he did, was testimony of a gameness difficult to extol too highly."

As a result of his injury, War Admiral did not race again until late October. After an allowance victory, he closed his sophomore campaign with victories in the Washington Handicap and the Pimlico Special.

At four, the Admiral won the Widener as he pleased, then went on to capture the Queens County and Saratoga Handicaps, the Whitney and Wilson Stakes, and Saratoga and Jockey Club Gold Cups. War Admiral was the 1-20 favorite in the Gold Cup and won under restraint.

War Admiral, Man o' War's best son.

On November 1, Seabiscuit and War Admiral met in a much-heralded match race in the Pimlico Special, in which Seabiscuit prevailed.

War Admiral remained in training at five, with the intention of sending him to stud after the Widener. He won his prep race for that event but missed the Widener itself because of a fever and a troublesome ankle. Retired to Faraway Farm to join his illustrious sire, War Admiral took with him a record of twenty-one wins in twenty-six starts. He had been Horse of the Year as well as champion three-year-old in 1937.

War Admiral was quite a successful stallion, becoming the leading sire in 1945 and twice the leading broodmare sire. His forty stakes winners included the great filly Busher and the champion Blue Peter as well as Busanda, Striking, Searching, and Admiral Vee. Although some of his sons became successful sires, his male line has not continued. But his outstanding daughters produced a host of top performers who have carried his name into modern pedigrees.

War Admiral moved to Hamburg Place in 1958, after the death of Samuel Riddle and the sale of Faraway Farm. He died there the following year, but his remains were returned to be buried in the small park next to Faraway Farm, at the feet of his sire.

WAR RELIC

Unraced at two, War Relic won stakes at three, raced briefly without winning at four, and then retired to stud at his owner's Faraway Farm. There he stood alongside his sire Man o' War and Triple Crown winner War Admiral. Although War Relic's fourteen stakes winners included the champion two-year-old Battlefield, War Admiral was by far the more successful sire. But War Relic supplied the links that have continued the male line of Man o' War: Intent and Relic.

A strained back kept War Relic off the track at two. He won his debut at three, then lost six races in succession. His third race produced a near-disaster when he shied to the left in the stretch and collided with the rail. Sent to Suffolk Downs, near Boston, Massachusetts, the big chestnut finally scored that elusive second victory in a six-furlong allowance race. Second at a mile in his next attempt, War Relic won twice more in allowance company.

Rather surprisingly, just two days after the Riddle colt started just two days after that third allowance win in the Massachusetts Handicap, taking on Fenelon, Foxbrough, and Market Wise, among others. War Relic carried a feather-light 102 pounds, while Fenelon was top-weighted at 130. In a shocker, War Relic won by three parts of a length from a game Foxbrough.

Despite the weight concessions, War Relic obviously was a much-improved colt. He next met Whirlaway in the Saranac Handicap and missed by the slimmest of noses. War Relic then won the Kenner at Saratoga by

three lengths. In the Narragansett Special, he turned the tables on Whirlaway, winning by four and one-half lengths, though in receipt of eleven pounds. War Relic finished out his season by winning the Governor's Handicap. He was retired after three starts at four.

Moved along with War Admiral to Hamburg Place near the end of his stud career, War Relic died on April 1, 1963. In accordance with Samuel Riddle's wishes, he, too, was returned to his birthplace and buried in the shadow of his sire's statue.

Chapter 12 – The Tradition Continues

Walmac Farm's 300 acres on the west side of Paris Pike outside of Lexington originally were part of a 2,000-acre land grant to Virginian Joseph Beckley. During Beckley's tenure, it was called Valley Farm. In 1910, it was absorbed into the vast acreage comprising James Ben Ali Haggin's Elmendorf. The farm gained its present name in 1936, after oilman Robert W. McIlvain purchased it.

McIlvain bred sixteen stakes winners at his Kentucky farm, the best being Bushwacker, Royal Native, Volcanic, Billings, and Gala Fete. Following McIlvain's death in 1959, various individuals leased the farm until present owner John T. L. Jones Jr. bought it in 1977. Jones changed the farm's name to Walmac International, reflecting the industry's expansion. Jones has established a large stallion station at Walmac, and through the years, acquired such stars as Alleged and Nureyev to head the roster. The farm also boards mares and markets yearlings at the major sales.

The stallions Sham and Brent's Prince are buried near the farm office, while the more recently deceased Risen Star rests near the barn housing Nureyev. The three graves are marked with simple headstones.

RISEN STAR

Like Man o' War and his best son, War Admiral, Secretariat and his best son did not look alike but shared some of the same verve on the racetrack. While Secretariat was a large horse, Risen Star was taller; however, he lacked his sire's prodigious bulk. Nevertheless, in the 1988 Belmont Stakes, Risen Star brought back memories of his famous sire by flashing down the stretch by a widening margin.

Bred in partnership by Arthur B. Hancock III and Leone Peters, the big bay colt out of the His Majesty mare Ribbon failed to meet his reserve at the 1986 Keeneland July select yearling sale. The next spring, he was consigned to Fasig-Tipton's sale of two-year-olds in training at Calder. Louis Roussel III went to $300,000 to secure the colt, which he raced in partnership with Ronnie Lamarque.

Risen Star was brought along patiently, making his debut on September 24, 1987. Trainer Roussel had chosen to bypass maiden and allowance events, sending the colt out in the Minstrel Stakes. The colt won, but could not catch Success Express in his next outing, the Sport of Kings Futurity. Success Express went on to take the Breeders' Cup Juvenile, so Roussel's colt was hardly disgraced. In his final appearance at two, Risen Star tried the turf and won impressively. Although he certainly had demonstrated ability, he nevertheless was ranked seventeen pounds below Forty Niner on the Experimental Free Handicap.

Risen Star began his three-year-old season on January 2, winning a one-and-one-sixteenth-mile allowance test by ten lengths. He finished second in the Lecomte Handicap at Fair Grounds, then won the Louisiana Derby Trial and the Louisiana Derby itself.

Sent next to Keeneland, Risen Star finished a head in front of Forty Niner in the Lexington Stakes. He started from the rail post position in the Kentucky Derby and encountered his share of traffic problems. Nevertheless, he closed well to finish third behind Winning Colors and Forty Niner. Two weeks later, in the Preakness, he benefited from Forty Niner's early duel with Winning Colors, sweeping past to win.

In the Belmont, he gave a display reminiscent of his sire's in that race, taking the lead after six furlongs and drawing away. As Ray Paulick wrote in the *Thoroughbred Times*, "As Risen Star galloped to the wire in isolated splendor, pulling away from his five opponents with remarkable ease, there was no way to hide from the image of the muscular chestnut star who captured the hearts of a nation."[1] The colt's time of 2:26 2/5 was second only to his sire's 2:24.

The Belmont was Risen Star's final start. A suspensory ligament that had begun troubling him between the Preakness and Belmont failed to heal, and he retired to stud at Walmac International.

Risen Star, named champion three-year-old at year's end, made little mark at stud, siring just fourteen stakes winners, among them the ill-fated Star Standard and the German champion Risen Raven. Plagued by bouts

of colic throughout his retirement, Risen Star died from an intestinal rupture on March 13, 1998.

SHAM

Secretariat's main rival in the 1973 Triple Crown races, Sham was unfortunate enough to have been foaled in the same year as Meadow Stable's great chestnut. A horse of tremendous ability, the Claiborne Farm-bred Sham was by the Santa Anita Handicap winner Pretense and out of Sequoia, by Princequillo. Sequoia won the Spinaway Stakes and was a full sister to the stakes winners How and Cherokee Rose.

At two, Sham faced the starter four times, racing three times for Claiborne before Sigmund Sommer bought him for $200,000 at the Hancock dispersal in November 1972. The big bay broke his maiden in his first outing in the Sommer colors under the tutelage of Frank "Pancho" Martin.

Sent to California, Sham won two allowance races, then got his first stakes win in the Santa Catalina. In the San Felipe Stakes, he was fourth to Linda's Chief. The Sommer colt's next engagement was the Santa Anita Derby, in which he ran coupled with stablemate Knightly Dawn, who set the pace. In the words of *The Blood-Horse* correspondent Robert Hebert, Sham "made a shambles of his field."

Despite the publicity that two-year-old champion and reigning Horse of the Year Secretariat was receiving as a result of his two facile wins at three, Sham and Knightly Dawn headed east to try the Meadow Stable runner in the Wood Memorial. Only Sham went postward for Sommer, and he finished ahead of Secretariat, but both were behind the latter's entry mate Angle Light.

Secretariat beat Sham by two and one-half lengths in the Kentucky Derby; Sham himself ran a sub-two-minute mile and one-quarter. The Preakness resulted in an identical margin and result, Secretariat leading his dark rival to the wire. In the Belmont, Sham raced with Secretariat for six furlongs, then fell back to finish fourth as Secretariat flew away to a thirty-one-length victory.

The Belmont was Sham's final race, as he fractured a cannon bone in a workout not long after. He underwent successful surgery to repair the leg and entered stud in 1974 at Spendthrift Farm. He moved to Walmac in 1992 and stood at stud there until his death from a heart attack on April 3, 1993. He proved a capable stallion, siring forty-seven stakes winners, including Sherry Peppers, Jaazeiro, Arewehavingfunyet, and Safe Play.

ASHFORD STUD

In the early days of this century, the property that today comprises Ashford Stud was part of Colonel Edmund H. Taylor Jr.'s 1,450-acre Hereford Farm. That establishment was famous for its imported cattle rather than Thoroughbreds. A 1923 real-estate advertisement in *The Thoroughbred Record* pictured the impressive stone gateway and gatehouse at the farm's entrance. The ad read in part, "The long, wide driveway, lined with young trees, groups of flowering shrubs and bordered with roses…is only one of the superb accomplishments…Here one finds natural shade, shelter, spring water from the underlying limestone strata, and blue grass in all its perfection, all so necessary in the production of bone, stamina, and greatness, no matter what breed of pure-bred livestock one carries on its fertile acres."[2]

It was not until 1978, when Texas veterinarian William Lockridge purchased 475 acres in partnership with Robert A. Hefner III, that the property was developed for Thoroughbreds and renamed Ashford Stud. The trees lining the drive were by now mature oaks, and Lockridge kept the original stone fences, adding a stone stallion barn and other equine facilities.

Today, Ashford Stud is part of Coolmore's worldwide racing and breeding empire, owned by partners Robert Sangster, Vincent O'Brien, and John Magnier. The cemetery lies along one of the farm's beautiful dry stone or mortarless walls, just outside the stone house that serves as the farm office. Shecky Greene was the first to be buried there, and he was followed by the mares Fairy Bridge, Sex Appeal, Secretariat's Love, and Fall Aspen.

FAIRY BRIDGE

Fairy Bridge's racing career was brief: she made just two starts at two, and won both. As a broodmare, she fulfilled the promise she had shown on the racecourse, producing four stakes winners. She certainly had the pedigree to become an outstanding producer.

By the Hail to Reason sire Bold Reason, Fairy Bridge descended in female line from Rough Shod II, the famous mare imported by Arthur B. Hancock Sr. Among Rough Shod II's foals were the stakes-winning

full siblings Ridan, Lt. Stevens, and Moccasin. Another full sibling to that remarkable trio was the stakes-placed filly Thong, who went on to produce the English champion miler Thatch and other stakes winners King Pellinore, Espadrille, and Lisadell. Thong's daughter (and Fairy Bridge's dam), Special, was unplaced in her only start but produced the superb racehorse and sire Nureyev and other stakes winners Bound and Number.

Fairy Bridge's first foal was the Northern Dancer colt Sadler's Wells. Trained by Vincent O'Brien, Sadler's Wells won the Irish Two Thousand Guineas, the Coral-Eclipse Stakes, the Phoenix Champion Stakes, and two other stakes in eleven starts. He was an immediate success at stud, and through early December 1999, had sired 142 stakes winners, and led the European sire list eight times through 1998.

Fairy Bridge's next foal was Fairy King, a full brother to Sadler's Wells who fractured sesamoids in his only start but enjoyed a successful stud career before his death on July 1, 1999. Tate Gallery, another colt by Northern Dancer, was Fairy Bridge's 1983 foal. Tate Gallery was a group I winner at two and also has been a successful sire.

Mated with Northern Dancer's English Triple Crown-winning son Nijinsky II, Fairy Bridge foaled the filly Fairy Dancer in 1984. Fairy Dancer placed in stakes at three before being retired. Returned to Northern Dancer the next two seasons, Fairy Bridge produced the stakes-winning fillies Fairy Gold and Puppet Dance. Of Fairy Bridge's final three offspring, only Perugino, by Danzig, was a winner. Fairy Bridge died in 1991.

Although her daughters are still young and have not yet shown that they can continue her female line, in producing Sadler's Wells, Fairy Bridge has assured herself prominence in Thoroughbred pedigrees for many years to come.

FALL ASPEN

Fall Aspen was a stakes winner who outdid herself as a broodmare. At the time of her death on February 3, 1998, she had produced fourteen foals. Of the twelve who had raced, eight had won stakes.

Fall Aspen was bred by Joseph M. Roebling, who also bred her fourth dam, Carillon. Portage, Carillon's daughter by War Admiral, produced four stakes winners, including Rainy Lake and Black Mountain. Bred to Swaps, Portage foaled Change Water, a winner and Fall Aspen's dam.

Sired by Pretense, Fall Aspen won eight of her twenty starts, earning $198,037. At two, she captured the Matron and Astarita Stakes, and at three added the Prioress. Roebling died when Fall Aspen was four, and his stock was dispersed. Fall Aspen sold for $600,000 to Spendthrift Farm and Frances Kernan. This partnership bred Fall Aspen's first two foals, the stakes winners Northern Aspen (by Northern Dancer) and Elle Seule (by Exclusive Native).

Fall Aspen changed hands again when the Spendthrift partnership consigned the mare, in foal to Raise a Native, to Keeneland's January horses of all ages sale. Robert Brennan's International Thoroughbred Breeders Inc. made the winning bid of $900,000. For ITB Inc., Fall Aspen produced the stakes winners

Fall Aspen was an outstanding producer, and her offspring include the Preakness Stakes winner Timber Country.

Mazzacano and Colorado Dancer as well as the stakes-placed Native Aspen.

In 1987, ITB Inc. sold Fall Aspen to English breeder David Jamison for $1.1 million at the Keeneland November breeding stock sale. The mare was in foal to Shareef Dancer at the time. For Jamison, Fall Aspen produced the stakes winners Hamas, Fort Wood, Timber Country, and Prince of Thieves. Timber Country won the Breeders' Cup Juvenile and went on to take the 1995 Preakness Stakes.

Just two days after Timber Country's Breeders' Cup Juvenile win, Fall Aspen again went through Keeneland's sales ring. Her sale price of $2.4 million was the second-highest paid for a broodmare in 1994. Coolmore's John Magnier was the successful bidder.

Fall Aspen produced three foals for Coolmore: the Danzig colt Bianconi, an English group II winner at three in 1998; the winning 1996 filly Aspen Leaves, by Woodman; and a Thunder Gulch colt foaled the day before her death in 1998.

Her daughters have begun to compile distinguished records as broodmares. Elle Seule has produced the stakes winners Mehthaaf and Elnadim, while Dance of Leaves has foaled the champion miler Charnwood Forest and the stakes winner Medaaly. Colorado Dancer is the dam of group I winner Dubai Millennium, and the unraced Sheroog has produced stakes winners Sharaf Kabeer and Kabool. The family seems set to continue its influence into future generations.

SEX APPEAL

A chestnut filly by Buckpasser out of the stakes-winning Traffic Judge mare Best in Show, Sex Appeal was consigned by her breeder, Mrs. Frank Forsythe, to

Keeneland's 1971 summer sale. Canadian E. P. Taylor bought her for $52,000. The filly was the first foal from her dam, who later produced the stakes winners Blush With Pride, Malinowski, Gielgud, and Monroe.

At four, the unraced Sex Appeal produced her first foal, the Protanto colt Kaskitayo. Like his dam, Kaskitayo never raced. Sex Appeal's second foal was the Northern Dancer colt Try My Best. Purchased by Robert Sangster from the Keeneland summer sale for $185,000, Try My Best won the Dewhurst Stakes in England and was named champion two-year-old in both England and Ireland. His three-year-old season was a disappointment, as he won but once then trailed home last in the classic Two Thousand Guineas. He never raced again and retired to Coolmore in Ireland, where he has been a successful sire.

In 1976, Sex Appeal foaled the Halo filly Solar. Raced only at two, Solar won the Park and the Railway Stakes. Returned to Northern Dancer, Sex Appeal produced the 1977 colt Northern Guest, who did not race. Her 1978 colt, Compliance, failed to win, although he placed in the Ballycorus Stakes. Neither Carillon Miss nor Northern Prancer, her 1979 and 1980 fillies by The Minstrel and Northern Dancer, respectively, raced.

El Gran Senor, her 1981 bay colt by Northern Dancer and bred by Taylor in partnership with Robert Sangster and Vincent O'Brien, was a champion at two and three. He won each of his four races at two, including the William Hill Dewhurst Stakes, one of England's prestigious two-year-old events. At three, he won the Two Thousand Guineas and the Irish Sweeps Derby but suffered a narrow loss at Epsom in the Derby to Secreto. Timeform's *Racehorses of 1984* summed up his career: "He developed quickly and was able to shine in some of the richly-endowed major two-year-old races; and he trained on to win classic races at both a mile and a mile and a half. He was very genuine, he possessed a superb temperament and a brilliant turn of foot, and furthermore he had the looks and pedigree to match his racing record."

At stud, El Gran Senor has sired individuals of the highest class, although his career has been hampered by fertility problems. Among his forty-four stakes winners are Breeders' Cup Sprint winner Lit de Justice, Helmsman, and Rodrigo de Triano.

Sex Appeal produced eight foals after El Gran Senor, but that colt was the last to win in stakes. Many of the mare's later fillies were raced lightly, if at all. Solar, Russian Ballet (by Nijinsky II), Carillon Miss, and Bella Senora (by Northern Dancer) have produced stakes winners. Sex Appeal's youngest daughter was foaled in 1992, so her legacy is by no means complete. Sex Appeal died in 1993, her final foal being a colt by Woodman named Kailey Senor.

OVERBROOK FARM

Lexington native William T. Young got a late start in the Thoroughbred industry but wasted little time in establishing Overbrook Farm as one of the most successful breeding operations in the Bluegrass. Young's first grade I winner was Storm Cat, who won the 1985 Young America Stakes at Meadowlands and narrowly lost the Breeders' Cup Juvenile. Storm Cat was Overbrook's first stallion, and his outstanding record has been one of the keys to Overbrook's success.

In the early 1980s, Young began acquiring property on the southeastern edge of Lexington, beginning with a 110-acre tract purchased from Lucas Combs. Today, Overbrook comprises some 1,500 rolling acres. As Kimberly S. Herbert wrote in a 1994 article in *The Blood-Horse*, "Overbrook reflects its owner's personality — his pursuit of perfection, his devotion to detail, his penchant for privacy."

Overbrook has been represented at the track by such stars as Kentucky Oaks winner Seaside Attraction, the champion two-year-old filly Flanders, Preakness and Belmont Stakes winner Tabasco Cat, and Kentucky Derby winner Grindstone. Young received the Eclipse Award in 1995 as the nation's leading breeder.

The cemetery lies in a peaceful area, winding among the trees on the bank high above Hickman Creek. Simple flat stones mark the graves of Grand Canyon, The Minstrel, Seaside Attraction, Country Cat, Mrs. Penny, and other notable Overbrook horses.

GRAND CANYON

Trainer D. Wayne Lukas purchased Grand Canyon, a Florida-bred son of Fappiano out of the L'Enjoleur mare Champagne Ginny, for $825,000 at Keeneland's 1988 July yearling sale. Lukas retained a one-quarter interest in the colt, selling the majority to Overbrook Farm.

Though always well-regarded by his connections, Grand Canyon did not begin to show the scope of his ability until the fall of his two-year-old season. He broke his maiden in his first start, then got his first stakes victory in mid-October, taking the grade I Norfolk by one and one-half lengths from Single Dawn. He contested the Breeders' Cup Juvenile in his next outing, finishing second to eventual two-year-old champion Rhythm.

Sent to Churchill Downs for the Kentucky Jockey Club Stakes, Grand Canyon won as much the best, coming home ten lengths clear. Grand Canyon's final race at two turned out to be the final race of his career. Sent out for the Hollywood Futurity on December 17, 1989, he ran the mile in 1:33 — believed to be the fastest mile ever by a two-year-old — to win impressively by six and one-half lengths. His late-season improvement gained him some support for championship honors, but Rhythm got the voters' nod.

Grand Canyon returned from the Hollywood Futurity with a bruised knee and remained sidelined by a series of problems. He missed the spring classics, then ruptured a blood vessel in a front leg in July, developed laminitis, and was euthanized on July 14, 1990.

MRS. PENNY

Marshall Jenney imported the Le Fabuleux mare Tananarive from France in 1976. At the time,

Grand Canyon electrified in his brief racing career.

Tananarive was in foal to Prix du Moulin de Longchamp winner Great Nephew, also the sire of champion Grundy. Tananarive's chestnut filly was subsequently consigned to the 1978 Saratoga yearling sale, where she went to Eric Kronfeld for $40,000.

Mrs. Penny raced for two and a half seasons abroad before closing out her career in the U.S. At two, she won three of her six starts in England, accounting for the Cheveley Park Stakes as well as the Cherry Hinton and the Lowther Stakes.

At three, Mrs. Penny failed to win in England, although she ran a good second in the King George VI and Queen Elizabeth Diamond Stakes and placed in the English and Irish One Thousand Guineas. It was in France that she gained classic success, winning the Prix de Diane (French Oaks). She also won the Prix Vermeille.

At four, Mrs. Penny ran twice abroad without distinguishing herself before returning to America for her final six starts. She won just once, accounting for the Queen Charlotte Stakes at the Meadowlands.

Mrs. Penny produced the stakes winners Northern

Park, by Northern Dancer, and Mrs. Jenney, by The Minstrel. Mrs. Jenney has produced the grade I winner Unaccounted For and the French stakes winner A Votre Sante. Mrs. Penny died in 1997 at Overbrook.

SEASIDE ATTRACTION

Bred by Warner L. Jones' Hermitage Farm near Louisville, Kentucky, Seaside Attraction was by the Triple Crown winner Seattle Slew and out of the Canadian Oaks winner Kamar, who also produced the stakes winners Key to the Moon, Hiaam, and Gorgeous. Young bought Seaside Attraction at the 1987 Hermitage dispersal as a weanling for $1.05 million.

Seaside Attraction started just three times at two, winning a maiden event in December at Hollywood Park. At three, she started nine times and won three races. Her only stakes win was the Kentucky Oaks, in which she defeated champion Go for Wand on a muddy track; she had previously been third to that filly in the Beaumont Stakes at Keeneland. Seaside Attraction also placed in the Acorn Stakes and the Churchill Downs Breeders' Cup Handicap.

Retired to the Overbrook broodmare band, Seaside Attraction's first foal was the Mr. Prospector filly Red

Carnival, who won stakes abroad. Her second foal, also by Mr. Prospector, was the 1995 champion two-year-old filly Golden Attraction. Seaside Attraction's 1994 colt, Mercer Mill (by Mr. Prospector's son Forty Niner), won two of his twenty starts. Cape Town, foaled in 1995, was by Seeking the Gold, another son of Mr. Prospector. Cape Town accounted for the Brown and Williamson Kentucky Jockey Club Stakes at two and the Florida Derby and Holy Bull Stakes at three. Seaside Attraction's final foal, Cape Canaveral, also by Mr. Prospector, became his dam's fourth stakes winner early in 1999 by taking the San Miguel Stakes. Seaside Attraction died in December 1996.

THE MINSTREL

Closely related to Nijinsky II, The Minstrel was bred by E. P. Taylor's Windfields Farm in Canada. Nijinsky II was a son of Northern Dancer out of the Bull Page mare Flaming Page; The Minstrel is by the same sire and out of Flaming Page's daughter, Fleur. But Nijinsky II was much larger and coarser than the smallish, refined The Minstrel.

Robert Sangster purchased The Minstrel as a yearling at the 1975 Keeneland July sale for $200,000.

Installed in the Irish yard of Vincent O'Brien, the colt won each of his three starts at two, including the Larkspur Stakes and the Dewhurst Stakes.

Regarded as a bright prospect for the spring classics, The Minstrel won his seasonal debut but then ran third in the Two Thousand Guineas. He followed that up with a second in the Irish Two Thousand Guineas. At this point, he seemed to have little hope of winning a classic race, as many of Northern Dancer's offspring were best at something less than the English Derby distance of twelve furlongs. Nonetheless, The Minstrel proved his class and courage with a hard-fought victory in the Derby from Hot Grove, then added the Irish Derby in July. In his final race, he con-

The Minstrel won the English Derby, then went on to success as a sire.

quered older rivals in the King George VI and Queen Elizabeth Diamond Stakes.

Syndicated for stud duty at $250,000 per share, The Minstrel was hastily repatriated to avoid a shipping ban due to an outbreak of contagious equine metritis. Initially standing at Windfields Farm in Maryland alongside his famous sire, The Minstrel was moved to Overbrook in 1988. He was a highly successful stallion, siring fifty-eight stakes winners. Among his outstanding performers were L'Emigrant, Minstrella, Treizieme, and Opening Verse. The Minstrel was euthanized on September 3, 1990, when he developed laminitis resulting from toxic enteritis.

THREE CHIMNEYS FARM

Three Chimneys, a commercial breeding operation established in the early 1970s by Robert Clay, continues the tradition of providing an equine cemetery for its finest horses. There are two burial sites. The first is next to the stallion complex and is where champion Chief's Crown, leading sire Nodouble, and Time for a Change lie. The second, used for mares, is on the broodmare division on the north side of Old Frankfort Pike.

Clay purchased the first hundred-acre parcel of

Three Chimneys in 1971. He has since added acreage to form the ninety-two-acre stallion division, a yearling division at Sheffield Farm, and most recently the former King Ranch property.

The stallion complex was completed in 1984, and the farm's first stallion, Slew o' Gold, took up residence the following year. Chief's Crown came to Three Chimneys in 1986, and since that time the stallion operation has grown steadily. Triple Crown winner Seattle Slew moved to Three Chimneys in 1986, and in 1999, dual classic winner Silver Charm was added to the roster. In addition to standing stallions, Three Chimneys boards mares and acts as an agent at the major auctions.

CHIEF'S CROWN

Chief's Crown's breeder was the fashion-industry mogul Carl Rosen, who died before the colt raced. From the first crop of the brilliantly fast but unsound Danzig, Chief's Crown was out of Six Crowns, Rosen's stakes-winning daughter of the Triple Crown winner Secretariat and the Filly Triple winner Chris Evert.

A two-year-old of 1984, Chief's Crown raced twice at Belmont before scoring his first win. He broke his

maiden by five lengths, then immediately moved into stakes competition. At Saratoga, he accounted for the Saratoga Special and Hopeful Stakes.

Chief's Crown encountered a sloppy track at Belmont for the Futurity, but he closed gamely in the stretch to lose by a length. He gained revenge in his next outing, taking the Cowdin by six. Heading West, the Chief won Santa Anita's Norfolk Stakes, then took the inaugural Breeders' Cup Juvenile. He earned the Eclipse Award as champion two-year-old male.

Chief's Crown was a champion racehorse and top sire.

At three, Chief's Crown ran off consecutive victories in the Swale, Flamingo, and Blue Grass Stakes. He appeared at his peak for the classics. Favored in all three Triple Crown races, he was beaten each time, running third to Spend a Buck in the Kentucky Derby, second to Tank's Prospect in the Preakness, and third to Creme Fraiche in the Belmont.

Chief's Crown won the Travers but then finished third in the Woodward, his first outing against older

rivals. In the Marlboro Cup, he defeated Track Barron and Vanlandingham — his conquerors in the Woodward — as well as the West Coast star Greinton. In his final race, the Breeders' Cup Classic, he finished fourth to Proud Truth. He was retired to Three Chimneys with a record of twelve wins in twenty-one starts and earnings of $2,191,168.

Chief's Crown was an immediate success at stud. As of early December 1999, forty-one of his offspring are stakes winners, among them Epsom Derby winner Erhaab, English champion two-year-old Grand Lodge, and Canadian Horse of the Year Chief Bearhart.

On April 29, 1997, Chief's Crown was euthanized after fracturing his patella in a paddock accident, then re-injuring himself following surgery. He was fifteen.

NODOUBLE

In four seasons of racing, the Arkansas-bred Nodouble traveled from coast to coast and back again, emerging at four and five as one of the nation's top handicap horses. "The Arkansas Traveler," as he became known, followed a similar pattern in his stud career, standing at five locations in California, Florida, and Kentucky. At stud, too, he reached the highest level, becoming America's leading sire in 1981.

Bred and raced by Gene Goff, Nodouble compiled a record of thirteen wins in forty-two starts, with earnings of $846,749. As a two-year-old of 1967, he won just twice in twelve outings but placed in four stakes. At three, his wins included the Arkansas Derby, Hawthorne Gold Cup, and Michigan Mile and One-Eighth Handicap. In the Gold Cup, he equaled the track record for one and one-quarter miles; in Michigan, he defeated the mighty Damascus.

At four, Nodouble won four of his twelve races and finished second six times, his victories coming in the Santa Anita and Brooklyn Handicaps, the Californian Stakes, and Hawthorne Gold Cup. Although he was second to eventual Horse of the Year Arts and Letters each time they met, Nodouble still shared champion older horse honors with that rival. At five, Nodouble took the San Pasqual and Metropolitan Handicaps, the latter in track-record time.

Nodouble entered stud in 1971, standing initially in California at El Rancho Murrieta. He also spent seasons in Lexington at Domino Stud and in Florida at Lasater Farm and Wooden Horse Stud before moving to Three Chimneys for the 1986 season. He was lead-ing sire in 1981, when he was represented by sixteen stakes winners, including Skillful Joy and Mairzy Doates. In all, he sired eighty-eight stakes winners. He was pensioned in 1988 due to declining fertility.

Nodouble was euthanized as a result of colic on April 26, 1990, at Three Chimneys. Wrote David Dink in the *Thoroughbred Times*, "Nodouble's traveling days are over now, but his influence on the breed is far from depleted."[3]

References

CHAPTER 1

1. *The Thoroughbred Record*, August 14, 1897, p. 76, "Domino is Dead" by Maj. B. G. Thomas

2. *The Thoroughbred Record*, August 7, 1897, p. 53, "Death of Domino"

3. *The Thoroughbred Record*, August 7, 1897, p. 66, "Death of Domino"

4. *The Thoroughbred Record*, May 9, 1896, p. 219, "Ben Brush by His Moustache"

CHAPTER 2

1. *The Thoroughbred Record*, November 9, 1929, p. 286, "Memories of John E. Madden" by 'Salvator'

2. *The Thoroughbred Record*, September 30, 1899, p. 161, "Imp Greatest of Mares"

3. *The Thoroughbred Record*, October 14, 1899, p. 182, "Imp Day in Chillicothe"

4. *The Thoroughbred Record*, January 24, 1920, p. 59, "Return of Sir Martin"

CHAPTER 3

1. *The Thoroughbred Record*, September 29, 1962, p. 30, "Mahmoud 1933-1962"

2. *The Thoroughbred Record*, April 21, 1934, p. 245, "Death of Regret"

CHAPTER 4

1. *The Thoroughbred Record*, September 30, 1944, p. 325, "All Racing Mourns Death of Mrs. Payne Whitney"

CHAPTER 5

1. *The Thoroughbred Record*, December 21, 1929, p. 402, "Fair Play Dies at Elmendorf"

2. *The Thoroughbred Record*, December 17, 1931, p. 245, "The Passing of Mahubah"

CHAPTER 6

1. *The Thoroughbred Record*, August 1987, p. 1805, "Gallant Man" by Timothy T. Capps

2. *The Thoroughbred Record*, February 10, 1982, p. 866, "Nashua 1952-1982" by Susan Rhodemyre

3. *The Thoroughbred Record*, August 29, 1984, p. 4309, "Contemporary Stallions—Prince John" by William G. Munn

CHAPTER 7

1. *The Thoroughbred Record*, September 24, 1938, p. 190, "Black Toney Dies at Idle Hour Farm"

2. *The Thoroughbred Record*, October 26, 1983, p. 5502, "Contemporary Stallions—Ribot" by John P. Sparkman

CHAPTER 8

1. *The Thoroughbred Record*, April 10, 1976, p. 1061, "American Matriarchs, Part VI—Easy Lass" by Bob Stokhaug

2. *The Thoroughbred Record*, August 4, 1982, p. 742, "Tim Tam Dead" by David Dink

CHAPTER 9

1. *The Thoroughbred Record*, July 17, 1971, p. 253, "Bold Ruler, April 6, 1954-July 12, 1971" by William Robertson

2. *The Thoroughbred Record*, March 15, 1978, p. 866, "Buckpasser 1963-1978" by William G. Munn

3. *The Thoroughbred Record*, July 18, 1984, p. 3481, "Contemporary Stallions—Buckpasser" by Timothy T. Capps

4. *The Thoroughbred Record*, May 28, 1980, p. 1948-9, "The Fighter" by William G. Munn

5. *The Thoroughbred Record*, December 21, 1983, p. 6768, "Contemporary Stallions—Round Table" by William G. Munn

6. "Contemporary Stallions—Round Table," p. 6765

7. *The Thoroughbred Record*, October 1989, p. 1218, "So Long Big Red" by Don Clippinger

8. *The Thoroughbred Record*, July 16, 1949, p. 35-6, "The King is Dead" by Frank Jennings

9. *The Thoroughbred Times*, August 19, 1995, p. 14, "Hero of an Age Past" by Mary Fleming Simon

CHAPTER 10

1. *The Thoroughbred Record*, June 10, 1981, p. 2485, "Pedigree of Belmont Stakes Winner Summing"

2. *The Thoroughbred Record*, June 5, 1985, p. 2711, "Contemporary Stallions—Hail to Reason" by John P. Sparkman

CHAPTER 11

1. *The Thoroughbred Record*, September 20, 1919, p. 134, "Man o' War Wins the Futurity"

CHAPTER 12

1. *The Thoroughbred Times*, June 17, 1988, p. 3, "Running in the Shadow of Greatness" by Ray Paulick

2. *The Thoroughbred Record*, June 2, 1923, p. 488

3. *The Thoroughbred Times*, May 4, 1990, p. 54, "Two-Time Champion Nodouble Dead" by David Dink

Appendix

EQUINE GRAVE MARKERS BY FARM

505 FARM/THE STALLION STATION

Blue Prince	b.h.	1951-1979	Princequillo—Blue Denim
Bold and Brave	br.h.	1963-1977	Bold Ruler—Bases Full
Bold Commander	b.h.	1960-1981	Bold Ruler—High Voltage
Bolero	ch.h.	1946-1975	Eight Thirty—Stepwisely
Bon Mot	ch.h.	1963-1988	Worden—Djebel Idra
Bupers	dk.b.h.	1961-1990	Double Jay—Busanda
Call Me Prince	b.h.	1965-1974	Princequillo—Flight Deck
Devil Diver	b.h.	1939-1961	St. Germans—Dabchick
Flushing II	gr.h.	1939-1962	Mahmoud—Callandar
Gallant Romeo	b.h.	1961-1986	Gallant Man—Juliets Nurse
Ludham	b.m.	1964-1986	Pampered King II—Sunward II
Poker	b.h.	1963-1986	Round Table—Glamour
Porterhouse	br.h.	1951-1971	Endeavour II—Red Stamp
Portersville	b.h.	1952-1964	Count Fleet—Artena
Rico Monte	b.h.	1942-1971	Saint Patrick—Rica Patria
Roman	b.h.	1937-1960	Sir Gallahad III—Buckup
Royal Coinage	br.h.	1952-1964	Eight Thirty—Canina
Royal Serenade	ch.h.	1948-1975	Royal Charger—Pasquinade
Sassafras	b.h.	1967-1988	Sheshoon—Ruta
Tomy Lee	b.h.	1956-1971	Tudor Minstrel—Auld Alliance
Traffic Judge	ch.h.	1952-1972	Alibhai—Traffic Court
Zonta	dk.b/br.m.	1973-1990	Dr. Fager—Santa Tina

ADENA SPRINGS

Mira Femme	b.m.	1964-1991	Dumpty Humpty—Mlle. Somebody

AIRDRIE STUD

Dance Spell	b.h.	1973-1979	Northern Dancer—Obeah
Key to the Kingdom	dk.b/br.h.	1970-1995	Bold Ruler—Key Bridge

ASHFORD STUD

Fairy Bridge	b.m.	1975-1991	Bold Reason—Special
Fall Aspen	ch.m.	1976-1998	Pretense—Change Water
Secretariat's Love	ch.m.	1981-1995	Secretariat—Flack Flack
Sex Appeal	ch.m.	1970-1993	Buckpasser—Best in Show
Shecky Greene	b.h.	1970-1984	Noholme II—Lester's Pride

BIG SINK FARM

Fanfreluche	b.m.	1967-1999	Northern Dancer—Ciboulette

BRECKINRIDGE FARM/NORTH RIDGE FARM

Desert Vixen	dk.b/br.m.	1970-1982	In Reality—Desert Trial

BROOKDALE FARM

Ballade	dk.b/br.m.	1972-1994	Herbager—Miss Swapsco
Brown Berry	b.m.	1960-1993	Mount Marcy—Brown Baby

Sweet Alliance	b.m.	1974-1996	Sir Ivor—Mrs. Peterkin

CALUMET FARM

Alydar	ch.h.	1975-1990	Raisea Native—Sweet Tooth
Amoret	br.m.	1952-1971	Bull Lea—Mar-Kell
Armed	b.g.	1941-1964	Bull Lea—Armful
Armful	blk.m.	1933-1962	Chance Shot—Negrina
Barbizon	dk.b.h.	1954-1983	Polynesian—Good Blood
Bardstown	dk.b.g.	1952-1972	Alibhai—Twilight Tear
Best Turn	dk.b/br.h.	1966-1984	Turn-to—Sweet Clementine
Bewitch	br.m.	1945-1963	Bull Lea—Potheen
Blue Delight	br.m.	1938-1966	Blue Larkspur—Chicleight
Bubbley	dk.b.m.	1950-1964	Bull Lea—Blue Delight
Bull Lea	br.h.	1935-1964	Bull Dog—Rose Leaves
Citation	b.h.	1945-1970	Bull Lea—Hydroplane II
Coaltown	b.h.	1945-1965	Bull Lea—Easy Lass
Commodore M.	b.h.	1951-1963	Bull Lea—Early Autumn
Dustwhirl	b.m.	1926-1946	Sweep—Ormonda
Easy Lass	blk.m.	1940-1968	Blenheim II—Slow and Easy
Gen. Duke	br.c.	1954-1958	Bull Lea—Wistful
Hill Gail	dk.b.h.	1949-1968	Bull Lea—Jane Gail
Hug Again	ch.m.	1931-1957	Stimulus—Affection
Hydroplane II	ch.m.	1938-1948	Hyperion—Toboggan
Iron Liege	b.h.	1954-1972	Bull Lea—Iron Maiden
Iron Maiden	b.m.	1941-1964	War Admiral—Betty Derr

Jane Gail	ch.m.	1944-1952	Blenheim II—Lady Higloss
Katonka	b.m.	1972-1990	Minnesota Mac—Minnetonka
Kennelot	b.m.	1974-1994	Gallant Man—Queen Sucree
Lech	b.h.	1988-1994	Danzig—Wedding Reception
Mar-Kell	b.m.	1939-1966	Blenheim II—Nellie Flag
Mark-Ye-Well	b.h.	1949-1970	Bull Lea—Mar-Kell
Miss Rushin	b.m.	1942-1958	Blenheim II—Lady Erne
Miz Clementine	b.m.	1951-1962	Bull Lea—Two Bob
Mon Ange	ch.m.	1962-1982	Tom Fool—Two Lea
Nellie Flag	ch.m.	1932-1953	American Flag—Nellie Morse
On-and-On	b.h.	1956-1970	Nasrullah—Two Lea
Penicuik II	ch.m.	1934-1958	Buchan—Pennycomequick
Pensive	ch.h.	1941-1949	Hyperion—Penicuik II
Plum Cake	ch.m.	1958-1975	Ponder—Real Delight
Ponder	dk.b.h.	1946-1958	Pensive—Miss Rushin
Potheen	br.m.	1928-1950	Wildair—Rosie O'Grady
Princess Turia	ch.m.	1953-1975	Heliopolis—Blue Delight
Real Delight	b.m.	1949-1969	Bull Lea—Blue Delight
Sagace	b.h.	1980-1989	Luthier—Seneca
Slow and Easy	ch.m.	1922-1944	Colin—Shyness
Some Pomp	b.m.	1931-1951	Pompey—Some More
Sun Again	ch.h.	1939-1965	Sun Teddy—Hug Again
Sweet Tooth	b.m.	1965-1988	On-and-On—Plum Cake
Tim Tam	dk.b.h.	1955-1982	Tom Fool—Two Lea
Twilight Tear	b.m.	1941-1954	Bull Lea—Lady Lark

Two Bob	ch.m.	1933-1953	The Porter—Blessings
Two Lea	b.m.	1946-1973	Bull Lea—Two Bob
Twosy	b.m.	1942-1975	Bull Lea—Two Bob
Unerring	br.m.	1936-1956	Insco—Margaret Lawrence
Waynoka	blk.m.	1949-1966	War Admiral—Leonissa
Whirlaway	ch.h.	1938-1953	Blenheim II—Dustwhirl
Whirl Some	gr.m.	1945-1958	Whirlaway—Some Pep
Wistful	ch.m.	1946-1964	Sun Again—Easy Lass
Yorky	b.h.	1957-1966	Bull Lea—Waynoka

CLAIBORNE FARM

Ambiorix	dk.b.h.	1946-1975	Tourbillon—Lavendula
Blenheim II	b.h.	1927-1958	Blandford—Malva
Bold Ruler	dk.b.h.	1954-1971	Nasrullah—Miss Disco
Buckpasser	b.h.	1963-1978	Tom Fool—Busanda
Court Martial	ch.h.	1942-1966	Fair Trial—Instantaneous
Double Jay	dk.br.h.	1944-1972	Balladier—Broomshot
Gallant Fox	b.h.	1927-1954	Sir Gallahad III—Marguerite
Herbager	b.h.	1956-1976	Vandale—Flagette
Hoist the Flag	b.h.	1968-1980	Tom Rolfe—Wavy Navy
Johnstown	b.h.	1936-1950	Jamestown—La France
Mr. Prospector	b.h.	1970-1999	Raise a Native—Gold Digger
Nasrullah	b.h.	1940-1959	Nearco—Mumtaz Begum
Nijinsky II	b.h.	1967-1992	Northern Dancer—Flaming Page
Princequillo	b.h.	1940-1964	Prince Rose—Cosquilla

Reviewer	b.h.	1966-1977	Bold Ruler—Broadway
Riva Ridge	b.h.	1969-1985	First Landing—Iberia
Round Table	b.h.	1954-1987	Princequillo—Knight's Daughter
Secretariat	ch.h.	1970-1989	Bold Ruler—Somethingroyal
Sir Gallahad III	b.h.	1920-1949	Teddy—Plucky Liege
Swale	dk.b/br.c.	1981-1984	Seattle Slew—Tuerta

CLAIBORNE/MARCHMONT

Ack Ack	b.h.	1966-1990	Battle Joined—Fast Turn
Alluvial	ch.m.	1969-1994	Buckpasser—Bayou
Cox's Ridge	b.h.	1974-1998	Best Turn—Our Martha
Damascus	b.h.	1964-1995	Sword Dancer—Kerala
Dearly Precious	dk.b/br.m.	1973-1992	Dr. Fager—Imsodear
Drone	gr.h.	1966-1987	Sir Gaylord—Cap and Bells
Easy Goer	ch.h.	1986-1994	Alydar—Relaxing
File	ch.m.	1976-1993	Tom Rolfe—Continue
Foreseer	dk.b/br.m.	1969-1998	Round Table—Regal Gleam
Forli	ch.h.	1963-1988	Aristophanes—Trevisa
Hawaii	b.h.	1964-1990	Utrillo II—Ethane
Marguerite	ch.m.	1920-1945	Celt—Fairy Ray
Moccasin	ch.m.	1963-1986	Nantallah—Rough Shod II
Numbered Account	b.m.	1969-1996	Buckpasser—Intriguing
Obeah	b.m.	1965-1993	Cyane—Book of Verse
Pure Profit	ch.m.	1982-1999	Key to the Mint—Clear Ceiling
Qui Royalty	dk.b/br.m.	1977-1999	Native Royalty—Qui Blink

Relaxing	b.m.	1976-1999	Buckpasser—Marking Time
Sir Ivor	b.h.	1965-1995	Sir Gaylord—Attica
State	b.m.	1974-1993	Nijinsky II—Monarchy
Thong	b.m.	1964-1986	Nantallah—Rough Shod II
Tom Rolfe	b.h.	1962-1989	Ribot—Pocahontas
Topsider	b.h.	1974-1992	Northern Dancer—Drumtop
Tuerta	dk.b/br.m.	1970-1985	Forli—Continue

CLOVELLY FARM

Ancient Regime	gr.m.	1978-1998	Olden Times—Caterina
Caterina II	gr.m.	1963-1986	Princely Gift—Radiopye
Clinkers II	b.m.	1960-1976	Relic—La Fresnes
Flower Boat	ch.m.	1977-1985	Barachois—Sweet Snowdrop
La Trinite	ch.m.	1976-1991	Lyphard—Promessa
Lady Lufton	ch.m.	1954-1977	Petition—Barchester
Loved	ch.m.	1967-1996	Jaipur—Cantadora II
Lupe II	b.m.	1967-1989	Primera—Alcoa
Misty Light	b.m.	1968-1993	Ribot—Hasty Cast
Parioli	b.m.	1981-1994	Bold Bidder—Rumbling Roman
Plume II	blk.m.	1947-1972	Vatellor—Platteville
Primary II	br.m.	1957-1973	Petition—Hymette
Rajput Princess	ch.m.	1961-1989	Prince Taj—Royal Arrival
Regal Exception	b.m.	1969-1990	Ribot—Rajput Princess
Southern Seas II	dk.b/br.m.	1975-1998	Jim French—Schonbrunn
Yahabeebe	dk.b/br.m.	1953-1975	Mid-Day Sun—Grilse

CRESTWOOD FARM/BROOKDALE

Eurasian	br.h.	1940-1963	Quatre Bras II—Tehani
Piet	ch.h.	1945-1968	Grand Slam—Valdina Lark

DARBY DAN FARM

Black Toney	br.h.	1911-1938	Peter Pan—Belgravia
Blossom Time	br.m.	1920-1946	North Star III—Vaila
Blue Swords	b.h.	1940-1955	Blue Larkspur—Flaming Swords
Bubbling Over	ch.h.	1923-1938	North Star III—Beaming Beauty
Darby Dunedin	b.m.	1942-1962	Blenheim II—Ethel Dear
Flower Bowl	b.m.	1952-1968	Alibhai—Flower Bed
Graustark	ch.h.	1963-1988	Ribot—Flower Bowl
His Majesty	b.h.	1968-1995	Ribot—Flower Bowl
Ribot	b.h.	1952-1972	Tenerani—Romanella
Roberto	b.h.	1969-1988	Hail to Reason—Bramalea
Summer Tan	b.h.	1952-1969	Heliopolis—Miss Zibby

DOMINO STUD

Al Hattab	gr.h.	1966-1983	The Axe II—Abyssinia II
Dewan	b.h.	1965-1984	Bold Ruler—Sunshine Nell
Oil Capitol	gr.h.	1947-1959	Mahmoud—Never Again II
Pet Bully	b.h.	1948-1971	Petrose—Camelina

EATON FARM

Comely Nell	dk.b.m.	1962-1985	Commodore M.—Nellie L

ECHO VALLEY FARM

All Rainbows	b.m.	1973-1996	Bold Hour—Miss Carmie

ELMENDORF FARM

Protagonist	ch.h.	1971-1976	Prince John—Hornpipe II
Speak John	b.h.	1958-1980	Prince John—Nuit de Folies
Verbatim	dk.b/br.h.	1965-1991	Speak John—Well Kept

GAINESWAY FARM

Arts and Letters	ch.h.	1966-1998	Ribot—All Beautiful
Apalachee	b.h.	1971-1996	Round Table—Moccasin
Blushing Groom	ch.h.	1974-1992	Red God—Runaway Bride
Bold Bidder	b.h.	1962-1982	Bold Ruler—High Bid
Cannonade	b.h.	1971-1993	Bold Bidder—Queen Sucree
Icecapade	gr.h.	1969-1988	Nearctic—Shenanigans
In Reality	b.h.	1964-1989	Intentionally—My Dear Girl
Key to the Mint	b.h.	1969-1996	Graustark—Key Bridge
Riverman	b.h.	1969-1999	Never Bend—River Lady
Silent Screen	ch.h.	1967-1993	Prince John—Prayer Bell
Stage Door Johnny	ch.h.	1965-1996	Prince John—Peroxide Blonde
Vaguely Noble	b.h.	1965-1989	Vienna—Noble Lassie

GAINESWAY/GREENTREE

Bebopper	b.m.	1962-1983	Tom Fool—Bebop II
Bimelech	b.h.	1937-1966	Black Toney—La Troienne

Blackball	dk.b.m.	1950-1967	Shut Out—Big Event
Bonus	b.m.	1919-1941	All Gold—Remembrance
Capot	br.h.	1946-1974	Menow—Piquet
Cherry Malotte	b.m.	1909-1924	Orlando—Dottie
Cherry Pie	b.g.	1920-1946	Chicle—Cherry Malotte
Coincidence	b.g.	1942-1966	Questionnaire—Small World
Dunce Cap II	dk.b/br.m.	1960-1982	Tom Fool—Bright Coronet
Easter Hero	ch.g.	1920-1948	My Prince—Easter Week
Jedina	dk.b/br.m.	1976-1997	What a Pleasure—Killaloe
Jolly Roger	ch.g.	1922-1948	Pennant—Lethe
La Troienne	b.m.	1926-1954	Teddy—Helene de Troie
Polite Lady	b.m.	1977-1995	Venetian Jester—Friendly Ways
Questionnaire	b.h.	1927-1950	Sting—Miss Puzzle
Shut Out	ch.h.	1939-1964	Equipoise—Goose Egg
St. Germans	b.h.	1921-1947	Swynford—Hamoaze
The Axe II	gr.h.	1958-1982	Mahmoud—Blackball
The Porter	b.h.	1915-1944	Sweep—Ballet Girl
Third Degree	b.h.	1936-1965	Questionnaire—Panache
Tom Fool	b.h.	1949-1976	Menow—Gaga
Twenty Grand	b.h.	1928-1948	St. Germans—Bonus

GAINESWAY/WHITNEY

Boojum	b.h.	1927-1949	John P. Grier—Elf
Broomstick	b.h.	1901-1931	Ben Brush—Elf
Counterpoint	ch.h.	1948-1969	Count Fleet—Jabot

Equipoise	ch.h.	1928-1938	Pennant—Swinging
Mahmoud	gr.h.	1933-1962	Blenheim II—Mah Mahal
Pennant	ch.h.	1911-1938	Peter Pan—Royal Rose
Peter Pan	b.h.	1904-1933	Commando—Cinderella
Prudery	br.m.	1918-1930	Peter Pan—Polly Flinders
Regret	ch.m.	1912-1934	Broomstick—Jersey Lightning
Silver Fog	gr.m.	1944-1966	Mahmoud—Equilette
Silver Spoon	ch.m.	1956-1978	Citation—Silver Fog
Top Flight	dk.b.m.	1929-1949	Dis Donc—Flyatit
Whisk Broom II	ch.h.	1907-1928	Broomstick—Audience

HAGYARD FARM

Dancing Maid	b.m.	1975-1982	Lyphard—Morana
Gold River	ch.m.	1977-1986	Riverman—Glaneuse
Hail to Reason	br.h.	1958-1976	Turn-to—Nothirdchance
Pistol Packer	ch.m.	1968-1986	Gun Bow—George's Girl II
Stymie	ch.h.	1941-1962	Equestrian—Stop Watch

HAMBURG PLACE

Ida Pickwick	b.m.	1888-1908	Mr. Pickwick—Ida K.
Imp	blk.m.	1894-1909	Wagner—Fondling
Lady Sterling	ch.m.	1899-1920	Hanover—Aquila
Miss Kearney	b.m.	1906-1925	Planudes—Courtplaster
Ogden	br.h.	1894-1923	Kilwarlin—Oriole
Pink Pigeon	ro.m.	1964-1976	T. V. Lark—Ruwenzori

Plaudit	b.h.	1895-1919	Himyar—Cinderella
Princess Mary	blk.m.	1917-1926	Hessian—Royal Gun
Sir Martin	ch.h.	1906-1930	Ogden—Lady Sterling
Star Shoot	ch.h.	1898-1919	Isinglass—Astrology
T. V. Lark	b.h.	1957-1975	Indian Hemp—Miss Larksfly

HIGHCLERE

Killaloe	b.m.	1970-1996	Dr. Fager—Grand Splendor

JONABELL FARM

Aflicker	gr.m.	1978-1987	Damascus—Aglimmer
Bedazzled	ch.m.	1969-1984	Nasomo—Dark Dazzler
Cicada	b.m.	1959-1981	Bryan G.—Satsuma
Dark Display	b.m.	1941-1965	Display—Dark Loveliness
Hail the Pirates	b.h.	1970-1988	Hail to Reason—Bravura
Honest and True	b.m.	1977-1999	Mr. Leader—Tell Meno Lies
Kerala	b.m.	1958-1984	My Babu—Blade of Time
Singing Grass	ch.m.	1944-1960	War Admiral—Boreale
Stellar Role	b.m.	1943-1965	Bimelech—Astralobe
Sumatra	ch.m.	1969-1995	Groton—Sunda Strait
Tell Meno Lies	gr.m.	1971-1985	The Axe II—Filatonga
Vigors	ro.h.	1973-1994	Grey Dawn II—Relifordie
Virginia Rapids	ch.h.	1990-1999	Riverman—Virginiana

KENTUCKY HORSE PARK

Allez France	b.m.	1970-1989	Sea Bird—Priceless Gem
Forego	b.g.	1970-1997	Forli—Lady Golconda
Jay Trump	dk.b.g.	1957-1988	Tonga Prince—Be Trump
Sefa's Beauty	b.m.	1979-1989	Lt. Stevens—Delightful Vie
Brushup	b.m.	1929-1956	Sweep—Annette K.
Man o' War	ch.h.	1917-1947	Fair Play—Mahubah
War Admiral	br.h.	1934-1959	Man o' War—Brushup
War Hazard	ch.m.	1938-1944	Man o' War—Artifice
War Kilt	ch.m.	1943-1956	Man o' War—Friar's Carse
War Relic	ch.h.	1938-1963	Man o' War—Friar's Carse

LANE'S END FARM/BOSQUE BONITA

Bally Ache	b.c.	1957-1960	Ballydam—Celestial Blue
Celestial Blue	b.m.	1943-1966	Supremus—Vanda Cerulea

MARE HAVEN FARM

Bejilla	gr.h.	1977-1989	Quadrangle—Dancing Angela
Chieftain	br.h.	1961-1982	Bold Ruler—Pocahontas
Native Charger	gr.h.	1962-1990	Native Dancer—Greek Blond
Proudest Roman	dk.b/br.h.	1968-1989	Never Bend—Roman Song
San's the Shadow	b.c.	1984-1989	San Feliou—Lucky Shadow

MARGAUX FARM/J. T. LUNDY FARM

Turn and Count	b.h.	1973-1980	Best Turn—Countess Alberta

MEREWORTH FARM

Allie's Tune	ro.m.	1977-1998	Drone—Allie's Serenade
Alpenstock III	br.m.	1936-1959	Apelle—Plymstock
Ariel	blk.h.	1925-1950	Eternal—Adana
Canina	b.m.	1941-1962	Bull Dog—Coronium
Cathy Baby	b.m.	1969-1998	Native Charger—Token of Love
Colfax Maid	b.m.	1958-1977	My Babu—Tsumani
Dance Fan	dk.b/br.m.	1960-1979	Dedicate—Evening Belle
Display	b.h.	1923-1944	Fair Play—Cicuta
Hairan	b.h.	1932-1956	Fairway—Harpsichord
Hasty Flapper	b.m.	1971-1997	Hitting Away—Hasty Doll
Lady Lark	b.m.	1934-1959	Blue Larkspur—Ladana
Miss Doreen	b.m.	1942-1967	Pilate—Princess Doreen
Ryelands	ch.f.	1993-1997	Naevus—Stage Door Model
Secret Story	br.m.	1954-1973	Spy Song—Belle Histoire
Snowflake	ch.m.	1927-1951	Mad Hatter—Snowdrop
Sunglow	ch.h.	1947-1964	Sun Again—Rosern
Swivel	b.m.	1930-1955	Swift and Sure—Toddle
Waltz Fan	dk.b/br.m.	1970-1995	Chieftain—Dance Fan
War Swept	br.m.	1936-1959	Man o' War—Brush Along

MERRICK PLACE

Merrick	ch.h.	1903-1941	Golden Garter—Bianca

MIDDLEBROOK FARM

Althea	ch.m.	1981-1995	Alydar—Courtly Dee
Courtly Dee	dk b/br.m.	1968-1995	Never Bend—Tulle

MT. BRILLIANT FARM/HIRA VILLA

Domino	br.h.	1891-1897	Himyar—Mannie Gray

NANTURA FARM

Longfellow	br.h.	1867-1893	Leamington—Nantura
Ten Broeck	b.h.	1872-1887	Phaeton—Fanny Holton

NORMANDY FARM

Alablue	b.m.	1945-1962	Blue Larkspur—Double Time
Blue Glass	br.m.	1917-1941	Prince Palatine—Hour Glass
Bonnie Beryl	ch.m.	1943-1963	Fighting Fox—Bonnie Maginn
Chance Shot	b.h.	1924-1952	Fair Play—Quelle Chance
Fair Play	ch.h.	1905-1929	Hastings—Fairy Gold
Firm Policy	b.m.	1959-1985	Princequillo—White Cross
Haste	b.h.	1923-1944	Maintenant—Miss Malaprop
La Roseraie	ch.m.	1928-1946	Niceas—Eblouissante
Mahubah	b.m.	1910-1931	Rock Sand—Merry Token
Nature	b.m.	1906-1931	Meddler—Correction
Nipisiquit	b.m.	1924-1947	Buchan—Herself
Offensive	b.m.	1941-1960	Sir Gallahad III—Buckup
Ormonda	ch.m.	1916-1944	Superman—Princess Ormonde

Osmand	ch.g.	1924-1951	Sweeper—Ormonda
Peace	gr.m.	1927-1945	Stefan the Great—Memories II
Pipette	br.m.	1944-1960	Piping Rock—Highclere
Qu'elle est Belle II	dk.br.m.	1909-1932	Rock Sand—Queen's Bower
Quelle Chance	b/br.m.	1917-1936	Ethelbert—Qu'elle est Belle II
Quick Pitch	ch.g.	1960-1983	Charlevoix—The Ghizeh
Rose Pompon	b.m.	1910-1933	Rock Sand—Martha Gorman
Sickle	br.h.	1924-1943	Phalaris—Selene
Stagecraft	b.m.	1929-1939	Fair Play—Franconia
Zephyretta	b.m.	1922-1948	Lemberg—Rose Pompon

NUCKOLS FARM

Mr. Leader	b.h.	1966-1999	Hail to Reason—Jolie Deja

OVERBROOK FARM

Always Mint	dk.b/br.m.	1982-1996	Key to the Mint—Always a Princess
Blacksburg	b.g.	1989-1996	Seattle Slew—Devil's Sister
Buzz My Bell	dk b/br.m.	1981-1998	Drone—Chateaupavia
Cinegita	b.m.	1977-1997	Secretariat—Wanika
Country Cat	b.f.	1992-1996	Storm Cat—La Affirmed
Grand Canyon	b.c.	1987-1990	Fappiano—Champagne Ginny
Hopespringseternal	ch.m.	1971-1986	Buckpasser—Rose Bower
Miss Betty	b.m.	1971-1994	Buckpasser—In the Clouds
Mrs. Penny	ch.m.	1977-1997	Great Nephew—Tananarive
My Yellow Bird	ch.m.	1979-1995	Raise a Native—Consequential

Mysterious	ch.m.	1970-1988	Crepello—Hill Shade
Seaside Attraction	b.m.	1987-1996	Seattle Slew—Kamar
Stellarette	b.m.	1978-1993	Tentam—Square Angel
The Minstrel	ch.h.	1974-1990	Northern Dancer—Fleur
Tizna	b.m.	1969-1989	Trevieres—Noris

PLUM LANE FARM

Sadair	b.h.	1962-1989	Petare—Blue Missy

SAXONY FARM

Free to Fly	b.m.	1974-1994	Stevward—Dancing Lark
Native Partner	b.m.	1966-1986	Raise a Native—Dinner Partner

SHADWELL

Al Azhar	ch.c.	1990-1991	Forty Niner—Bolt from the Blue
Al Bayan	dk.b/br.m.	1981-1987	Northern Dancer—Bold Melody
Ashayer	b.m.	1985-1993	Lomond—Good Lassie
Desirable	gr.m.	1981-1998	Lord Gayle—Balidaress
Gesedeh	ch.m.	1983-1998	Ela-Mana-Mou—Le Melody
Give Thanks	b.m.	1980-1998	Relko—Parthica
Goalwah	b.m.	1992-1997	Sadler's Wells—Al Bahathri
Hasbah	ch.m.	1987-1992	Kris—Al Bahathri
Hayajan	dk.b/br.c.	1995-1996	Dayjur—Basma
Hooriah	ch.m.	1986-1995	Northern Dancer—Where You Lead
Kesar Queen	b.m.	1973-1995	Nashua—Meadow Saffron

Kit's Double	ch.m.	1973-1998	Spring Double—Kit's Play
Linda's Magic	dk.b/br.m.	1984-1997	Far North—Pogonip
Majjthub	b.c.	1994-1998	Slew o' Gold—Jathibiyah
Manal	b.m.	1979-1989	Luthier—Top Twig
Salsabil	b.m.	1987-1996	Sadler's Wells—Flame of Tara
Unnamed	b.c.	1993-1993	Lyphard—Asl
Unnamed	dk.b/br.c.	1990-1990	Arctic Tern—Bar J. Gal
Unnamed	gr.c.	1987-1987	El Gran Senor—Desirable
Unnamed	ch.f.	1986-1987	Majestic Light—Glamour Girl
Unnamed	dk.b/br.c.	1996-1996	Dayjur—Glamourous Bride
Unnamed	b.c.	1997-1998	Riverman—Height of Fashion
Unnamed	ch.c.	1995-1995	Diesis —Kazoo
Unnamed	dk.b/br.f.	1997-1997	Gone West—Kazoo
Unnamed	b.f.	1988-1988	Diesis—Khwlah
Unnamed	ch.c.	1988-1988	Topsider—Kit's Double
Unnamed	b.c.	1992-1992	Diesis —Linda's Magic
Unnamed	dk.b/br.f.	1997-1997	Bahri—Linda's Magic
Unnamed	dk.b/br.f.	1995-1995	Riverman—Mafatin
Unnamed	b.f.	1987-1987	Chief's Crown—Manal
Unnamed	b.f.	1995-1995	Mr. Prospector—Muhbubh
Unnamed	b.f.	1996-1996	Dayjur—Saffaanh
Unnamed	b.f.	1992-1992	Gulch—Shicklah
Unnamed	b.c.	1986-1986	Seattle Slew—So Fine
Unnamed	dk.b/br.f.	1996-1996	Storm Cat—Sweet Roberta
Unnamed	b.c.	1997-1998	Diesis—Treble

Zaahi	dk.b/br.h.	1989-1994	Slew o' Gold—Alghuzaylah
Zawahir	ch.f.	1987-1991	Nureyev—Solariat
Talb	dk.b/br.h.	1989-1996	Caro—Go March

SOUTH CREEK OFFICE PARK/BEAUMONT FARM

Ornament	ch.h.	1894-1916	Order—Victorine

SPENDTHRIFT FARM

Beau Pere	br.h.	1927-1947	Son-in-Law—Cinna
Caro	gr.h.	1967-1989	Fortino—Chambord
Cornish Prince	br.h.	1962-1985	Bold Ruler—Teleran
Creme dela Creme	b.h.	1963-1977	Olympia—Judy Rullah
Exclusive Native	ch.h.	1965-1983	Raise a Native—Exclusive
Fleet Nasrullah	dk.b.h.	1955-1979	Nasrullah—Happy Go Fleet
Gallant Man	b.h.	1954-1988	Migoli—Majideh
Intrepid Hero	b.h.	1972-1980	Forli—Bold Princess
Majestic Prince	ch.h.	1966-1981	Raise a Native—Gay Hostess
Nashua	b.h.	1952-1982	Nasrullah—Segula
Never Bend	dk.b.h.	1960-1977	Nasrullah—Lalun
Prince John	ch.h.	1953-1979	Princequillo—Not Afraid
Proud Clarion	b.h.	1964-1981	Hail to Reason—Breath O' Morn
Rainy Lake	ch.h.	1959-1980	Royal Charger—Portage
Raise a Native	ch.h.	1961-1988	Native Dancer—Raise You
Valdez	ch.h.	1976-1985	Exclusive Native—Sally Stark

SPENDTHRIFT/GREEN GATES

Affectionately	dk.b.m.	1960-1979	Swaps—Searching
Amiga	gr.m.	1947-1977	Mahmoud—Miss Dogwood
Anchors Aweigh	b.m.	1949-1968	Devil Diver—True Bearing
Armada	ch.m.	1924-1944	Man o' War—Crepuscule
Cantadora II	ch.m.	1957-1983	Canthare—Madiana
Dinner Time	ch.m.	1929-1952	High Time—Seaplane
Egret	b.m.	1961-1979	Tudor Minstrel—Miss Fleetwood
Eight Thirty	ch.h.	1936-1965	Pilate—Dinner Time
Evening	dk.b.m.	1929-1948	St. James—Crepuscule
Evening Belle	b.m.	1945-1967	Eight Thirty—Evening
Francine M.	b.m.	1964-1977	Sir Gaylord—Fleece
Gay Hostess	ch.m.	1957-1976	Royal Charger—Your Hostess
Gold Digger	b.m.	1962-1990	Nashua—Sequence
High Fleet	ch.m.	1933-1952	Jack High—Armada
Jamestown	b.h.	1928-1953	St. James—Mlle. Dazie
Lady Tramp	b.m.	1965-1980	Sensitivo—La Morlaye
Last Straw	ch.m.	1918-1940	Ultimus—Broom Flower
Masked Lady	b.m.	1964-1981	Spy Song—Spinosa
Mideau	b.m.	1942-1967	Bull Dog—Wild Waters
Miss Dogwood	dk.b.m.	1939-1968	Bull Dog—Myrtlewood
Miss Fleetwood	b.m.	1954-1977	Count Fleet—Miss Dogwood
Requested	ch.h.	1939-1969	Questionnaire—Fair Perdita
Salacia	br.m.	1921-1942	Ultimus—Queen of the Water
Seaneen	ch.h.	1954-1972	Royal Charger—Tir an Oir

Sequence	dk.b.m.	1946-1977	Count Fleet—Miss Dogwood
Source Sucree	br.m.	1940-1968	Admiral Drake—Lavendula
St. James	b.h.	1921-1943	Ambassador IV—Bobolink II
Straight Deal	b.m.	1962-1982	Hail to Reason—No Fiddling
Tatanne	br.m.	1931-1953	St. James—Titanite
Tedmelia	br.m.	1935-1958	Teddy—Sunmelia
Turn-to	b.h.	1951-1973	Royal Charger—Source Sucree
Yorktown	ch.h.	1957-1968	Battlefield—Joodles

STONE FARM

Cougar II	dk.b/br.h.	1966-1989	Tale of Two Cities—Cindy Lou II
Harlan	dk.b/br.h.	1989-1999	Storm Cat—Country Romance
Herculean	dk.b/br.h.	1971-1986	Bold Ruler—Fool's Play

STONELEIGH

Lisanninga	b.m.	1963-1984	Whodunit—Haute Roche

STONER CREEK STUD

Count Fleet	br.h.	1940-1973	Reigh Count—Quickly
Quickly	blk.m.	1930-1944	Haste—Stephanie
Reigh Count	ch.h.	1925-1948	Sunreigh—Contessina

STONEREATH FARMS

Best in Show	ch.m.	1965-1990	Traffic Judge—Stolen Hour

THREE CHIMNEYS FARM

Bold Example	b.m.	1969-1994	Bold Lad—Lady Be Good
Chief's Crown	b.h.	1982-1997	Danzig—Six Crowns
Dancing Tribute	b.m.	1986-1996	Nureyev—Sophisticated Girl
Icing	b.m.	1973-1996	Prince Tenderfoot—Cake
Little Baby Bear	dk.b/br.m.	1990-1997	Broad Brush—In Jubilation
Nodouble	ch.h.	1965-1990	Noholme II—Abla-Jay
Royal Folly	ch.m.	1966-1995	Tom Fool—Golden Sari
Time for a Change	ch.h.	1981-1996	Damascus—Resolver
Virunga	b.m.	1970-1995	Sodium—Vale

THREE CHIMNEYS FARM/KING RANCH

Bee Mac	b.m.	1941-c.1964	War Admiral—Baba Kenny
Dotted Line	ch.m.	1953-c.1975	Princequillo—Inscribe
Gallant Bloom	b.m.	1966-1991	Gallant Man—Multiflora
Green Finger	dk.b.m.	1958-1991	Better Self—Flower Bed
Igual	ch.m.	1937-c.1962	Equipoise—Incandescent
Monade	br.m.	1959-1991	Klairon—Mormyre

UNIVERSITY OF KENTUCKY/COLDSTREAM STUD

Bull Dog	b/br.h.	1927-1954	Teddy—Plucky Liege
My Auntie	b.m.	1933-1949	Busy American—Babe K.

UNIVERSITY OF KENTUCKY/HARTLAND FARM

Ben Brush	b.h.	1893-1918	Bramble—Roseville

Esher	br.h.	1883-1901	Claremont—Una
Peter Quince	ch.h.	1905-1930	Commando—Fair Vision
Rosa Mundi	ch.m.	1911-1930	Plaudit—Hindoo Rose
Rose of Sharon	br.m.	1926-1929	Light Brigade—Rosa Mundi

UNIVERSITY OF KENTUCKY/MAINE CHANCE FARM

| Blue Fantasy | b.m. | 1944-1965 | Blue Larkspur—Risk |
| Myrtle Charm | b.m. | 1946-1964 | Alsab—Crepe Myrtle |

VALKYRE STUD

Ebb and Flow	dk.b/br.m.	1968-1996	Fleet Nasrullah—Sea-Change
Fondre	dk.b/br.m.	1975-1991	Key to the Mint—Miss Manalapan
Isolt	b.m.	1961-1982	Round Table—All My Eye
Kota Call	ch.m.	1969-1984	Jet Man—Dove Call
Light Verse	b.m.	1970-1985	Reverse—Brighton View
Point of Balance	ch.m.	1970-1984	Fulcrum—Honor Point
Vivacious Girl	b.m.	1978-1992	Royal Landy—Bornforglory
West Bramble	dk.b/br.m.	1960-1980	Krakatao—Dented Bell

VINERY

Loss or Gain	dk.b/br.m.	1975-1993	Ack Ack—Gain or Loss
No Robbery	b.h.	1960-1985	Swaps—Bimlette
Timeless Moment	ch.h.	1970-1998	Damascus—Hour of Parting

WALMAC INTERNATIONAL

Brent's Prince	dk.b/br.h.	1972-1986	Proud Clarion—Brent's Princess
Risen Star	dk.b/br.h.	1985-1998	Secretariat—Ribbon
Sham	b.h.	1970-1993	Pretense—Sequoia

WIMBORNE FARM

| Lord At War | ch.h. | 1980-1998 | General—Luna de Miel |

WINDWARD OAKS FARM

| Queen Sucree | b.m. | 1966-1998 | Ribot—Cosmah |

XALAPA FARM

Mystery Mood	ch.m.	1972-1994	Night Invader—Moaning Low
Prince Palatine	b.h.	1908-1924	Persimmon—Lady Lightfoot
Witherite	ch.m.	1958-1988	Ky. Colonel—Whither Wander

Maps

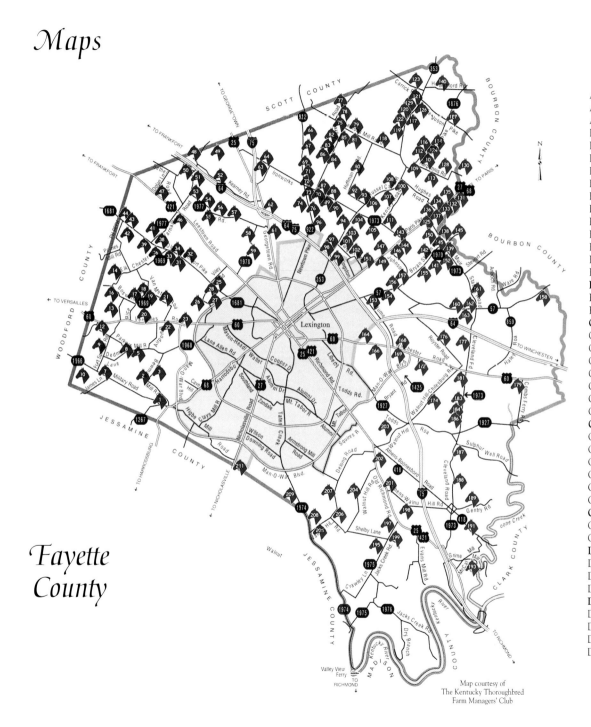

Fayette
County

Map courtesy of
The Kentucky Thoroughbred
Farm Managers' Club

Bourbon County

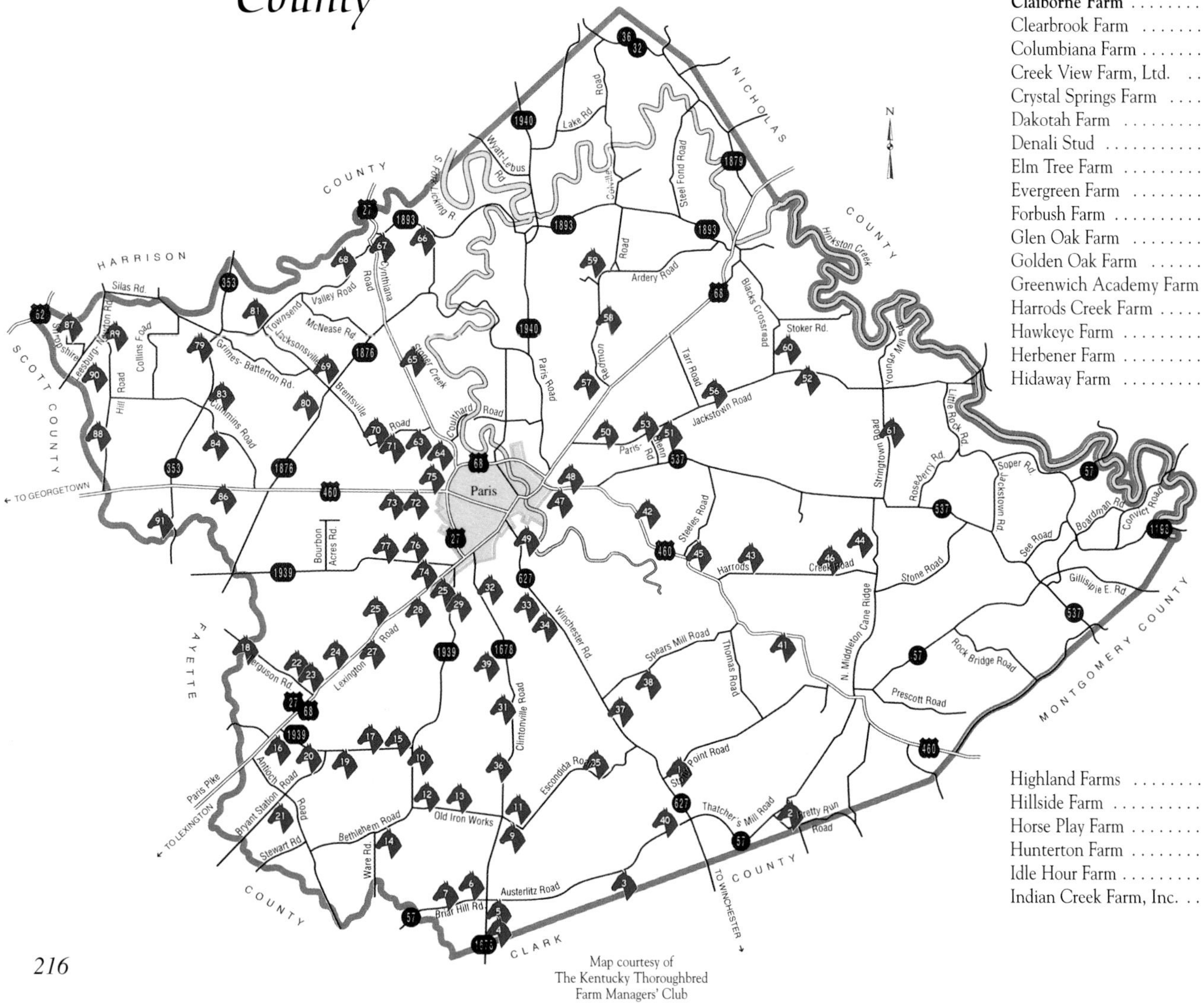

Map courtesy of
The Kentucky Thoroughbred
Farm Managers' Club

Ann Marie Farm 76
Ashleigh Stud Farm 84
Beech Spring Farm 68
Biggs Farm 79
Blandford Stud 52
Bourbon Lane Farm 25
Bradyleigh Farm 26
Brandywine Farm 53
Briar Hill Farms 07
Briarbrooke Farm 58
Canefield Farm 28
Cedar Point Farm 14
Cherry Valley Farm 33
Circle O Farm 09
Claiborne Farm 49
Clearbrook Farm 39
Columbiana Farm 31
Creek View Farm, Ltd. 45
Crystal Springs Farm 73
Dakotah Farm 16
Denali Stud 72
Elm Tree Farm 77
Evergreen Farm 11
Forbush Farm 10
Glen Oak Farm 02
Golden Oak Farm 88
Greenwich Academy Farm 22
Harrods Creek Farm 46
Hawkeye Farm 24
Herbener Farm 87
Hidaway Farm 48
Highland Farms 35, 37, 40
Hillside Farm 42
Horse Play Farm 32
Hunterton Farm 47
Idle Hour Farm 23
Indian Creek Farm, Inc. 59
Innisbrooke Farm 03
John Penn Farm 43
Katalpa Farm 51
Knockgriffin Farm 63
Loch Lea Farm, Inc. 50
Lochness Farm 06
Locust Grove Farm 18
Locust Ridge Farm 04
Lynnwood Farm 74
Marsetta Farm 57
Martingale Farm 56
Meadow Haven Farm 13
Meadowlark Valley Farm 69
Mt. Auburn Farm 44
Mt. Carmel Farm 66
Muckross Farm 38
Paris Hills Farm 90
Pleasant Retreat Farm 29
Raceland Farm 75
Runnymede Farm, Inc. 65
Ruthland Farm 21
Sa'Long Farm 83
Shenanigan Farm 89
Silver Springs Farm 70
Southern Cross Farm 60
Springland Farm, Inc. 36
Springwell Farm 15
Steeple Hill Farm 20
Step Ahead Farm 71
Stone Farm 01
Stoneleigh Farm 27
Stonereath Farms 86
Stoney Brook Farm 21
Sugar Grove Farm 80
Sunny Oak Farm 81
Sunnyside Farm 64
Taaffe Farm 12
Threave Main Stud 17
Triad Farm 61
Tri-County Farms, LLC 91
Trilogy Farm 05
Westview Farm 67
Wimborne Farm 34
Xalapa Farm 41

(Farms in **bold face** are listed in the Appendix.)

(Farms in **bold face** are listed in the Appendix.)

Woodford County

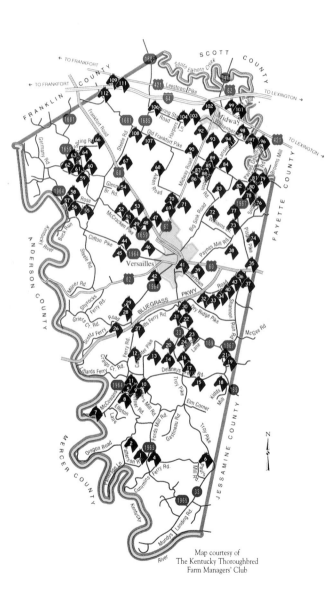

Map courtesy of
The Kentucky Thoroughbred
Farm Managers' Club

217

Index

Photo Credits

Chapter 1 — Markers: Longfellow, Ten Broeck, Merrick, Ornament, Ben Brush (Lucy Zeh); Domino (Barbara D. Livingston)
Horses: Domino (Widener collection); Ben Brush (The Blood-Horse)

Chapter 2 — Markers: cemetery (Barbara D. Livingston); Imp, Sir Martin (Lucy Zeh)
Horses: T. V. Lark (The Blood-Horse)

Chapter 3 — Markers: cemetery, Broomstick, Equipoise, Mahmoud (Barbara D. Livingston);
Peter Pan (Lucy Zeh)
Horses: Equipoise (C. Cook); Regret (Keeneland-Cook)

Chapter 4 — Markers: cemetery (Barbara D. Livingston); Bimelech, La Troienne, Tom Fool, Twenty Grand (Lucy Zeh)
Horses: Bimelech (Turf Pix); Tom Fool (Bert Morgan); Shut Out (H. C. Ashby)

Chapter 5 — Markers: columns (Anne M. Eberhardt); Fair Play, Fair Play statue, Mahubah (Barbara D. Livingston);
Clovelly barn, Lupe II (Lucy Zeh)

Chapter 6 — Markers: Lion's Circle, Affectionately, Eight Thirty, Straight Deal, Turn-To, Gallant Man, Nashua, Never
Bend (Lucy Zeh)
Horses: Affectionately (Turfotos); Gold Digger (The Blood-Horse); Gallant Man (Bert and Richard Morgan)

Chapter 7 — Markers: Black Toney, Althea, Courtly Dee (Barbara D. Livingston); Flower Bowl, Graustark, His Majesty,
Roberto (Lucy Zeh)
Horses: Graustark (The Blood-Horse); Roberto (John C. Wyatt)

Chapter 8 — Markers: cemetery, Alydar, Citation (Barbara D. Livingston); Armed, Blue Delight, Twilight Tear (Lucy Zeh)
Horses: Bull Lea, Pensive (The Blood-Horse); Two Lea (Arlington Park)

Chapter 9 — Markers: cemetery, Bold Ruler, Buckpasser, Nasrullah, Round Table, Secretariat (Barbara D. Livingston); Mr. Prospector, (Lucy Zeh); Marchmont cemetery, Marguerite (Tom Hall)
Horses: Bold Ruler (Bert and Richard Morgan); Gallant Fox, Sir Gallahad III, Ack Ack, Sir Ivor (The Blood-Horse); Nijinsky II (P. Bertrand et Fils)

Chapter 10 — Markers: Display, Lady Lark, Devil Diver, Roman, Cicada, Vigors, Stoner Creek Stud cemetery, Count Fleet, Hail to Reason, Stymie, Bally Ache, Desert Vixen (Lucy Zeh)
Horses: Devil Diver, Stymie (Bert Morgan); Count Fleet (The Blood-Horse)

Chapter 11 — Markers: Allez France, Forego, Jay Trump, War Admiral, War Relic (Lucy Zeh); Man o' War, Faraway Farm, Man o' War's stall (Barbara D. Livingston);
Horses: Forego (The Blood-Horse); War Admiral (Morgan Photo Service)

Chapter 12 — Markers: Risen Star, Fairy Bridge, Fall Aspen, Seaside Attraction, The Minstrel (Lucy Zeh); Chief's Crown, Nodouble (Barbara D. Livingston)
Horses: Fall Aspen (Anne M. Eberhardt); Grand Canyon (Four Footed Photos); The Minstrel (Chris Maguire); Chief's Crown (Anne M. Eberhardt)

Cover images — Barbara D. Livingston

Acknowledgments

Etched in Stone would not have been possible without assistance from many quarters. Many farm owners, managers, and employees have allowed visits to be made and photographs to be taken. They also have expressed interest in this project, and in many cases suggested other locations. Kim Graetz, editor of *The Horse*, provided guidance and encouragement, as did Judy Marchman of *The Blood-Horse*. Vickie Neiduski read much of the manuscript and made suggestions and corrections, as did Diane Viert of *The Blood-Horse*. The Keeneland librarians, Cathy Schenck and Phyllis Rogers, were generous with their assistance. Others, far too many to list, lent a hand or encouragement along the way. To think, it all started so innocently, with a visit to Domino's grave.

Note from author: Some Thoroughbred memorials are accessible to the public, but many exist on private property. While some farms allow visitors, others do not. The author encourages all potential visitors to respect the policies of each farm.

For more information on farms and their visitor's policies, contact the Kentucky Thoroughbred Farm Manager's Club at (606) 296-4279 or at kyfarmclub@aol.com.

Editors — Jacqueline Duke, Judy L. Marchman
Book Design — Jeff Flannery
Copy Editor — Jennifer O. Bryant
Proofreaders — Tom Hall, Hiro Tonegawa,
Diane L. Viert

Also from The Blood-Horse, Inc.

Baffert: Dirt Road to the Derby

Cigar: America's Horse (revised edition)

Country Life Diary (revised edition)

Crown Jewels of Thoroughbred Racing

Four Seasons of Racing

Kentucky Derby Glasses Price Guide

Man o' War: Thoroughbred Legends

Matriarchs: Great Mares of the 20th Century

Royal Blood

Thoroughbred Champions:
Top 100 Racehorses of the 20th Century

Whittingham